Passenger and Merchant Ships of the Grand Trunk Pacific and Canadian Northern Railways

PASSENGER AND MERCHANT SHIPS OF THE GRAND TRUNK PACIFIC AND CANADIAN NORTHERN RAILWAYS

DAVID R.P. GUAY

DUNDURN
TORONTO

Editor: Michael Carroll
Design: Laura Boyle
Cover Design: Sarah Beaudin
Cover Images: Clockwise from top left: The sternwheeler *Operator*, British Columbia Archives C-05493; map, University of Alaska-Fairbanks UAF-G3511 P53 1910 P6; the steamer *Acadian*, Historical Collection of the Great Lakes 000060, Bowling Green State University; the *Royal Edward*, Author's Collection; advertising card for the Uranium Steamship Line, Ian Lawler Collection; the steamer *Garden City*, Library and Archives Canada PA-020788.
Printer: Webcom

Library and Archives Canada Cataloguing in Publication

Guay, David R. P., 1954-, author
Passenger and merchant ships of the Grand Trunk Pacific and Canadian Northern Railways / David R.P. Guay.

Includes bibliographical references and index. Issued in print and electronic formats.

ISBN 978-1-4597-3555-2 (paperback).--ISBN 978-1-4597-3556-9 (pdf).--ISBN 978-1-4597-3557-6 (epub)

1. Grand Trunk Pacific Railway Company. 2. Canadian Northern Railway Company. 3. Ship-railroads--Maritime Provinces--History. 4. Railroads--Maritime Provinces--History. I. Title.

HE2808.G83 2016   385.09715   C2016-901743-5
                                             C2016-901744-3

1 2 3 4 5   20 19 18 17 16

We acknowledge the support of the **Canada Council for the Arts** and the **Ontario Arts Council** for our publishing program. We also acknowledge the financial support of the **Government of Canada** through the **Canada Book Fund** and **Livres Canada Books**, and the **Government of Ontario** through the **Ontario Book Publishing Tax Credit** and the **Ontario Media Development Corporation**.

Printed and bound in Canada.

VISIT US AT

Dundurn.com | @dundurnpress | Facebook.com/dundurnpress |Pinterest.com/dundurnpress

Dundurn
3 Church Street, Suite 500
Toronto, Ontario, Canada
M5E 1M2

To my wife, Maureen, and son, Matthew

CONTENTS

PREFACE

Much has been written with regard to the histories of Canada's great transcontinental railways. However, with the exception of the Canadian Pacific and Canadian National Railways, the story behind their involvement with maritime affairs on salt and fresh water has gone relatively untold. This book attempts to correct this oversight by identifying and describing the various shipping enterprises of the Grand Trunk Pacific and Canadian Northern Railways between 1900 and 1920.

Each chapter after the introduction in the first chapter covers a particular aspect of the maritime operations of one railway on either salt or fresh water. Within this framework, steamer operations are individually described following a chronological and/or geographical order as befits the circumstances.

In order to improve readability of the text, and at the same time provide salient details of the vessels owned/operated, tables have been provided at the end of each chapter describing the most important vessels discussed in that chapter.

As a general rule of thumb, the author has attempted to present at least one photograph or drawing of every vessel that is the subject of a descriptive table, along with a selection of illustrations representing related maritime infrastructure. In some cases, either no photographs were ever taken or none have, as yet, come to light. Photographic quality has also presented some problems. Ideally, only the sharpest and clearest photographs should be used in a book, since these are easily reproduced and readily understood. The author has chosen to include a small number of "marginal" photographs, if for no other reason than that they represent the only photographs available at the time of writing.

The author has provided appendices that describe the house flags and funnels of the steamship lines reviewed in this book, a listing of sources of scale model kits and ship plans available to those who wish to scale model vessels and infrastructure described in this book, and a glossary of nautical abbreviations and terms.

ACKNOWLEDGEMENTS

The author wishes to thank the staff of the University of Minnesota Bio-Medical Library for providing the author access to otherwise unavailable articles, periodical volumes, and books. The assistance of Jacques Marc and Peter Laister and the administrative assistance of Dede Johnston in word processing and then pulling this labour of love together into its final form are gratefully acknowledged, as well.

The author wishes to thank the following individuals and organizations for providing illustrations:

- Archives of Ontario, Toronto, Ontario.
- British Columbia Archives, Victoria, British Columbia.
- Carla Tofinetti.
- Cathy Chapin.
- Centre d'archives de la MRC du Doumaine-du-Roy, Roberval, Quebec.
- City of Vancouver Archives, Vancouver, British Columbia.
- Clydebuilt Ships database (clydesite.co.uk).
- Delta Museum and Archives, Delta, British Columbia.
- Donal Baird.
- Fotocollectie Het Leven, Dutch National Archives, The Hague, Netherlands.
- Historical Collection of the Great Lakes, Bowling Green State University, Bowling Green, Kentucky.
- John O. Greenwood.
- Leonard Gray and John Lingwood.
- Library and Archives Canada, Ottawa, Ontario.
- McCord Museum, Montreal, Quebec.
- Milo S. Ketchum (deceased).
- Niagara Falls Public Library, Niagara Falls, Ontario.
- Peter Searle (searlecanada.org).

- Prince Rupert City and Regional Archives, Prince Rupert, British Columbia.
- Saguenay Historical Society, Chicoutimi, Quebec.
- Salem Public Library, Salem, Oregon.
- Thunder Bay National Marine Sanctuary Database, Alpena County Public Library, Alpena, Michigan.
- Toronto Public Library, Toronto, Ontario.
- Tyne built ships database.
- University of Alaska-Fairbanks, Fairbanks, Alaska.
- University of Washington Archives, Seattle, Washington.
- Vancouver Maritime Museum, Vancouver, British Columbia.
- Vancouver Public Library, Vancouver, British Columbia.
- Wrecksite.eu database.

The author wishes to thank the following organizations for their assistance in completing Appendix 2:

- Dundee City Archives, Dundee, Scotland.
- Glasgow City Archives, Glasgow, Scotland.
- Royal Maritime Museum, Greenwich, England.
- Tyne & Wear Archives, Newcastle, England.
- Vancouver Maritime Museum, Vancouver, British Columbia.
- Wisconsin Maritime Museum, Manitowoc, Wisconsin.

The author also wishes to thank Michael Caroll, Kathryn Lane, Cheryl Hawley, and Kirk Howard of Dundurn Press for their unfailing support of this project.

Any inaccuracies in this book are solely the responsibility of the author.

1

CANADIAN MARITIME TRADE IN THE EDWARDIAN ERA (1900–1914)

INTRODUCTION

The first 13 years of the 20th century were a period of unbridled economic growth, stability, and optimism for the young Dominion of Canada. Prime Minister Sir Wilfrid Laurier pronounced that the 20th century would belong to Canada. The immigration boom of the 1890s and 1900s, under the auspices of Minister of the Interior Sir Clifford Sifton, had filled the "Last Best West" with eager individuals fleeing the pogroms and strife of Continental Europe and Russia. Canada's future role as one of the pre-eminent "granaries of the world" seemed assured.

The railway boom of the 1890s and 1900s also marched along at full blast, thanks in large part to the federal Liberal government's policy of tremendous financial backing, especially for the second and third transcontinental lines of the Grand Trunk Pacific/National Transcontinental and Canadian Northern Railways. Western Canadians had long complained about the rates charged by the Canadian Pacific Railway (CPR), which had a monopoly on railway transportation. Even before the CPR's exclusivity period of 20 years was over, the race was on to bring in competitive rail lines to lower rates. It was also the role of the new transcontinental lines to facilitate immigrant settlement of Prairie lands to the north of the "border-hugging" CPR. This they would do splendidly.

Excellent books are available that describe the political, construction, and economic aspects of the Canadian Northern and Grand Trunk Pacific Railways — see T.D. Regehr, *The Canadian Northern Railway: Pioneer Road of the Northern Prairies, 1895–1918* (Toronto: Macmillan, 1976); G.R. Stevens, *Canadian National Railways: Volume*

2: Towards the Inevitable (Toronto: Clarke, Irwin, 1962); R.B. Fleming, *Railway King of Canada: Sir William Mackenzie, 1849–1923* (Vancouver: University of British Columbia Press, 1994); F. Leonard, *A Thousand Blunders: The Grand Trunk Pacific Railway and Northern British Columbia* (Vancouver: University of British Columbia Press, 1996); and A.W. Currie, *The Grand Trunk Railway of Canada* (Toronto: University of Toronto Press, 1957).

As most Canadians should remember from their school years, both lines would become massively debt-encumbered in the late 1910s, without the possibility of relief by the banking barons of a Britain that was spending itself into pauper status due to the First World War. The Grand Trunk Pacific (and parent Grand Trunk) and Canadian Northern Railways would be bailed out by Sir Robert Borden's Conservative government and combined, along with Canadian Government Railways (former Intercolonial and National Transcontinental Railways), into the government-owned Canadian National Railways (later Canadian National Railway or CNR).

The railway aspects of these lines have been reasonably well studied. However, those aspects surrounding their marine (or maritime) arms have not heretofore been the subject of comprehensive study and publication in a single document until now.

Railway personnel over the years have been interested in the potential symbiotic relationship of combined land and water transportation modes under one corporate banner. This was certainly the case in the United States, at least until 1915 when the Panama Canal Act forbade U.S. railways from owning shipping lines (including ocean-, coastal-, lake-, and river-based shipping lines) due to antitrust considerations. Canadian railways did not suffer this fate. Some lines continued to own their own shipping lines late into the 20th century (Canadian National Marine being sold in 1986) or early 21st century (Canadian Pacific Ships being sold in 2005). Although Algoma Central Corporation still operates Great Lakes and ocean-going bulk carrier and tanker fleets established under Algoma Central Railway ownership, the railway is no longer involved in this endeavour, having been sold in 1995 to Canadian National Railway.

During the formative years of the Grand Trunk Pacific and Canadian Northern Railways, the concept of an integrated transportation network across the British Empire from the United Kingdom to the Far East and India excited the imaginations of empire politicians and transportation business executives. The CPR already had, by 1910, the framework of an integrated transportation network in place, with its Atlantic and Pacific Ocean maritime arms complementing its transcontinental railway. The new transcontinental railways then under construction would be judged on this basis, as well. The pressure on both companies to add maritime arms was enormous as they "tried to make up for lost time" in competition with the CPR.

The balance of this chapter will describe the well-established competitors of the Grand Trunk Pacific and Canadian Northern in the Atlantic and Pacific Oceans and Great Lakes/St. Lawrence River Basin. These are divided as follows:

- Competition for the Grand Trunk Pacific Coastal British Columbia Passenger/Freight Services.

- Competition for the Canadian Northern Transatlantic Passenger/Freight Services.
- Competition for the Canadian Northern and Grand Trunk Pacific Railbarge/Ferry Services in Coastal British Columbia.
- Competition for the Canadian Northern Great Lakes/ St. Lawrence River Basin Passenger/Freight Services.

The chapter will conclude with a discussion of the potential for these new transcontinental lines to expand into the American market via U.S. subsidiary lines.

COMPETITION FOR THE GRAND TRUNK PACIFIC COASTAL BRITISH COLUMBIA PASSENGER/FREIGHT SERVICES

Canadian Pacific British Columbia Coastal Steamships (BCCS)

With the Cariboo Gold Rush and the entry of the Hudson's Bay Company into the fur trade west of the Rocky Mountains, development of coastal British Columbia and Vancouver Island quickened and the need for reliable, scheduled maritime services became paramount. Major coastal operators during the 1870s included an independent (William Moore), the Hudson's Bay Company, and Captain John Irvine's Pioneer Line. However, competition was still "wide open" as fully 40 percent of Victoria, British Columbia–registered tonnage at the time was owned by single or small-party private investors (merchants, traders, manufacturers).

Cigarette cards from the early 20th century, illustrating the house flags and funnels for the Canadian Pacific and Allan Lines. (Ogden's Cigarettes, 1906. Author's Collection.)

The Canadian Pacific Navigation Company (not related to the railway of the same name) was formed in January 1883 by the amalgamation of the Hudson's Bay Company and Pioneer Lines under the management of Captain Irvine, producing a seven-vessel fleet. Competition was still intense, with Joseph Spratt's East Coast Mail Line being the most formidable (Spratt was the original owner of the Albion Iron Works in Victoria). Within a year the East Coast Mail Line was taken over by Canadian Pacific Navigation, while People's Steam Navigation Company provided competition on the Vancouver to/from Nanaimo run between 1884 and 1889.

Canadian Pacific Railway officials realized the need for a transoceanic maritime service on the Pacific Ocean early on to take advantage of the lucrative silk trade and British/Canadian postal subsidies. After a short period of chartering vessels, trans-Pacific services using a trio of CPR-owned "Empress" ships (*Empress of China*, *Empress of India*, and *Empress of Japan*) began in 1891 between Vancouver and Yokohama, Japan (later adding Hong Kong as a destination).

Officials at the CPR also understood the need for a good maritime service to connect the end of rail at Vancouver to Vancouver Island as well as isolated settlements along the B.C. coast. In 1893 an order was placed for a new vessel named *Prince Rupert*. Before the vessel could even reach the West Coast, opposition from Canadian Pacific Navigation and other local interests forced the railway to reconsider. The railway decided to bide its time. When the *Prince Rupert* reached Tenerife, it was recalled and laid up in Plymouth, England, before joining the Canadian Pacific Bay of Fundy steamship service in 1911–12.

By 1898 Vancouver to/from Victoria service had deteriorated and sentiment toward the railway had improved. During the Klondike Gold Rush, Canadian Pacific Navigation had gambled on the Stikine River route to the goldfields and lost out to the Skagway, Alaska–Whitehorse, Yukon route. The CPR had, as well, but could weather the losses. The Hudson's Bay Company, which still had a considerable holding in Canadian Pacific Navigation, was anxious to sell. On January 10, 1901, the CPR secured a controlling interest in Canadian Pacific Navigation. Formal transfer occurred on May 15, 1903, when the red-and-white-checkered house flag was hoisted on the 14 vessels in the fleet: nine propeller steamers and five sidewheeler steamers.

These 14 vessels had 72 ports of call on seven scheduled routes (for details, see table 1.1). The first ship built for the coastal service, *Princess Victoria*, was launched on November 18, 1902, in the U.K. yard of Swan Hunter & Wigham Richardson. An instant success, it was the fastest vessel in coastal service until the *Princess Charlotte* arrived in 1909. Upon the purchase in 1905 of the Esquimalt and Nanaimo Railway on Vancouver Island by the CPR, the former company's passenger steamers, *City of Nanaimo* and *Joan*, were added to the CPR's fleet.

The "triangle service" evolved from the fertile mind of Captain J.W. Troup, general superintendent of BCCS, and the speed of the *Princess Victoria*. This service, between Vancouver, Victoria, and Seattle, was established in September 1908, with the *Princess Victoria* and *Princess Royal* sailing in opposite directions. The Seattle leg was operated at night. For the next 40 years, this would be one of the most important and lucrative services of BCCS.

Beginning in May 1911, the *Princess Alice* and *Princess Adelaide* were operated on a night route between Vancouver and Victoria, a very attractive service to businessmen. Formerly the *Queen Alexandra*, the *Princess Patricia* was purchased in 1911 after catching fire at Greenock in Scotland. Fully reconditioned with an enlarged superstructure to provide enclosed lounges, it entered the Vancouver to/from Nanaimo service on May 11, 1912. One of the most beloved ships on the coast was the *Princess Maquinna*, which served more than 40 ports of call on the west coast of Vancouver Island for many years, starting on July 20, 1913.

By 1913 there were 12 "Princess" steamers, 10 having been built new for BCCS service. The service comprised 22 vessels, including one tow/tugboat and one sternwheeler (*Beaver*), with an aggregate gross tonnage of 30,804. This was quite an accomplishment in only a dozen years by Superintendent Troup (for details, see table 1.1).

Union Steamships of British Columbia

The other major Canadian coastal B.C. steamship company was Union Steamships of British Columbia. This firm was founded by Captain William Webster and John Darling, the latter being a former director and general superintendent of the Union Steamship Company of New Zealand. Officially incorporated on November 16, 1899, it acquired Burrard Inlet Towing Company of Vancouver. Initially, the firm's primary goal was to supply cargo to remote coastal B.C. communities, thus avoiding competition with the CPR's BCCS service. As with other coastal shipping firms, the possibilities of the Klondike Gold Rush could not be ignored and so the company expanded into the Alaskan port trade.

In 1911 J.H. Welsford and Company, a cargo line based in Liverpool, England, purchased controlling interest in the company. Under new management it expanded into the day excursion and resort business by offering passenger services and then building and operating the Selma Park and Sechelt picnic grounds and the Bowen Island resort. The latter included Mount Strahan Lodge, six picnic grounds, more than 150 rental cottages, an octagonal dance pavilion that could handle 800 couples, beach and saltwater pool swimming, and accommodations for many types of sports. A number of large organizations held annual picnic events at Bowen Island Resort. The company remained under British ownership for 26 years. From 1889 until the beginning of the First World War, the company owned 16 vessels, all being propeller steamers and five being tow/tugboats (aggregate gross tonnage of 6,836; for details, see table 1.1).

Alaska Steamship Company

Of American shipping lines with Alaskan ports of call, the Alaska Steamship Company was the most important and would eventually enjoy a near monopoly on passenger and freight service to Alaska. Founded by Charles Peabody, Captain George Roberts, Captain Melville Nichols, George Lent, Frank E. Burns, and Walter Oakes (incorporated on January 21, 1895), the company was sustained initially by the shipment of supplies for construction of the U.S. Government Railroad (eventually to become the Alaska Railroad) from Seward on the coast to Anchorage and Fairbanks in the interior, which encouraged tourism and prospecting for precious metals. The company was reorganized late in 1897.

Timing could not have been better, considering the need to expand the fleet quickly with the onset of the Klondike Gold Rush. The Puget Sound Navigation Company was formed as an inland water subsidiary in Seattle, "great takeoff point for the Gold Rush." As the original small steamers of the Alaska Steamship Company became obsolete for the challenging Alaskan routes, they were transferred to the Seattle area to serve out the rest of their careers. La Conner Trade and Transportation Company was purchased in 1903 and merged with Puget Sound Navigation. Initially rechristened the Inland Navigation Company, the name eventually reverted to the familiar Puget Sound Navigation Company.

A Port Townsend, Washington, to/from Port Angeles, Washington, to/from Victoria route was established by Puget Sound Navigation in 1902. The Pacific Coast Steamship Company (see next section below) could not compete, since all of its ships were still committed to Klondike-related service as the Gold Rush subsided. Canadian Pacific BCCS elected not to compete with Puget Sound Navigation for the time being, although Puget Sound Navigation would be a strong competitor in the Washington State–British Columbia service for many years.

The Alaska Syndicate (funded equally by J.P. Morgan and the Guggenheim Company) purchased the Alaska Steamship Company for the sole purpose of shipping copper ore/concentrates south for smelting from the Bonanza mine at Kennecott via the port of Cordova at the south end of the 195-mile-long Copper River and Northwestern Railway. The company was merged with the Northwestern Steamship Company Limited in 1909, keeping the Alaska Steamship name. This merger gave the company a virtual monopoly in the Alaskan shipping industry. The fleet was expanded to 18 vessels and the service area ranged from Ketchikan, Alaska, in the south to Kotzebue in the far north. In fact, the line served 34 ports of call in southeastern and southwestern Alaska, the Seward Peninsula, the Bering Sea, St. Michael, and Nome (1915). Seattle was the only port of call south of Alaska. In 1912 day-to-day management passed from Charles Peabody to S.W. Eccles of the Guggenheim Company. In 1915 the Kennecott Copper Company was formed and began acquiring Alaska Steamship stock.

Vessels present in the Alaska Steamship Company fleet in 1910 included 14 propeller vessels with an aggregate gross tonnage of 34,308, while the Puget Sound Navigation Company fleet in the same year included five propeller vessels with an aggregate gross tonnage of 3,906 (for details, see table 1.1).

Pacific Coast Steamship Company

This firm began in 1867 as Goodall, Nelson & Perkins and was reorganized in February 1875 as the Goodall, Nelson & Perkins Steamship Company. On October 17, 1876, after yet another reorganization, the Pacific Coast Steamship Company was formed. Although, in the beginning, the firm was primarily involved in the California coastal trade, the Pacific Coast Steamship Company became heavily engaged in the Klondike Gold Rush, transporting prospectors and their goods to Skagway, Alaska, gateway to the goldfields via the Chilkoot and White Passes and the Yukon River. In fact, the company established the first direct regular service between Seattle and

Skagway with the *Ancon*, which left on its first voyage to Skagway on May 17, 1896. The ship returned with $35,000 in gold, a harbinger of things to come.

Although this company ran ships coastwise along the entire western coast of the continental United States, it is the Seattle to/from Alaska route that is of most interest to readers of this book. After 1909 the significance of this line on the Seattle to/from Alaska route was much diminished by the dominance of the Alaska Steamship Company. On November 1, 1916, the Pacific Coast Steamship Company merged with the Pacific-Alaska Steamship Company to form the Pacific Steamship Company.

In 1913 the line had eight propeller and two stern-wheeler vessels engaged in maritime services relevant to this book, with an aggregate gross tonnage of 28,127 (for details, see table 1.1).

Bottom Line

The Grand Trunk Pacific Railway would be entering into a coastal B.C. passenger and freight steamship trade already saturated with vessels of the Canadian Pacific BCCS and Union Steamships of British Columbia lines. It would also be competing with the juggernaut of the Alaska Steamship Company in terms of trade at Alaskan ports. Lastly, the Grand Trunk Pacific would be at loggerheads with U.S. federal law if it attempted to compete in the Alaskan port-to-port trade, since U.S. federal law prohibited non-U.S.-registered vessels from trading between U.S. ports of call. However, as will be discussed subsequently, this would not dissuade the railway from engaging in the Alaskan trade via legal means and otherwise in its attempt to generate eastbound freight at its railway terminus in Prince Rupert, British Columbia.

COMPETITION FOR THE CANADIAN NORTHERN TRANSATLANTIC PASSENGER/FREIGHT SERVICES

Canadian Pacific Railway Atlantic Service

By 1884, well before the transcontinental line of the Canadian Pacific Railway had been completed, arrangements had been made with the Beaver Line for the handling of traffic to and from Liverpool, England, and through the Robert Redford Company of Montreal with the shipping lines that it represented (Donaldson Line and Great Western, Thompson, and Ross Lines).

William Van Horne and George Stephen knew that the CPR would have to establish a first-class line of mail and passenger steamships between Canada and the United Kingdom. The CPR's line would have to be "fully equal in speed and character to any crossing the Atlantic." Obviously, it would contribute greatly to its transcontinental railway and complement its trans-Pacific service. The railway had no interest in owning or chartering inferior ships or cattle carriers in order to obtain a large subsidy. It was hoped that the railway would not have to look to New York City or Boston. Fortunately, it did not. All vessels mentioned in this section were propeller steamers.

Beaver Line

The Canada Shipping Company of Montreal, later named Beaver Line Associated Steamers, was founded in 1867 and began services in 1868 with two sailing ships, *Lake Erie* and

Lake Ontario. From 1872 the company chartered steamers until bringing its own steamers into the fold in 1875 (*Lake Champlain, Lake Nepigon,* and *Lake Megantic*). Apart from a series of maritime disasters, the company held its own until 1894 when the consequences of the financial panic of 1893 made times especially hard for the transatlantic shipping trade. In that year the company went into liquidation and sailings were suspended until 1895 when new managers were hired (Messrs. D. and C. McIver, Liverpool). In 1897 a new company was formed: Beaver Line Associated Steamers. However, this company also ran into financial difficulties, with the last "Lake" sailing taking place in 1898. In 1899 the company was fully taken over by Elder Dempster and Company, which operated it as the Beaver Line of Steamers (see "African Steam Ship Company/Elder Dempster and Company" section below).

China badging from the Beaver Line. (Manufacturer: Cauldon. Author's Collection.)

The railway would initiate its foray into the transatlantic trade by purchasing from Elder Dempster Shipping Limited its Canadian "Beaver Line" fleet of eight passenger and seven cargo ships (for details, see table 1.1). Aggregate gross tonnage of these vessels was 100,869. With speeds of only 12 or 13 knots, none of these steamers approached the ideal of "20 knots to Canada." However, with one stroke, one competitor had been eliminated and the railway finally had an Atlantic service of its own.

The *Lake Manitoba* made the last sailing for the Beaver Line on March 31, 1903. On April 6, on board the *Lake Champlain* in Liverpool, the transition of the line to the CPR was signalled by the hoisting of the red-and-white-checkered house flag of the railway. Together with the *Lake Erie* and *Lake Manitoba,* 33 trips were made from Liverpool that year, carrying 860 first-class, 1,634

second-class, and 23,400 third-class (steerage) passengers. Twenty sailings were also made from Bristol, England. Although primarily a freight service, 325 second-class passengers were carried in 1903 out of Bristol.

The following year the service from Bristol was switched to London and Antwerp, Belgium, with seven vessels sailing regularly out of Antwerp from 1904 until 1914, carrying 188,000 emigrants in third class. When vessels arrived in Montreal, the berths were often dismantled and replaced with portable stalls to carry up to 1,200 head of cattle to London's Deptford Cattle Market!

In 1910 the CPR announced that a number of its older ships would become "one-class cabin steamers." Obviously, first class in these older steamers had ceased to attract passengers who now gravitated to newer and more luxurious ships. To compensate, first class was downgraded to a new designation of "cabin class" with an appropriate downward adjustment in fare charged. The *Lake Champlain* and *Lake Manitoba* were the first such vessels for the CPR.

Atlantic "Empresses"

The railway was well aware that purchasing a ready-made fleet was only a beginning and that fast, new passenger liners would be needed to take full advantage of the through route from Liverpool to Yokohama/Hong Kong. In addition, they would be needed to compete with the Allan Line (discussed in the next section). Contracts were signed in November 1904 for the construction of two 18-knot, 14,190-ton (gross) liners — the *Empress of Britain* and the ill-fated *Empress of Ireland*. The latter was doomed to sink in the St. Lawrence River in the early hours of May 29, 1914, after colliding with the Norwegian collier *Storstad*, leaving 1,012 dead. These were the first liners ordered for the railway's transatlantic service. Although "20 knots to Canada" was still a dream, the railway was inching ever closer to this goal. Further details are available in table 1.1.

Introduction of the new liners soon justified the contention that a "fast line" would help to generate traffic. Apparently, immigrants preferred faster ships, too (perhaps because of fewer potential days with seasickness). Third-class passengers sailing westbound from Liverpool in 1905, 1906, and 1907 numbered 13,871, 23,815, and 34,036, respectively. Third class was no longer steerage on these ships. Although still crowded and plain, dormitory style had given way to cabins and lounges, while dining saloons were provided with real china to replace "eating irons."

China badging from the Canadian Pacific Ocean Services (Atlantic and Pacific). (Manufacturer: Spode. Author's Collection.)

Allan Line

The Allan Line began as the Montreal Ocean Steam Ship Company, founded in 1854 by Hugh Allan, formerly from Glasgow, Scotland. However, much as the British and North American Royal Mail Steam Packet Company became known as the Cunard Line, after its founder Samuel Cunard, the same would happen to the Montreal Ocean Steamship Company. The firm formally became the Allan Line Steamship Company in 1897. The first Allan Line vessel was the *Canadian*, which inaugurated the Liverpool to/from Quebec City to/from Montreal (summer) and to/from Portland, Maine (winter), routes in September 1854. From the line's very beginning, virtually all vessel names ended in *ian*. A pioneer in maritime navigation, the Allan Line could claim a number of

Samples of china badging from British Columbia Coastal Steamships of Canadian Pacific and Allan Line. (Respective Manufacturers: Grindley and Doulton/Burslem. Author's Collection.)

"firsts": the first steel-hulled ship on the Atlantic (*Buenos Ayrean*, 1880), the first ship with bilge keels (*Parisian*, 1881), and the first ships to have three screws (propellers) on the Atlantic (*Victorian* and *Virginian*, 1905).

In 1906 the Allan Line negotiated a new mail contract for a weekly London, England, to/from Canada 17- to 18-knot mail service. It called for two new liners to complement the turbine liners *Victorian* and *Virginian*. This clause gave the CPR its chance. Although the Allan Line had a large fleet, it was aging and many ships had to be replaced soon. It was not in a financial position to do this plus build the two new liners required for the mail service. The two "Empresses" were available, and the railway was able to persuade the Allan family to sublet the mail contract.

In 1908, in great secrecy, a number of meetings took place between the two parties, with Royal Trust acting on behalf of the railway and F.E. Meredith, KC, DCL, of Montreal carrying through the arrangements for ownership transfer. On September 9, 1909, a formal agreement was signed between Meredith and the Allan Line board. The vast majority of shares (57,000) were purchased for £1.6 million, with five Allan Line–affiliated individuals retaining 500 shares each. Allan Line ships continued to sail under the Allan Line house flag and advertising continued using the Allan Line name. Both companies chartered each other's ships in order to maintain advertised schedules. Secrecy was maintained until 1915! Sixteen Allan Line vessels were taken over on January 10, 1915, with an aggregate gross tonnage of 150,811 (for details, see table 1.1).

Another example of china badging from the Allan Line.
(Manufacturer: Ashworth Bros. Author's Collection.)

Other Important North Atlantic Passenger/Freight Lines

African Steam Ship Company/Elder Dempster and Company

The first Elder Dempster Company was formed in 1852 by Macgregor Laird and was named the African Steam Ship Company. The company employed four individuals: Alexander Elder, John Dempster, John Holt, and Alfred Jones. In 1868 the British and African Steam Navigation Company (B&ASN) was formed to compete with the African Steam Ship Company. Since there were no suitable agents in Liverpool other than Fletcher and Parr (who were agents for the African Steam Ship Company), B&ASN asked John Dempster to set up a new agency. Dempster did so, inviting colleague Alexander Elder to join him, and thus Elder Dempster and Company was formed on October 1, 1868. In 1878 Alfred Jones decided to compete with B&ASN using chartered vessels. However, he was subsequently convinced to join Elder Dempster and Company as a junior partner. In 1879 the firm became managers of B&ASN. By 1884 Jones was the senior partner and Elder Dempster and Company began to acquire shares in the African Steam Ship Company. Elder Dempster and Company bought its first vessel in 1887 (*Clare*). In 1891 Elder Dempster and Company became managers of the African Steam Ship Company. This led to both competing companies being managed basically as one by Elder Dempster.

In 1894 the firm entered into the Canadian trade by taking over some of the Canadian routes of the Dominion Line (see "Dominion Line" section below). Four years later the Beaver Line was purchased, securing Liverpool to/from Canada routes. In 1899 the famous Elder Dempster Shipping Limited line was formed. The Imperial Direct West India Mail Services Company was created to commence services to the Caribbean (West Indies). In 1903 Elder Dempster sold its Beaver Line interests along with 15 vessels to the CPR (as previously discussed). After the death of the managing director (Alfred Jones) and sale of company assets to Lords Kylsant and Pirrie in 1910, Elder Dempster and Company Limited was formed.

By 1910 Elder Dempster had only five vessels (aggregate gross tonnage of 17,772) serving Canada on the United Kingdom to/from Quebec City to/from Montreal (summer) and to/from Halifax to/from Saint John, New Brunswick (winter), routes (for details, see table 1.1).

Cairn Line/Cairns, Noble & Company

This line initially was involved in the cargo tramp steamer trade to the Black, Mediterranean, and Baltic Seas and was founded in 1883 by Cairns and Noble of Newcastle, England, and was managed, in turn, by Cairns and Young; Cairns, Young & Noble; and from 1903 onward, the Cairn Line of Steamships (the last named having been founded in 1892). In 1908, after several years of association with the Thomson Line of Dundee, Scotland, the two lines merged as the Cairn Thomson Line. Passenger services of the Thomson Line had begun with the Mediterranean to/from New York City routes with the Southampton to/from Canada route added later. The Thomson Line was the first to carry livestock from Canada to Leith and the Tyne. After the Cairn Thomson Line sold its three passenger liners to the Cunard Line in 1911, it could only carry a maximum of 12 passengers per ship (the maximum that could be carried without a physician on board). Details of the nine vessels on the Canadian routes (aggregate gross tonnage of 39,093) are available in table 1.1.

Dominion Line

The Liverpool and Mississippi Steamship Company was formed in 1870 to trade between Liverpool and New Orleans under the management of Flinn, Main & Montgomery (former sailing ship owners). This was followed by a name change to the Mississippi and Dominion Steamship Company in 1872. Originally, its routes covered Liverpool to/from New Orleans via Bordeaux, France; Lisbon, Portugal; and Havana, Cuba (1870). As immigration was steadily increasing to North America, a Liverpool to/from Quebec City to/from Montreal summer route was added in 1872 under the moniker Dominion Line. This was followed by cancellation of the New Orleans route and the addition of Boston and later Philadelphia and Halifax as destinations in the winter.

In 1885, after being awarded a portion of the Canadian mail contract, the company advertised itself as Dominion Line Royal Mail Steamers. At that time winter sailings occurred between Liverpool and Avonmouth (Bristol) to/from Halifax and Portland, Maine, and between Avonmouth to/from New York City. All but one vessel (*Vancouver*) carried livestock. In the early 1890s, the Dominion Line experienced financial difficulties, resulting in its sale on December 12, 1894, to Richards, Mills & Company in Liverpool, which also owned the British and North Atlantic Steam Navigation Company and its five cargo steamers that plied the Liverpool to/from Boston route, managed by the Warren Line. At that time the British and North Atlantic Steam Navigation Company amalgamated with the Dominion Line. In 1894 Elder Dempster purchased the Avonmouth (Bristol) to/from Canada routes from the Dominion Line.

The giant American-owned cartel known as the International Mercantile Marine Company was formed in 1902 and included several shipping lines (Leyland, Dominion, American, Atlantic Transport, Red Star, and White Star Lines, plus others). Much reallocation of ships and routes then took place. From 1909 onward, the Dominion Line's passenger services became a joint service with the White Star Line, being known as the White

Star–Dominion Line Joint Service. Passenger services in Dominion Line vessels ceased in 1914. For details of the three ships (aggregate gross tonnage of 25,059) on the routes to Canada in 1910, see table 1.1.

Donaldson Line

In 1855 the Donaldson brothers, William and John, founded the firm of Donaldson Brothers. The next year Donaldson Brothers managed the Clyde Line of Packets, which commenced its South American trade with the bark *John Taylor*. A steamer (*Astarte*) was brought into service in 1870 on the routes between Glasgow and eastern South American ports; in 1874 regular services were begun to Canada. Although service to Baltimore started in 1880, the focus of the firm remained on South America and Canada. Passenger services to Canada were initiated in 1905 with the *Athenia*. In 1916 a joint company was formed with the Anchor Line, known as Anchor-Donaldson Limited. All vessels employed by the joint company were owned by Donaldson Brothers. For details of the 10 vessels employed on Canadian routes in 1910 (aggregate gross tonnage of 55,959), see table 1.1.

Furness-Warren Line/Furness, Withy & Company

This shipping line was a successor to the failed White Diamond Steamship Company in 1857. The Liverpool to/from Boston route was continued as George Warren's Line of Liverpool and Boston Packets. Passenger services were begun in 1865 under the name George Warren & Company. In 1898 the line became known as the White Diamond Steamship Company. Four years later Furness, Withy & Company bought a controlling interest in the firm, which now became known as George Warren & Company (Liverpool) Limited. Although predominantly active on the Liverpool to/from Boston route, vessels also called at the ports of Halifax and Philadelphia. For details of the five ships on Canadian routes in 1910 (aggregate gross tonnage of 14,314), see table 1.1.

Hamburg-American Packet Company

Founded in 1847, this firm initiated services from Hamburg, Germany, to New York City via Southampton, with a sailing time of approximately 40 days. The route of Hamburg to/from Quebec City to/from Montreal was one of the earliest North Atlantic routes established for a steamship service (1856). In 1875 the firm acquired the Adler Line and, in 1886, amalgamated with the Carr-Union Line. Control of passenger services to/from Canada of the Hamburg–South America Line, German East Africa Line, and Hansa Line was assumed in 1888. Five vessels from the Eagle Line were purchased upon that firm's collapse. The year 1890 witnessed the takeover of the Hansa Line.

At the same time as the above actions proceeded the firm was also committed to broadening its services worldwide. By 1872 its ships were making weekly voyages to New York, and the company had extended services to include Baltimore, the West Indies, Mexico, South America, China, Japan, and Australia. The year 1873 witnessed the advent of the routes of Hamburg to/from Antwerp to/from Montreal (summer) and Hamburg to/from Antwerp to/from Boston (winter). Later on Saint

John, New Brunswick, and Halifax were added as winter destinations. Details of the five ships serving on Canadian routes in 1910 (aggregate gross tonnage of 29,063) are available in table 1.1.

Manchester Lines

This firm was formed in 1898, subsequent to the opening of the Manchester Ship Canal in 1894, by Christopher Furness of Furness, Withy & Company to operate cargo vessels between Manchester and North American ports. The names of all ships commenced with the word *Manchester*. Routes primarily involved Canadian ports of call (Montreal and Quebec City in summer and Saint John, New Brunswick, and Halifax in winter), especially for the cattle trade, but also eastern U.S. ports as well as Galveston, Texas, and New Orleans for the cotton trade to supply Lancashire textile mills. In 1901 a joint service was established with R.W. Leyland & Company to Philadelphia. Five years later a joint service was established with the same firm to the River Plate in South America. Unfortunately, both services were unsuccessful and regular sailings were discontinued by 1908. Manchester Lines was primarily a cargo-hauling firm, but many of its ships had accommodations for limited numbers of passengers. For details of the seven vessels on Canadian routes in 1910 (aggregate gross tonnage of 29,946), see table 1.1.

North German Lloyd

This firm was founded in 1857 by Bremen merchants Hermann Henrich Meier and Eduard Crüsemann after the dissolution of the Ocean Steam Navigation Company, a joint German-American enterprise. Initially, the route of Bremen, Germany, to/from London was served by a fleet of 500-ton steamers. Transatlantic services to/from New York City began in June 1858, to/from Baltimore in March 1868, and to/from New Orleans in 1869. By 1874 weekly sailings to/from New York City averaged 11 days, 13 hours in duration. A Central American service was initiated in 1871 but was withdrawn in 1874. Bremen to/from Brazil to/from the River Plate and Genoa, Italy, to/from Brazil to/from the River Plate services were inaugurated in 1878, but the latter was withdrawn in 1881. In 1882 the New Orleans service was extended to Galveston, but the entire service was withdrawn by 1886. The year 1886 witnessed the initiation of the Bremen to/from Far Eastern ports and to/from Australia services via the Suez Canal, while the Italy to/from New York City service began in October 1891. A fortnightly service between Bremen and New York City started in 1893 on the Roland Line, the company's wholly owned subsidiary. This service was targeted to the conveyance of cargo and third-class passengers.

The Bremen to/from United Kingdom service was sold in 1897 to the Argo Steamship Company along with seven vessels. The Bremen to/from Galveston service was resurrected in 1898–99. New routes were initiated in 1904 and 1909. The former involved Marseille, France, to/from Naples, Italy, to/from Alexandria, Egypt, while the latter was a joint service (Bremen to/from Hamburg to/from Quebec City to/from Montreal) with the Hamburg-America, Red Star, and Holland America Lines. For details of the two vessels on Canadian routes in 1910 (aggregate gross tonnage of 12,293), see table 1.1.

White Star Line

This company traced its origins back to 1849 when John Pilkington and Henry Threlfell Wilkinson advertised sailings under the moniker White Star Line of Boston Packets. After the discovery of gold in Australia in 1851, the partners began sailings to Australia under the moniker of White Star Line of Australian Packets. For a number of years the partners prospered, operating famous clipper ships to the goldfields. In 1863 the company acquired its first steamer (*Royal Standard*). Unfortunately, the partners made a number of unwise business decisions and were forced into bankruptcy, and liquidation of the firm occurred late in 1867.

Thomas Ismay purchased the "goodwill" and trade name of the company on January 18, 1868. He then commenced sailings with his own vessels to Australia and New Zealand. In conjunction with a Liverpool businessman, Gustav Christian Schwabe, Ismay expanded the firm in 1869 and renamed it the Oceanic Steam Navigation Company. Most vessels had names ending in *ic*. Due to intense competition on the transatlantic routes, Ismay sought to diversify by commencing service through the newly opened Suez Canal to Calcutta, India, and in 1872 with service to South America via Cape Horn. The latter service was terminated in 1874. Joint services with Shaw, Savill and Albion to New Zealand via Cape Town were commenced in 1883 and to Melbourne and Sydney, Australia, in 1899.

Although carriage of passengers across the Atlantic Ocean was of prime importance, from 1888 onward the transport of livestock from North America assumed greater importance over time, and since the movement of passengers and livestock in the same vessels was not ideal, the firm purchased several cargo-only vessels. The participation of the line in the International Mercantile Marine Company of J. Pierpont Morgan, starting in 1902, was discussed earlier (see the previous "Dominion Line" section).

During the late 19th and early 20th centuries, White Star Line steamers left Liverpool for the far corners of the globe, including New York City, Boston, Philadelphia, New Zealand, Valparaiso, San Francisco, Yokohama, Hong Kong, the Azores, Gibraltar, Naples, and Genoa. The last route added prior to the First World War was Liverpool to/from Belfast/Glasgow to/from Quebec City to/from Montreal in 1909. Details of the two vessels on the Canadian routes in 1910 (aggregate gross tonnage of 29,770) are available in table 1.1.

Westbound Transatlantic Voyages in 1910

A perusal of table 1.2 provides a sobering picture of the utilization of Canadian ports of call in 1910 according to passenger lists from Library and Archives Canada. Seven Atlantic ports of call were provided in the passenger lists: Quebec City alone, Montreal alone, Halifax alone, Saint John (New Brunswick) alone, Quebec City followed by Montreal, Halifax followed by Saint John (New Brunswick), and Halifax followed by St. John's (Newfoundland). Only 37 (actual) or 53 (adjusted) calls of 507 total calls at Canadian ports in 1910 were made by vessels under Canadian Northern control (respective percentages of 7.3 and 10.5). The term *adjusted* refers to mathematical adjustment of the actual number of calls to compensate for the entry of the two "Royals" (*Royal Edward* and *Royal George* of Canadian Northern Steamships) into active service halfway through 1910. This fact alone illustrates the tremendous competition for the immigrant traffic out of Europe and the difficult position of the Canadian Northern in trying to break into this market. In addition, an Atlantic steamship cartel made life rather ugly for the predecessor steamship companies of Canadian Northern Steamships (for details, see chapter 5).

Competition for the Canadian Northern and Grand Trunk Pacific Railbarge/Ferry Services in Coastal British Columbia

Victoria Terminal Railway and Ferry/ Great Northern Railway

This railbarge/ferry operation between the Lower Mainland and Vancouver Island/Vancouver is reviewed in detail elsewhere (see chapter 2).

Esquimalt and Nanaimo Railway/ Canadian Pacific Railway

In 1898 a railbarge/ferry slip was built at Ladysmith on Vancouver Island for use by both the Wellington Colliery and Esquimalt and Nanaimo Railways for traffic exchange with the Canadian Pacific Railway. The first loaded car transfer occurred on November 7, 1898, when a car containing flour, consigned to Simon Leiser & Company at Union Bay, was unloaded on Vancouver Island. A formal agreement was concluded between the Esquimalt and Nanaimo Railway and the CPR concerning the railbarge transfer service in 1901.

This service utilized the tow/tugboat *Czar*, a 152-ton 1897 product of T.H. Trahey of Victoria, equipped with a powerful quadruple-cylinder, triple-crankshaft steam engine (11-, 14-, 20-, and 31-inch piston diameters and 24-inch stroke). The *Czar* towed the wooden railbarge *Transfer No. 1*. These vessels were transferred to CPR ownership upon the 1905 acquisition of the Esquimalt and Nanaimo Railway. The railbarge service was administered under the British Columbia Coastal Steamship (BCCS) service banner. Traffic inbound (to Vancouver Island)/outbound in 1907 was a respectable 3,471/2,891 cars.

Increasing traffic volumes required additional tow/tugboats. The *Nanoose* was built new for the railbarge service in 1908 by the British Columbia Marine Railway Company in Esquimalt (305 tons with a compound steam engine with 17- and 40-inch piston diameters and 27-inch stroke). The *Qualicum* (ex-*Colima*), a 1904 product of Heafie and Levy of Philadelphia, was purchased in 1911. The *Nitinat* (ex–*William Joliffe*), an 1885 product of Readhead and Company in the United Kingdom, was purchased in 1914. Tow/tugboats were also chartered on occasion, examples being the *Pilot* and *Lorne* (more details regarding the latter are provided in chapter 4).

Increasing traffic volumes also required additional railbarges. The *Transfer No. 2* was built in 1907. An additional railbarge/ferry slip was constructed in 1908 in Nanaimo. On August 28, 1911, a new steel railbarge (*Transfer No. 3*) was launched. It was built using a new system of longitudinal plating (Isherwood system), being the first such vessel on the Canadian West Coast. This unit was a 254-foot-long, 42-foot-wide, and four-foot-deep monster, with three tracks and a 1,200-ton cargo capacity (in addition to 15 loaded railcars). A new railbarge/ferry slip was erected in Esquimalt in April 1913. This allowed Ladysmith to/from Vancouver railbarge traffic. The *Transfer No. 4*, a virtual carbon copy of the *Transfer No. 3*, was launched on October 23, 1913. The *Transfer Nos. 1–4* were all products of the British Columbia Marine Railway Company. In February 1917, an announcement was made in the *Victoria Daily Colonist* that the Canadian Pacific BCCS would soon let contracts for two additional wooden railbarges, each 156 feet long and 46 feet wide with three tracks, holding up to nine cars.

Bottom Line

Railbarge services were in their infancy on the Canadian West Coast when the Grand Trunk Pacific and Canadian Northern Railways entered the scene. However, the substantial development of the Vancouver to/from Vancouver Island service of the CPR, even at this early date, certainly would limit the potential for such services by these two new transcontinental lines. The Grand Trunk Pacific railbarge service would be limited and based far away from Vancouver Island. This railway would wisely avoid anything to do with the overcrowded (in terms of railway mileage) Vancouver Island. In contrast, Mackenzie and Mann would develop an island branch line and a limited railbarge service, both being in direct competition with pre-existing lines and railbarge services.

COMPETITION FOR THE CANADIAN NORTHERN GREAT LAKES/ ST. LAWRENCE RIVER BASIN PASSENGER/FREIGHT SERVICES

The competitive pressures on a new freight (cargo) steamship line were enormous on the Great Lakes at the turn of the 20th century. Nowhere else in North America was the density of cargo steamships as great as that on the Great Lakes. This was, obviously, due to the rich rewards available to successful owners/managers.

In the interest of space, only a brief survey can be made of the principal lake lines existing from 1900 to 1914, the time period when Canadian Northern initiated and expanded its Great Lakes/St. Lawrence River freight services. Data regarding these competitor lake lines are provided in table 1.3. All vessels mentioned in this section were propeller steamers. It should be noted that there were many more cargo ships owned by one or more individuals in the absence of incorporation or ownership by a joint stock company. These also would be competitors of the Canadian Northern Railway.

Bottom Line

The time period of 1900 through 1914 was one characterized by phenomenal growth in the Great Lakes shipping industry. This was due to the opening of the Canadian West and the economic upturn known as the "Laurier boom." Grain shipments from the Lakehead (Prince Arthur–Fort William, Ontario, today's Thunder Bay) increased almost ninefold (389,300 tons in 1900 versus 3,447,900 tons in 1914). Coal and other commodities kept pace. Shipping tonnage grew even faster, from 30,000 to 300,000 tons over the same period. This translated into more than 130 additional lake vessels (25 lakers, 109 canallers). It was into this environment that Mackenzie and Mann attempted to establish a cargo line to work collaboratively with their railway.

POTENTIAL FOR U.S. SUBSIDIARY SHIPPING LINES

Another issue that needs to be discussed is the impact of the passage of the Sherman Antitrust and Panama Canal Acts by the U.S. Congress in 1890 and 1912, respectively, on the maritime affairs of the Grand Trunk Pacific and Canadian Northern Railways. Although this might be viewed as a rather odd consideration for Canadian railways, the prospects of securing a portion of the lucrative east-west transcontinental U.S. trade to supplement their hard-fought portions of transcontinental Canadian trade held a powerful attraction.

For many years railways on both sides of the U.S./Canadian border had realized the symbiotic relationship of ship- and rail-based transportation modalities on both salt and fresh water. They had joined together in a variety of cartels, one of which was the Association of Lake Lines, predominantly for railway-owned or -controlled shipping lines based on the Great Lakes and the St. Lawrence River. The Minneapolis, St. Paul and Sault Ste. Marie Railroad (aka the Soo Line), a CPR U.S. subsidiary, and the Grand Trunk Railway of Canada had their own American shipping lines. For the Soo Line these included the Minneapolis, St. Paul, & Buffalo Steamship Company

(MStP&BSSCo) and the Lower Lakes Steamship Company (LLSSCo), while for the Grand Trunk this was the Canada Atlantic Transit Company (U.S.).

The Association of Lake Lines was formed at the beginning of the 1895 shipping season. Its other members (with their railway affiliations in parentheses) included the Western Transit Company (New York Central), Union Steamboat Line (Erie), Erie and Western Transportation Company (Pennsylvania), Northern Steamship Company (Great Northern), Lake Erie Transportation Company (Wabash), Lehigh Valley Transportation Company (Lehigh Valley), and Lackawanna Transportation Company (Delaware, Lackawanna, and Western), as well as a number of other lines.

The purposes of this trade association were threefold:

- To orchestrate, in an economical and orderly fashion, all traffic for which its members competed.
- To establish and maintain uniform, reasonable rates, rules, and regulations to prevent unfair discrimination in charges and facilities.
- To co-operate with contracting carriers and adjacent transportation associations.

All members had several characteristics in common:

- They were owned by corporations.
- They were affiliated by ownership or otherwise with connecting railways from which business was interchanged.
- They had close traffic relationships with eastern and western railways, forming a connecting link between

eastern and western lake ports, thereby becoming part of a through route for merchandise, flour, grain, coal, et cetera, between eastern and western North America.

It should be noted that all of the involved lines were American. However, there was no law against Canadian railways incorporating U.S. subsidiary shipping lines as the Canada Atlantic Railway did when it incorporated both Canadian and U.S. shipping arms prior to the railway's acquisition by the Grand Trunk. The Grand Trunk Pacific Railway would do likewise when it incorporated the Grand Trunk Pacific Alaska Steamship Company (see chapter 3).

Most of 1895 was spent on reaching traffic agreements for the division (by percentage) of both eastbound and westbound cargo among member lines. Agreements were also secured over the division of freight rates between the connecting railways and member lines ("lake and rail" rates) and between Erie Canal lines and member lines ("canal and lake" rates). The freight rate structure was formulated by the Trunk Line Association, which served the interests of the regional railways. Thus, with the indirect help of the railways, the Association of Lake Lines operated a tightly knit cartel in which freight rates were set and maintained, and a strict division of U.S. tonnage was followed.

Although considered illegal by the U.S. federal government, this system did prevent ruinous rate wars from developing between member lines. "Canadian" participants were small players among the lake lines. For example, the MStP&BSSCo/LLSSCo allocation of U.S. shipping was 7.3 percent of all eastbound freight, 4 percent of all westbound freight, and 7 percent of pooled eastbound/westbound freight. In 1895 this represented 104,420 eastbound tons and 5,290 westbound tons (total of 109,710 tons). The overall annual tonnages carried eastbound and westbound remained remarkably stable over the lifetime of the association at approximately 1.4 to 1.5 million and 125,000 to 150,000 tons, respectively. The MStP&BSSCo/LLSSCo ranked seventh out of the top eight lines in tonnage carried. It should be noted that this arrangement had no effect at all on Canadian tonnages and freight rates as applied to the Canadian shipping arms of Canadian railways.

Despite the widespread adoption of the railway-shipping line ownership model in the 1890s, by 1900 it was becoming increasingly clear that legislators in Washington, D.C., took a dim view of this model and its logical extension, the Association of Lake Lines. In fact, the U.S. Congress felt that the association (by now swollen to 44 individual units) was engaged in the unlawful activity of maintaining joint freight rates considered "restraint of trade" as forbidden by federal antitrust legislation ("Preliminary Report on Trusts and Combinations," Industrial Commission, House of Representatives, 56th U.S. Congress, 1908).

By 1905 or thereabouts, several scandals involving U.S. railways had been exposed by the "muckraking press." The power and scope of the Interstate Commerce Commission (ICC) had been augmented by the U.S. federal government and affirmed by the courts. It was against this background that the Soo Line (and probably its CPR managers) decided the "writing was on the wall" and it was time to divorce itself from the U.S. Great Lakes steamship business. The 1907 sale of its remaining four ships saw the end of the Soo Line's brief foray into the shipping business.

In 1907 the Grand Trunk Pacific Railway was still two years away from initiating its maritime activities with the leased vessels of the Mackenzie Brothers Steamship Company (see chapter 2). By this time the Canadian Northern Railway had an established presence limited to the Great Lakes and the St. Lawrence River with a handful of cargo vessels. Neither railway was in a position to establish a U.S. shipping subsidiary at this time. Both had missed the golden opportunity.

The year 1912 left no doubt as to the U.S. federal government's view of railway-steamship line associations. Passage of the Panama Canal Act that year forbade U.S. railways from owning, leasing, operating, or controlling common carriers functioning on water (i.e., steamship lines) through canals or elsewhere "with which said railroad or other carrier aforesaid does or may compete for traffic." In 1913 legislation directing the ICC to regulate the railways finally became law.

On May 15, 1915, the ICC dealt a fatal blow to U.S. railway ownership/control of U.S. shipping lines on the Great Lakes when it refused the application of the appellant railways to retain their ownership/control of shipping lines operating on the Great Lakes between Buffalo and other lake ports. The ICC ruled that these railways had to dispose of their lake lines by December 1, 1915. These eight railways, which owned/controlled seven lake lines, were the Pennsylvania, Northern Central, Lehigh Valley, New York Central, Rutland, Erie, Grand Trunk (of Canada), and Delaware, Lackawanna, and Western.

The ICC held that "none of the several existing specified services by water is being operated in the interest of the public or is of advantage to the convenience or commerce of the people within the meaning of the [Panama Canal] act, and that an extension of the respective interests of the petitioners therein will prevent, exclude, and reduce competition on the Great Lakes."

The commission emphasized in its decision that the physical fact of ports of call being served in common by the ships and paralleling rails of the owner/controller railways established a case for competition existing between the two entities. The case was the same when the railway owning/controlling the lake line also owned, through stock control, another railway or was an integral part of a system of rail lines whose paralleling rails served ports of call in common with the lake lines. This was in direct contravention of the Panama Canal Act, which had already forced the railways to divest their saltwater shipping lines. Now the divestiture would be universal.

Bottom Line

It is against this background that the Grand Trunk Pacific and Canadian Northern Railways had to make decisions regarding the development, by acquisition or *de novo*, of U.S. subsidiary shipping lines. Unfortunately, both were late in entering the fray and had missed their opportunities. By 1915 the Canadian Northern was in worsening financial condition due to the absence of British venture capital because of the First World War. The railway was already contracting its various Canadian maritime operations on fresh and salt water. It certainly could not launch any U.S. maritime operation due to the ICC ruling.

The Grand Trunk Pacific was virtually exclusively involved, from a maritime perspective, along the West

Coast from Seattle, Washington, to Skagway, Alaska. The Antitrust and Panama Canal Acts were not issues for the Grand Trunk Pacific, which had only one West Coast terminal (i.e., Prince Rupert, British Columbia). It actively fought the U.S. government with respect to the Alaska port-to-port trade and created several U.S. holdings to foster that battle (Grand Trunk Pacific Alaska Steamship Company, U.S.-registered motor vessel *Tillamook*, and Grand Trunk Pacific Coast Dock Company in Seattle). See chapter 3 to view how this struggle played out.

Table 1.1
Details Regarding Competing Shipping Lines Covered in the Text

Name of Line	Routes	Vessels[a]
Canadian Pacific BCCS	• Vancouver to/from Victoria daily • New Westminster to/from Ladner to/from Steveston daily • Victoria to/from New Westminster thrice weekly • New Westminster to/from Chilliwack thrice weekly • Victoria to/from western coast of Vancouver Island thrice monthly • Victoria to/from Vancouver to/from northern BC thrice monthly • Victoria to/from Vancouver to/from Alaska twice monthly (1903+)	*Beaver*,[b] *Charmer, Joan, Nanoose, Otter, Princess Adelaide, Princess Alice, Princess Beatrice, Princess Charlotte, Princess Ena, Princess Irene, Princess Maquinna, Princess Margaret, Princess Mary, Princess May, Princess Patricia* (I)*, Princess Royal, Princess Sophia, Princess Victoria, Queen City, Tees, Will W. Case* (1913)
Union Steamships of British Columbia	In early days, serviced ports on Howe Sound, along the mainland coast, and logging camps and salmon, etc., canneries along the central coast. Also entered Vancouver to/from Skagway trade during gold rush era. By vessel: • *Coquitlam* (I): primarily in cannery service in Rivers Inlet and Skeena River • *Coquitlam* (I) and *Capilano* (I): Vancouver to/from Skagway (gold rush and beyond) (1889–1914+) • *Cassiar* (I): primarily serviced logging camps on mainland coast (1901–14+) • *Camosun* (I): serviced Vancouver to/from Prince Rupert route and other northern BC ports (1905–14+) • *Cowichan*: serviced logging camps as well as Nanaimo, Denman Island, Union Bay, and Comox (1908–14+) • *Cheakamus*: serviced mainly logging camps and local routes out of Vancouver (1910–14+) • *Chelohsin*: serviced Vancouver to/from Prince Rupert and later on logging camp route to Port Hardy (1911–14+) • *Venture* (I): serviced the northern canneries and Skeena River seasonally (1911–14+)	*Camosun* (I)*, Capilano* (I)*, Cassiar* (1)*, Chehalis, Chelohsin, Cheslakee/Cheakamus, Clutch, Comox* (I)*, Coutli, Coquitlam* (I)*, Cowichan, Leonora, Senator, Skidegate, Vadso, Venture* (I) (1889–1914+)

Table 1.1 Cont'd

Name of Line	Routes	Vessels
Alaska Steamship Company (subsidiary Puget Sound Navigation Company)	• Alaska Steamship Company: Seattle, Washington, to/from only Alaskan ports (1895–1914+)	Alaska Steamship Company: *Alameda, Aleutian* (I), *Cordovo, Dirigo, Dolphin, Dora, Edith, Jefferson, Northwestern, Olympia, Santa Ana, Seward, Victoria, Yucatán* (1910)
	• Puget Sound Navigation Company: Port Townsend, Washington, to/from Port Angeles, Washington, to/from Victoria (1902+)	Puget Sound Navigation Co.: *Chippewa, Whatcom, Iroquois, Rosalie, Indianapolis* (1910)
Pacific Coast Steamship Company	• San Francisco, California, to/from Victoria to/from Port Townsend to/from Seattle • Seattle to/from Prince Rupert, BC, to/from six Alaskan ports, ending at Skagway, Alaska • Seattle to/from Nome, Alaska, to/from St. Michael, Alaska (1913+)	*City of Puebla, City of Seattle*[b], *City of Topeka*[b], *Governor, President, Queen, Senator, Spokane, State of California, Umatilla* (1913)
Beaver Line	• During Elder Dempster ownership: see below under Elder Dempster entry • Pre-Elder Dempster ownership: Liverpool to/from Quebec to/from Montreal and also to/from Portland, Maine/Baltimore, Maryland (until 1894) • Liverpool to/from Quebec to/from Montreal (summer) and to/from Halifax/Portland (winter) (1895–98) • During Canadian Pacific ownership: Liverpool/Avonmouth to/from Quebec to/from Montreal (summer) and to/from Saint John, NB (winter) (1903+)	*Lake Champlain, Lake Erie, Lake Manitoba, Lake Michigan, Milwaukee, Monmouth, Montcalm* (I), *Monteagle, Monterey, Montezuma* (I), *Montfort, Montreal* (I), *Montrose* (I), *Mount Royal, Mount Temple* (I) (1903)
Canadian Pacific Atlantic Service	• Liverpool to/from Quebec to/from Montreal (summer) and to/from Saint John, NB (winter) (1903+)	*Empress of Britain, Empress of Ireland* (1903+)
Allan Line	• Liverpool to/from Quebec to/from Montreal (summer) (1854–1914+) • Liverpool to/from Halifax to/from Portland (winter) (1854–1903) • Glasgow to/from St. John's, NF, to/from Quebec to/from Montreal (1861–1914+) • Liverpool to/from Queenstown to/from Halifax to/from Norfolk, Virginia, to/from Baltimore (1871–92) • London/Le Havre to/from Quebec to/from Montreal (summer) and to/from Saint John, NB (winter) (1888–1914+) • Liverpool to/from Halifax to/from Saint John, NB (winter) (1901–14+)	*Alsatian, Calgarian, Carthaginian, Corinthian, Corsican, Grampian, Ionian, Pomeranian, Pretorian, Sardinian, Scandinavian, Scotian, Sicilian, Tunisian, Victorian, Virginian* (1915)

Table 1.1 Cont'd

Name of Line	Routes	Vessels
Elder Dempster	• Liverpool/Tyne to/from Montreal (summer) and to/from New Orleans, Louisiana (winter) • London to/from Quebec to/from Montreal (summer) and to/from Halifax to/from Saint John, NB (winter) • Avonmouth (Bristol) to/from Quebec to/from Montreal (summer) and to/from Halifax to/from Saint John, NB (winter) (1893–1910+)	*Bornu, Canada Cape, Sobo, Sokoto, Yola* (1910)
Cairn Thomson Line	• Southampton, U.K., to/from Quebec to/from Montreal (1910+)	*Bellona, Cairndon, Cairnrona, Cairntorr, Cervona, Devona, Hurona, Iona, Tortona* (1910)
Dominion Line	• Liverpool to/from Queenstown, Ireland, to/from Quebec to/from Montreal (1872–1914) • Liverpool/Avonmouth to/from Halifax to/from Portland, Maine/Philadelphia (1872–1914)[d] • Liverpool to/from Belfast/Londonderry, Northern Ireland, to/from Quebec to/from Montreal (1886–96)	*Canada, Dominion, Southwark*[c] (1910)
Donaldson Line	• Glasgow to/from Quebec to/from Montreal (summer) and to/from Saint John, NB (winter) (1880–1910+) • Avonmouth to/from Montreal (1894 only)	*Athenia, Cassandra, Indrani, Kastalia, Lakonia, Orthia, Parthenia, Salacia, Saturnia, Tritonia* (1910)
Furness-Warren Line/ Furness, Withy & Company	• Liverpool to/from Boston with calls at Halifax, Saint John, NB, and Philadelphia on some trips (1910+)	*Amanda, Kanawha, Rappahannock, Almeriana, Dahome* (1910)
Hamburg-American Packet Co.	• Hamburg to/from Antwerp, Belgium, to/from Quebec to/from Montreal (summer) and to/from Halifax/Boston (winter) (1873–1910+)	*Badenia, Pallanza, Pisa, Prinz Adelbart, Prinz Oskar* (1910)
Manchester Lines	• Manchester, U.K., to/from Quebec to/from Montreal (summer) and to/from Saint John, NB (winter) (1910+)	*M. Commerce, M. Exchange, M. Importer, M. Mariner, M. Port, M. Shipper, M. Spinner* (1910)[e]
North German Lloyd	• Bremen to/from Hamburg to/from Quebec to/from Montreal (summer) and to/from Halifax (winter) (1909–10+)	*Brandenburg, Willehad* (1910)
White Star Line	• Liverpool to/from Belfast/Glasgow to/from Quebec to/from Montreal (summer) and to/from Halifax (winter) (1909–10+)	*Laurentic, Megantic* (1910)

[a] (I) Refers to the first time (of two or more) that name has been used in the fleet.
[b] Paddlewheeler.
[c] Chartered from American Steamship Company at this time.
[d] Avonmouth route ceased after 1894 after sale of route to Elder Dempster.
[e] M. = Manchester.

Table 1.2
1910 Canadian Ports of Call for Transatlantic Steamship Companies[a]

Line	Ports of Call (Number of Landings)						
	Quebec	Quebec-Montreal	Montreal	Halifax	Halifax–Saint John, NB	Halifax–St. John's, NL	Saint John, NB
Canadian Pacific Railway							
1. "Lake" Ships							
Lake Champlain	--	8	--	--	--	--	1
Lake Erie	--	5	--	1	--	--	2
Lake Manitoba	1	6	--	--	--	--	2
Lake Michigan	4	1	--	--	--	--	2
2. "Empress" Ships							
Empress of Britain	8	--	--	3	5	--	1
Empress of Ireland	7	--	--	3	2	--	5
3. "Mont" Ships							
Montcalm	--	6	--	--	--	--	3
Montezuma	4	1	--	--	--	--	2
Montfort	4	1	--	--	--	--	1
Montreal	5	--	--	--	--	--	3
Montrose	2	3	--	--	--	--	--
4. Miscellaneous							
Monmouth	1	1	2	--	--	--	3
Mount Royal	--	1	--	--	--	--	--
Mount Temple	--	4	--	--	--	--	3
5. Allan Line (MOSS)							
Carthaginian	--	--	--	3	--	4	--
Corinthian	--	5	--	1	--	--	2
Corsican	--	8	--	--	5	--	--
Grampian	--	5	--	1	2	--	--
Hesperian	1	6	--	1	4	--	1
Ionian	7	1	--	2	--	--	--
Mongolian	--	--	--	5	--	1	--
Numidian	--	--	--	3	--	--	--
Parisian	--	--	--	2	--	--	--
Pomeranian	1	3	--	--	1	--	3
Pretorian	--	7	--	4	--	--	--
Sardinian	--	5	--	--	--	--	3
Siberian	--	--	--	5	--	--	--
Sicilian	--	5	--	--	--	1	--
Tunisian	--	7	--	--	6	--	--
Victorian	--	7	--	2	1	--	--
Virginian	--	7	--	1	2	--	--

Table 1.2 Cont'd

Line	Ports of Call (Number of Landings)						
	Quebec	Quebec-Montreal	Montreal	Halifax	Halifax–Saint John, NB	Halifax–St. John's, NL	Saint John, NB
African Steam Ship Co. (Elder Dempster)							
Bornu	--	--	--	--	2	--	--
Canada Cape	--	--	--	--	--	--	1
Sobo	--	--	--	--	--	--	7
Sokoto	--	1	1	--	--	--	1
Yola	--	--	--	--	--	--	1
Cairn/Thomson Line							
Bellona	--	1	--	--	--	--	--
Cairndon	--	--	1	--	--	--	--
Cairnrona	--	5	--	--	--	--	--
Cairntorr	--	--	1	--	--	--	--
Cervona	--	3	--	--	--	--	--
Devona	--	1	2	--	--	--	--
Hurona	--	2	--	--	--	--	--
Iona	--	--	3	--	--	--	--
Tortona	--	4	--	--	--	--	--
Hamburg-American Packet Co.							
Badenia	--	--	--	1	--	--	--
Indrani	--	--	--	--	--	--	1
Pallanza	--	--	--	1	--	--	--
Pisa	--	--	--	1	--	--	--
Prinz Adelbart	2	3	--	--	--	--	--
Prinz Oskar	--	2	--	--	--	--	--
Manchester Liners							
Manchester Commerce	--	--	--	--	--	--	2
Manchester Exchange	--	1	--	--	--	--	--
Manchester Importer	--	5	--	--	--	--	--
Manchester Mariner	1	2	--	--	--	--	--
Manchester Port	--	1	--	--	--	--	--
Manchester Shipper	--	5	--	--	--	--	1
Manchester Spinner	--	2	--	--	--	--	--
North German Lloyd Co.							
Brandenburg	--	--	--	1	--	--	--
Willehad	--	4	--	--	--	--	--

Table 1.2 Cont'd

Line	Ports of Call (Number of Landings)						
	Quebec	Quebec-Montreal	Montreal	Halifax	Halifax–Saint John, NB	Halifax–St. John's, NL	Saint John, NB
White Star Line							
Laurentic	1	6	--	2	--	--	--
Megantic	--	7	--	--	--	--	--
Anglo-Algerian Steamship Co.							
Luristan	--	--	--	--	--	--	1
Furness, Withy							
Amanda	--	--	--	4	--	--	--
Kanawha	--	--	--	1	--	--	1
Rappahannock	--	--	--	--	--	--	2
Furness Line							
Almeriana	--	--	--	1	--	--	--
Dahome	--	--	--	1	--	--	4
Bowring (CT) & Co.							
Florizel	--	--	--	1	--	--	--
Dominion Line							
Canada	--	7	--	8	--	--	--
Dominion	--	8	--	8	--	--	--
Southwark[b]	--	2	--	2	--	--	--
Colchester Steamship Co.							
Briardene	--	--	--	--	--	--	1
Cunard Steamship Line							
Campania	--	--	--	5	--	--	--
West India Line (Pickford & Black)							
Boston	--	--	--	5	--	--	--
Lunishun	--	--	--	1	--	--	--
Ocama	--	--	--	--	--	--	9
Oruro	--	--	--	2	--	--	6
Crown Steamship Co.							
Crown of Navarre	--	1	--	--	--	--	--

Table 1.2 Cont'd

Line	Quebec	Quebec-Montreal	Ports of Call (Number of Landings)				
			Montreal	Halifax	Halifax–Saint John, NB	Halifax–St. John's, NL	Saint John, NB
Donaldson Line							
Athenia	--	6	--	--	--	--	3
Cassandra	--	6	--	--	--	--	3
Kastalia	--	--	--	--	--	--	2
Lakonia	--	5	--	--	--	--	3
Orthia	--	--	--	--	--	--	1
Parthenia	--	1	--	--	--	--	--
Salacia	--	3	--	--	--	--	4
Saturnia	3	2	--	--	--	--	--
Tritonia	--	--	--	--	--	--	1
Miscellaneous Private Vessels							
Roma	--	--	--	1	--	--	--
E.A. Sabian	--	--	--	1	--	--	--
Victoria	--	--	--	1	--	--	--
TOTALS	52	199	10	85	30	6	92
Canadian Northern Steamships							
Royal Edward	--	7	--	1	--	--	--
Royal George	1	6	--	1	--	--	--
Campanello	--	--	--	3	--	--	--
Napolitan Prince	--	--	--	1	--	--	--
Uranium	--	--	--	9	--	--	--
Volturno	--	--	--	8	--	--	--
TOTALS	1	13	--	23	--	--	--

[a] Restricted to Canadian ports of call from overseas embarkation points (i.e., Quebec City, Montreal, Halifax, Saint John, New Brunswick). Sydney, Nova Scotia, and Newfoundland ports of call without also calling at one or more of these four ports of call were not included. In 1910 Newfoundland was not part of Canada. It was a Crown colony.

[b] Was chartered from the American Steamship Company at this time.

Abbreviations: NB = New Brunswick, NL = Newfoundland and Labrador, MOSS = Montreal Ocean Steam Ship Company.

Table 1.3
Details Regarding Competing Great Lakes and St. Lawrence River Freight Shipping Lines in 1910

Name of Line	Organization or Incorporation Date	Names of Vessels
Richelieu and Ontario Navigation Company[c]	1874	*Rochester, Rapids King, Montreal, Kingston, Toronto, Quebec, Brockville, Prescott, Saint-Irénée, Murray Bay, Tadoussac, Hamilton, Belleville, Berthier, Chambly, Cornwall, Terrebonne, Laprairie, Longueil, Boucherville, Varennes, Beaupré, Chicoutimi, Corsican, Fire Fly, Hosanna, Montreal* (2)[b], *St. Lawrence,* and *Sorel* (N = 29).
Canadian Pacific Railway Upper Lake Steamships[c,e]	1884	*Alberta, Athabasca, Manitoba, Assiniboia, Keewatin*[d], and two RORO ferries, *Michigan* and *Ontario* (N = 7)
Midland Navigation Company	1900	*Empress of Midland, Midland King, Midland Prince, Midland Queen,* and *Mount Stephen* (N = 5)
Inland Navigation Company	1908	*Dundurn, Dunelm, Neepawah, Wahcondah, Dundee, Glenellah, Rosedale, Winona, Donnacona,* and *Strathcona* (N = 10)
Northern Navigation Company[c,e]	1899	*Hamonic, Doric, Huronic, Majestic, Germanic, City of Midland, Britannic, City of Toronto, Ionic, Saronic,* and *City of Windsor* (N = 11)
Mathews Steamship Company	1905	*Haddington, Edmonton,* and *Beaverton* (N = 3)
A.W. Hepburn[c]	1883	*Aberdeen, Lloyd S. Porter, Alexandria, Niagara, Reliance,* and *Water Lily* (N = 6)
St. Lawrence and Chicago Steam Navigation Company	1888	*E.B. Osler, G.R. Crowe, W.D. Matthews, Iroquois,* and *Algonquin* (N = 5)
Rathbun Company[e]	1883	*Armenia, Deseronto, Nile, Ranger,* and *Rescue* (N = 5)
Lake Ontario and Bay of Quinte Steamboat Company	1893	*Aletha, North King,* and *Caspian* (N = 3)
Montreal Transportation Company	1869	*Active, Advance, Bartlett, Bothnia, D.G. Thompson, Emerson, Fairmount, Glenmount, Kinmount, Glide, Jessie Hall, Mary P. Hall, Rosemount, Stormount, Westmount, Windsor, Augustus, Brighton, Cornwall, Dunmore, Hamilton, Hector, Hilda, Hiawatha, Huron, John Gaskin, Kildonan, Lapwing, Melrose, Muskoka, Quebec, Selkirk, Senator, Thrush, Ungava, Valencia,* and *Winnipeg* (N = 37)
Farrar Transportation Company	1903	*Collingwood* and *Meaford* (N = 2)
Algoma Central Steamship Line[e]	1900	*Leafield, Paliki, King Edward, Ossifrage, Minnie M, Agawa, Barium, Philadelphia,* and *J.S. Austin* (N = 9)
Canada Atlantic Transit Company[e]	1898	*Geo. N. Orr, Arthur Orr,* and *Kearsarge* (N = 3)

Table 1.3 Cont'd

Name of Line	Organization or Incorporation Date	Names of Vessels
Niagara Navigation Company	1878	*Chippewa, Corona, Chicora, Ongiara,* and *Cayuga* (N = 5)

[a] Not including lines affiliated with Canadian Northern Railway or Steamships or smaller lines.
[b] Refers to the number of times (of two or more) that the name has been used in the company's fleet.
[c] Mixed passenger/package freight/grain.
[d] Still extant. Museum ship in Port McNicoll, Ontario, since 2012.
[e] Railway-affiliated.
Abbreviations: RORO = Roll-on, roll-off.

2

GRAND TRUNK PACIFIC COAST STEAMSHIPS: MACKENZIE BROTHERS LIMITED

Generally overlooked by maritime historians of British Columbia and the Pacific Northwest, Mackenzie Brothers Limited was actively engaged in marine transportation activities for nearly 20 years. Divestiture of the firm in 1910 to the newly incorporated Grand Trunk Pacific Coast Steamship Company kick-started the latter firm's entry into the highly competitive coastal trade of the Pacific Northwest, British Columbia, and Alaska. In addition, the firm was involved in providing railcar barge services for the Great Northern Railway on both the Lower Mainland and Vancouver Island. Captain Simon Mackenzie twice became the general manager of the companies associated with these services!

The Mackenzie brothers came from a family of nine — five of whom were sons and all of whom were born in Inverness on the east coast of Scotland. The company was founded by three brothers, who together emigrated from Scotland in 1888: Simon Francis (1857–1924), Duncan (1863–1943), and William (1868–1947).

Of the three hard-working brothers, Simon was the driving force and guiding light in the business. He continually worked on promotions and schemes in his drive to create wealth. Some did not come to fruition, while others might have had he stayed with them to conclusion. However, his drive to make money led him from one scheme to another, causing occasional financial difficulties. In these times his persuasiveness usually resulted in financial assistance from his brothers and others. Simon managed and developed the firm with an able staff while he carried out the day-to-day affairs, negotiated contracts, chartered ships, and made sure the company's activities were well publicized in local and regional

Simon Francis Mackenzie (far left) and Captain Duncan Mackenzie (far right) on the bridge of the *Prince Rupert*. Identities of other gentlemen and date are unknown. (British Columbia Archives C-07448.)

newspapers. Duncan and William were virtual polar opposites of Simon, both having a quiet, easygoing demeanour. They generally trusted Simon's decisions and were content to serve as officers aboard the company's ships.

Simon began his life on the sea at the age of 13 when he went to work on the steamer *Ocean Wave* wherein his father was the master. This ship was involved in the coastal freighting trade between Inverness and ports on Scotland's west coast, using the Caledonian Canal. The canal was composed of 23 miles of canals, four lakes, and 29 locks, making up a 60-mile system.

After a few years, Simon left to work aboard a freight/passenger steamer (name unknown) travelling to northern Scotland. The year 1878 saw Simon immigrate to the United States where he first worked in the Detroit area and then in the Duluth, Minnesota, region in lake boats, ferries, lumber camps, and construction camps of the Northern Pacific Railway.

During 1880, after some urging from his brother, Duncan also immigrated to the United States. Soon after his arrival, Duncan was offered a fireman's job on a Great Lakes freighter working out of Duluth. In 1884 the two brothers moved west upon learning that Donald, another of their brothers who was working his way to the Pacific coast aboard a British freighter, had died in a Portland, Oregon, hospital. After attending to Donald's affairs, Simon and Duncan decided to remain in Oregon. Simon built the schooner *Venture* for halibut fishing while living in Portland. Duncan was employed as a fireman aboard the tug *Columbia* operating out of Astoria. Simon and Duncan partnered on the *Venture* for many successful trips, and as a result they decided to sell the craft and build a larger schooner. This vessel, called the *Dolphin*, was schooner-rigged and was also fitted with a steam engine. Unfortunately, it was not a successful fishing vessel. Simon had experienced financial difficulties during its construction, which led to its forced sale.

The two brothers then proceeded to Ketchikan, Alaska, where Simon had contracted to construct a cannery building for a Portland-based firm. During the summer of 1888, the brothers returned to Scotland via Vancouver and the transcontinental Canadian Pacific Railway. There is some controversy as to the circumstances surrounding Simon's departure from Ketchikan in terms of whether or not the building had been completed. At home in Inverness, Simon married and together with his wife, Annie, and brothers, Duncan and William, left again for Canada, arriving in Vancouver toward the end of 1888.

Simon initially found work with the Vancouver Co-Op Grocery and Supply Company. Later, after securing financial backing from his brothers and others, he turned again to shipbuilding. He built two coastal steamers, the *Agnes* and *Clyde*, both employed in towing and freighting. The *Agnes* (official no. 94895) was a 67-foot, 23-ton screw (propeller) steamer built in 1889. The *Clyde* (official no. 94898) was an 80-foot, 68-ton screw steamer built in 1889, as well. Both ships were powered by simple single-cylinder steam engines (eight-inch piston diameters) built by Polson Iron Works of Toronto. Both ships were managed and marketed by an agent under the name of an unregistered company, the Vancouver Steam Navigation Company. The two ships generally ventured between False Creek and the north arm of the Fraser River, on occasion going as far as Texada Island, Bute Inlet, and Squamish.

In 1890 the *Clyde* proceeded to the Queen Charlotte Islands (today known as Haida Gwaii) with materials to build a fishing station. Simon and Duncan were master and engineer of the *Clyde*, respectively, while William was engineer aboard the *Agnes*.

Late 1890 saw the initiation of construction of a steam schooner for the pelagic sealing trade. The term *pelagic* referred to the harvesting of seals while at sea. In April 1891, the vessel was launched and christened the *Eliza Edwards* after the daughter of the man financing construction. The *Eliza Edwards* (official no. 100196) was an 82-foot, 55-ton screw steamer. Vancouver City Foundry supplied the dual-expansion steam engine (10- and 18-inch piston diameters and 14-inch stroke). The registered owner was Pacific Traders and Navigation Company Limited, which had been incorporated on March 6, 1891. The three Mackenzie brothers and four others owned this company. William was one of three directors. By this time, the brothers had sold the *Agnes* and *Clyde*. The *Eliza Edwards* departed on June 4, 1891, for the sealing grounds with Simon as master and his two brothers as engineers.

What now happened was the worst possible outcome for the Mackenzie brothers. On June 7 while hunting, the *Eliza Edwards* was stopped by the U.S. Revenue cutter *Thetis*. It was then announced that pelagic sealing would become prohibited effective June 15, 1891. The *Eliza Edwards* then proceeded to Unalaska in the Aleutian Islands where the commander of HMS *Nymph* allowed it to take on coal for the homeward journey. Despite universal advice to the contrary, Simon decided to hunt seals off the Siberian coast. Fortunately, before reaching the area, he took to heart the advice of the captain of the schooner *Henry Dennis* who

warned of the universal seizure of whaling vessels by Russian authorities. As a result, it was decided to end the seal hunt and head for home with the 70 seals already taken.

PELAGIC SEALING

Due to the rapidly depleting number of fur-bearing seals around the Pribilof Islands rookeries, U.S. authorities in 1890 attempted to stop all pelagic sealing, claiming sovereignty over Bering Sea waters. Great Britain protested this unilateral action. Also embroiled in the controversy were the Japanese, Russians, and Canadians. By 1893 an international tribunal struck down the U.S. position and stated that the United States could only control those waters within its three-mile limit. The entire matter was not settled until 1911 when all pelagic sealing was banned, with the exception of the U.S. seal harvesting on the Pribilof Islands. Prior to that, there had been a general agreement that there would be no sealing during the 1891 season. Thus, as it turned out, the Mackenzie brothers were denied sealing during the only year it was banned until 1911. Long before 1911, they had retired from the sealing business.

Upon returning, it was decided to place the *Eliza Edwards* in the passenger/freight business between Vancouver and the Fraser River, after completing an agreement with the Union Steamship Company of British Columbia. By the end of August 1891, fitting-out for its new work assignment had been completed. The deck house had been expanded to accommodate passengers and a wheelhouse had been added. The vessel then began trading out of the Union Steamship dock at the foot of Carrall Street in Vancouver to the farming region of the Fraser River delta. At that time it was quicker and less expensive to use the water route between the two destinations rather than the land route with its few execrable roads then available. Usual cargoes were hay, straw, farm produce, and canned salmon. Traffic on this route did not develop, in the main, because of the increased competition by coasters forced to enter this market by the closure of the pelagic sealing trade.

Therefore, Simon was determined to find a more lucrative trade for the vessel. By late 1891, the *Eliza Edwards* began transporting supplies to Texada Island from Vancouver by way of Nanaimo, where coal was loaded for the mining operations in the vicinity of Vananda (now Van Anda). Still, Simon was not satisfied with this trade and decided to re-enter the halibut fishery after obtaining the backing of two Vancouver businessmen. One was a shareholder in Pacific Traders and Navigation. The *Eliza Edwards* was fitted out with two dories. At this time there was little local demand for halibut. However, Simon Mackenzie felt that there was an opportunity to market winter-harvested fish in the eastern United States where fish stocks were known to be dwindling.

The *Eliza Edwards* made for the fishing grounds in Hecate Strait in mid-December 1891. Moderately successful, they landed 5,000 pounds of halibut. After two weeks, the *Eliza Edwards* returned to Vancouver with 30,000 pounds of halibut. As the fish were unloaded, they were placed in boxes and packed in ice. The next day several CPR refrigerator cars were attached to the *Atlantic Express* for what would be the first shipment of B.C. halibut to the U.S. Atlantic Seaboard. When the shipment headed east, an employee of Mackenzie Brothers accompanied the cargo in order to complete the sale to Boston fish merchants and to arrange future shipments.

Fortunately, the shipment arrived in good condition and fetched a reasonable price. The CPR, seeing the possibility of developing another traffic source, had given the shipment high priority, assuring its fast delivery as well as supplying fresh ice along the route. Unfortunately, no further halibut shipments east were arranged, despite the fact that Simon had journeyed that way later in 1892 to seek markets and to lobby Ottawa for assistance in developing a halibut fishery on Canada's West Coast. Meetings with the New England Fish Company in Boston produced no benefit to the Mackenzie brothers, since that company established its own operation in Vancouver in 1894.

In mid-1892, another money-making opportunity arose. A syndicate of American and Canadian businessmen required a vessel to support a treasure hunt on Cocos Island, 540 miles west by south of Panama (5°35'S, 87°02'W). After refitting and provisioning, the *Eliza Edwards* left Vancouver on June 26, 1892, with the three Mackenzie brothers and a crew of seven.

When asked by the press where the ship was bound, Simon gave misleading information to keep the purpose of the trip a secret. Upon arriving at the island in August, digging began. After two gruelling months, nothing was found.

Following this endeavour, work was found for the *Eliza Edwards* in the Central American-Panamanian-Colombian coastal trade. Simon left the ship in the competent hands of his brothers while he made his way back to Vancouver. April 1893 saw his return to Panama where it was expected that the brothers would continue operations until contracts were fulfilled and then all would head back to Vancouver in the vessel.

At this point the brothers began to disagree on what should be done. On the one hand, Simon felt the *Eliza Edwards* should be sold since it was "not in fit condition to return home." He insisted that the mechanical plant would cause them many problems. Neither Duncan nor William agreed with this assessment and argued against the sale. However, over time, Simon won over Duncan and the vessel was sold to a Panamanian buyer. The other five shareholders in the Pacific Traders and Navigation Company (including his brother, William) were not pleased with Simon's decision to sell, since it had been agreed by all concerned that the vessel would be brought back to Vancouver for further coastal trading.

Duncan and Simon made their way back to the Pacific Northwest via New York City and Chicago (perhaps using the proceeds from the *Eliza Edwards* sale to pay their way). William refused to travel with Simon and made his way back via San Francisco to Astoria where he went to work. Shortly after arriving back in Vancouver, Duncan

moved to Seattle where he gained an engineer's certificate and joined the crew of the 92-foot American coaster *W.H. Harrison* (official no. 081291) of Astoria.

In 1893, when home in Vancouver, Simon began building a small wooden freighter. This was done on land he had purchased with the assistance of his brothers at 1531 Westminster Avenue (now Main Street), which had frontage on False Creek. The shallow-drafted craft christened the *Staffa* was launched on August 29, 1893. The vessel started freighting duties in October. The *Staffa* (official no. 100677) was an 82-foot, 51-ton screw steamer equipped with a simple single-cylinder steam engine (nine-inch piston diameter, 12-inch stroke) manufactured by B.C. Iron Works in Vancouver.

The *Staffa* was registered under the name of Mary MacLean, the Mackenzie brothers' secretary (she later became William's spouse). Most of the time the *Staffa* traded in the areas of Vancouver, the north arm of the Fraser River, the Fraser River delta, and Boundary Bay. The *Staffa*, with only a four-foot draft and a flat bottom, could navigate in the shallow waters of Boundary Bay and up the Serpentine and Nicomekl Rivers as well as some of the sloughs/backwaters of the Fraser River. This facilitated the vessel's navigation on the tidal sections of rivers where it could be loaded directly from small wharves at the edges of farmers' fields, thus saving farmers long and slow wagon trips with produce over poor roads to the Fraser at either Ladner or Brownsville (opposite New Westminster). It was not unusual for the *Staffa* to be caught in a falling tide and settle on the river bottom. There was nothing to fear, however, so loading proceeded. The coaster would then depart on the rising tide. Its cargoes of farm products were taken to New Westminster, Vancouver, Nanaimo, and less frequently, Victoria.

Due to the financial panic of 1893 in the United States, 1894 was not a good year for coastal steamships, and numerous maritime-related businesses went bankrupt or cut wages/services in an attempt to "wait it out." Simon was among those in economic distress. In his case he could not pay the crew members of the *Staffa*, who instigated a lien on the ship for back pay. As a result, Simon was temporarily out of business.

This incident actually was the catalyst for the development of Mackenzie Brothers Limited. To settle the lien against the *Staffa*, Simon had to seek financial assistance from his brothers, who were still working in the United States. After paying off the lien, Duncan and William came on as joint owners of the *Staffa*. Later on the distribution of ownership changed to Annie Mackenzie (Simon's wife) with 32 shares and Duncan and William each with 16 shares. Why Duncan and William put up with Simon's fiscal shenanigans for so many years is unknown. Obviously, filial love and/or loyalty must have played a role in the interrelationships of the Mackenzie family.

In addition to the freighting of farm produce, the *Staffa* also did general freighting between the three ports, carrying bricks, cement, coal, canned fish, lumber, and anything else that had to be moved. Over the next few years, the business climate slowly improved, leading to the construction of two new coasters: the *Fingal* in 1895 and the *Clansman* in 1898. The *Fingal* (official no. 103152) was an 85-foot, 91-ton screw steamer equipped with a single-cylinder steam engine made by B.C. Iron Works

in Vancouver (10-inch piston diameter, 14-inch stroke). The *Clansman* (official no. 107711) was an 82-foot, 72-ton screw steamer. All three coasters were kept busy serving not only the three ports mentioned above but also Texada Island where copper ore or limestone was loaded for delivery to Vancouver.

The year 1895 witnessed the expansion of Mackenzie Brothers' interests into a non-maritime venture when it bought shares in the Gilman Coal Company. This firm supplied the residential coal needs for Vancouver, using Vancouver Island coal. The three ships were used to transport coal from the mines at Wellington (near Nanaimo) to a yard on False Creek. By 1897 Mackenzie Brothers had secured control of Gilman Coal and began to expand it, handling items such as limestone, fertilizers, sand, and bricks. Over time the shipping component of Mackenzie Brothers demanded more and more attention. This, along with competition from other building supply companies, which reduced margins every year, led the brothers to sell off Gilman Coal in 1900.

In 1896 Simon learned that Chilliwack-area farmers were unhappy with the service provided by other firms engaged in the river steamer trade in terms of sending their produce to New Westminster and Vancouver. He offered to supply a steamer, but his proposal was felt to be too expensive and was rejected outright.

He next attempted to start a steamer service between Vancouver and Skagway for which he planned to use three steamers capable of a speed of 14 knots. Seeking the backing of the Vancouver Board of Trade to help promote the idea, he was flatly turned down and the scheme went no further.

At this time the brothers decided to incorporate their business activities. And so was founded Mackenzie Brothers Limited on April 11, 1900. The company took over all assets and liabilities of the proprietors of Mackenzie Brothers, an unincorporated business. It is unclear what happened to the unregistered Vancouver Steam Navigation Company and the incorporated Pacific Traders and Navigation Company in which the Mackenzie brothers were involved. Stated activities of the new firm were wide-ranging, including the ownership and chartering of ships to carry passengers, freight, and mail. The articles of incorporation also demonstrated the wide-ranging tasks to be performed by the incorporators, including conducting business as barge owners, lightermen, freight contractors, conveyers by land and sea, forwarding agents, and general traders. Shares in the firm were held by Annie Mackenzie (2,330 or 50 percent), Duncan Mackenzie (1,165 or 25 percent), and William Mackenzie (1,165 or 25 percent). Simon would be the manager of the firm with a salary of $75 per month ($900 annually). Duncan and William would be paid $65 per month ($780 annually) and $60 per month ($720 annually), respectively.

Among the transportation proposals in 1899 and 1900 for a ferry-railway connection between Vancouver Island and the mainland, the first real interest from the Vancouver populace came from the Mackenzie brothers. The *Victoria Daily Colonist*, perhaps believing that the honour of bringing this project to fruition should go to a Victoria firm/syndicate, was skeptical about the Mackenzie brothers' proposal. As things turned out, the newspaper's skepticism was well founded.

Early in September 1899, Simon Mackenzie visited Victoria to discuss his ideas with the Victoria citizens' transportation committee. While the brothers had in mind a fast-running ferry from the mainland to the Victoria and Sidney Railway terminus at Sidney, they had not resolved where the mainland terminal would be located. Nor was it clear when this and other details would be worked out or when a proposal in contract form would be submitted for the approval of taxpayers who would be asked to subsidize the project to the tune of $125,000 ($12,500 annually for 10 years). With details lacking, the transportation committee rejected the plan outright. The brothers, not wishing to lose their chance, immediately set to work on a refinement of the proposal.

In the meantime, the Great Northern Railway forwarded a proposal to extend its line into Victoria through the use of fast railcar ferries and the Victoria and Sidney Railway. On October 16, 1900, Victoria City Council and the Board of Trade met to consider the proposal. The Great Northern proposed to run railcar ferries initially from Liverpool on the Fraser River to Sidney and then run trains down the Victoria and Sidney Railway (which would become a Great Northern subsidiary) to Victoria. In time the Great Northern would extend its line westward from Liverpool to a suitable coastal location and move the ferry terminal there. Victoria, in turn, had to allow a permanent right-of-way to the Market Building downtown (location of the new Victoria depot), a lease of the Market Building for 50 years at a nominal rent of $100 annually, a tax exemption for that period, and a $15,000 annual cash bonus for 20 years. The Victoria Terminal Railway By-Law, 1900, was passed by City

Council in late October and the voters ratified it on November 29 by a vote of 1,728 for to 319 against.

Within a month or so, Simon Mackenzie, one of the investors in the new project, purchased the barge *Georgian* for temporary use on the Liverpool to/ from Sidney run. This barge had been in use between Vancouver Island and Skagway in the coal trade with the White Pass and Yukon Railway. It had an 800-ton capacity and was 169 feet long but needed some structural changes to make it ready for its new role as a railbarge. On April 13, 1901, the *Victoria Daily Times* covered the preparations for the ferry service, including conversion of the barge to a three-track, 12-railcar-capacity barge:

The Victoria Ferry
Preparations for Temporary
Service via Great Northern

The cars of the Great Northern will be landed in Victoria, at least as far as the present accommodation of the line of the Victoria and Sidney Railway will allow, in a very short time. The big barge on which the tracks are to be placed for the cars to ferry them over from the present terminus of the Great Northern at Liverpool will be taken up next week for the purpose of preparing and fitting her for the work. The detail of a tug has been arranged for, and as soon as the barge is fitted up there will be another great transcontinental line sending its freight in its own cars direct to this city without breaking bulk.

Yesterday, Captain Mackenzie, of the Victoria Ferry Company, and Mr. Paterson, of the Victoria and Sidney Railway, made a special trip over the road to Sidney and there made arrangements for the barge to be pulled up for the work of preparation. The gentlemen were accompanied by Mr. J.D. Lynch, a gentleman from New York, who is said to be here representing the interests of Mr. Hill, of the Great Northern, and Mr. J. Pierpont Morgan, of the syndicate which is said to have a hand in the scheme for control of all the great continental railways. Mr. Lynch evinced great interest in the details of the proposed ferry service and looked carefully over the ground which is proposed to be the terminus. He left last night for Vancouver, accompanying Captain Mackenzie. The latter gentleman said he was not yet able to say when the ferry for freight service would be inaugurated, but it was only a question of a short time, as the preparing of the barge for the tracks to carry the cars was not a task of great magnitude.

In addition, Mackenzie purchased the tow/tugboat *Mystery* to tow the barge *Georgian*. The *Mystery* (official no. 94816) was an 81-foot, 65-ton vessel built in Victoria by W.J. Stephen in 1890. Power was supplied by a two-cylinder compound steam engine (12- and 24-inch piston diameters and 18-inch stroke) built by Albion Iron Works in Victoria. The company also planned for a passenger steamer to operate over the same route. Despite Mackenzie's optimistic assertions, completion of these arrangements would take time. For most of 1901, things would remain much as they had been in 1900 and earlier.

The tow/tugboat *Mystery* grounded on Galiano Island in October 1919. (British Columbia Archives F-02591.)

Finally, the Victoria Terminal Railway and Ferry Company (VTR&F) began to move "into high gear" in October. On October 15, the *Victoria Daily Times* announced that (Simon) Mackenzie had ordered steel rails from England for the new line from Liverpool to the mouth of the Fraser River. On October 16, the *Victoria Daily Colonist* announced that the:

Ladner-Sidney Ferry scheme, which is to give the Great Northern Railway a terminus in Victoria, is progressing favourably. Rails for 13 miles railway from Westminster south to a point just below Ladner have been ordered in England and will come by sailing ship. It is reported that during the summer the line will be completed to the water's edge from the Great Northern Railway station at South Westminster (Liverpool). This winter the attention of the promoters will be directed to putting on fast steamers for the ferry service.

The first general meeting of the VTR&F Company was held in October 1901, and E.V. Bodwell, the principal shareholder, was elected president. Other shareholders included Simon Mackenzie, A.E. Henry, and James Anderson, the general manager designate, who would take over from Thomas Paterson as head of the Victoria and Sidney Railway and Sidney and Nanaimo Transportation Company operations after a period of familiarization.

The Saanich Land Company, which was still the holding company for the Victoria and Sidney Railway and VTR&F Companies, also had new officials: Simon Mackenzie as president, Duncan Mackenzie as vice-president, and Samuel Rounding as company secretary (as well as Victoria station agent!).

On October 22, 1901, after many months of inactivity, the VTR&F finally announced the immediate commencement of the railway extensions. The delay was attributed to difficulty in obtaining funding because the Great Northern was unwilling, initially, to enter into a long-term traffic agreement for the delivery of railcars for a period exceeding 10 years. Eventually, agreement on a period of 25 years was achieved. To speed the process along, it was decided to delay construction of the new railcar ferry and instead use a tow/tugboat and railbarge service for the present. Ground was broken on the Victoria Market Building extension on November 7, 1901.

The VTR&F formally took over the assets of the Victoria and Sidney Railway on October 31, 1901. The commencement of a thrice daily ferry service to the mainland was announced on the same day. Despite the takeover, the two companies continued to operate as separate legal entities. It was stated that an announcement on construction of the ferry and the mainland extension was imminent. The mainland extension was destined never to be built, at least as originally intended.

Thomas Paterson, the guiding light behind the Victoria and Sidney Railway from its construction days, left the company on February 1, 1902. He was succeeded as general manager by Simon Mackenzie. Mackenzie busied himself with directing the renovations of the Victoria Market Building. Carpenters converted one end of the building into a large waiting room, ticket office, and two private offices for company staff. He was also busy on the maritime front, announcing that the steamer *Iroquois* (official no. 107822) would be withdrawn from the Gulf Islands run temporarily to be put on the daily run to the new smelter town of Crofton. The *Iroquois*'s replacement on the islands run was to be the tow/tugboat *Mystery*, which had originally been purchased to team up with the railbarge *Georgian*. The vessel had been temporarily reassigned to the Gulf Islands until the ferry slips at Sidney and Liverpool were completed. After another vessel was found for the Crofton run, the *Iroquois* and *Mystery* were restored to their original assignments.

In an unexpected move, Simon Mackenzie was replaced as general manager by James Anderson. No reason was given for this change. Mackenzie had proven himself a capable manager during his short time in charge.

Work on the ferry dock and barge slip at Sidney was begun in mid-January 1902 and was expected to be completed by mid-February to mid-March. In early March, the area was struck by a severe storm. The dock at Sidney was dangerously exposed to southeasterly winds and the piledriver had been tied to the unfinished barge slip wharf. When heavy seas drove into the wharf, the piledriver crashed into the wharf and both were essentially destroyed. A new piledriver was brought in, and work quickly resumed on the ferry slip, although completion by the scheduled April 1 commencement of the ferry service was unlikely.

It is unknown when exactly the *Mystery* and *Georgian* began railbarge service between Liverpool and Sidney, but April-June 1902 is a reasonable guesstimate. In May 1902, the VTR&F and Sidney and Nanaimo Transportation Company changed owners. The railway and ferry interests were sold to a Victoria syndicate represented by E.V. Bodwell. Under the new ownership, Simon Mackenzie was transferred to Vancouver to look after the VTR&F mainland railcar barge/ferry service. It is possible that Bodwell at this time had bought out the Mackenzies' investment in the companies. In addition, the Great Northern announced another new railbarge service to Vancouver from Liverpool where the Mackenzie Brothers had built a ferry slip at their False Creek yard. The tow/tugboat *Mystery* and the railbarge *Georgian* made the first trip to this slip in June 1902 from Liverpool.

In August 1902, the Great Northern began to negotiate the purchase of the VTR&F through its intermediaries John Hendry and J. Jaffray of Vancouver and A.H. Guthrie of St. Paul, Minnesota. Negotiations for the sale were conducted by General Manager James Anderson, acting on behalf of E.V. Bodwell, and Simon Mackenzie, acting for Guthrie, Hendry, and Jaffray. It should come as no surprise that Mackenzie became the new general manager (for a second time) on October 9, 1902. Exact details of the takeover leaked out over the next few weeks.

The new owners wanted a six-month extension in which to carry out the original terms of the 1900 agreement. They also wanted to substitute a separate fast passenger ferry (18 knots) and slower railcar ferry (10 knots) for the agreed-upon combination ferry. Before agreeing to this, Victoria City Council wanted some answers regarding the role of James J. Hill in the VTR&F. All they received was double talk. Then another complication ensued: Simon Mackenzie resigned as general manager on December 23 after only a short stint and was replaced by Frank Van Sant. Both Mackenzie brothers resigned from the board, as well, and sold their interests in the VTR&F. Simon was involved in litigation against the VTR&F until an amicable resolution was announced in May 1905.

Since this was the end of Mackenzie Brothers' direct involvement with the Victoria and Sidney Railway and VTR&F, we close this chapter in the brothers' lives. Mackenzie Brothers provided the Liverpool to/from False Creek railbarge service until February 1903, at which time the firm stated that the minimal volume of car traffic provided to it was not worth the effort. In any case, on October 1, 1904, a railway bridge over the Fraser River was opened, thus allowing through rail service to Vancouver. This rendered the Liverpool to/from Vancouver railbarge service untenable. The Liverpool to/from Sidney railbarge service was provided, at the latest, until the *Victorian*, a combination passenger and railcar ferry (official no. 161655 [U.S.]/111783 [Canada]), was placed in service on May 7, 1903. It is likely that February 1903 was also the date of cessation of the Liverpool to/from Sidney service, as it was for the Liverpool to/from False Creek service. Beginning about 1903–04, the Victoria Terminal Railway and Ferry Company chartered tow/tugboats (identities unknown) to tow its railbarge *Sidney* on the Liverpool to/from Sidney route. Later, in 1908, the VTR&F bought the tow/tugboat *Earl* (official no. 94906) and built a new railbarge, *Sidney No. 2*, to augment the service.

When the tow/tugboat *Mystery* and the barge *Georgian* were not engaged in the Victoria and Sidney service, they were used to haul coal and coke from Union Bay on Vancouver Island (near Courtenay) to smelters at Ladysmith and Crofton also on Vancouver Island, as well as in the CPR barge service in competition with the VTR&F. The tow/tugboat and railbarge combination also transported railcars carrying coke from the Great Northern rail yard at Seattle to the Crofton smelter. The *Georgian* was employed in these activities until it was lost on March 22, 1905 (see below).

The steamer *Victorian* before its conversion to a passenger/railcar ferry for the Victoria Terminal Railway and Ferry (VTR&F) Company. Photograph was taken at Victoria's inner harbour, circa 1880. (British Columbia Archives A-00151.)

Rear three-quarter view of the *Victorian* passenger and railcar ferry at the Port Guichon dock of the VTR&F Company in 1903. (Delta, British Columbia Museum and Archives 1970-1-1062-1.)

Another of Simon's promotions of 1902 was a plan to develop a pulp mill on the coast. He conceived this plan after hearing that the provincial government wished to bring industry to the province by offering timber grants and water licences to firms that agreed to erect and operate a paper or pulp mill. Simon spent considerable time acquiring timber and water rights as well as having surveys undertaken for what would become known as the Bella Coola Leases. He obtained a Crown Grant of 250 acres for a townsite and then negotiated financial backing from Toronto financiers. Later these same financiers withdrew their support because they felt British Columbia, in their opinion, did not have the potential for a pulp-and-paper industry! Mackenzie's holdings were on Cousins Inlet near the entrance to Dean Channel. In time others acquired the leases and built a paper mill at that site, which became Ocean Falls.

The year 1902 saw an announcement that had major implications for the future of Mackenzie Brothers: the Grand Trunk Railway would build a second transcontinental railway to help settle the Canadian West. This venture would be an alternative to the Canadian Pacific, which had had a virtual monopoly up to that time. In 1903 the Grand Trunk Pacific Railway was incorporated to build and operate the line. The western terminus of the line was to be Prince Rupert on Kaien Island, 600 miles north of Vancouver.

Early in 1902, Mackenzie Brothers successfully bid on a contract to deliver Nanaimo coal to Juneau, Alaska, after underbidding the Alaska Steamship and Pacific Coast Steamship Companies. For this, and in coordination with the regular heavy summer freight schedule north, they chartered the Norwegian Wilhelmsen Line ship *Thordis* for a six-month period. The 339-foot long, 3,735-ton, single-screw steamer had been built in 1899 by Osbourne Graham & Company in Sunderland, England (yard no. 108). Arriving from Japan on April 4, the *Thordis* proceeded to Ladysmith to load coal for Juneau. When it returned to Vancouver, the vessel was loaded with livestock and lumber to be delivered to Whitehorse and Dawson, Yukon Territory, via Skagway.

Effective June 1, 1902, Mackenzie Brothers chartered another Wilhelmsen Line ship, the *Transit*, for five months with an extension option. The ship had been in Nanaimo for five months idle, waiting for a charter. The 1,691-ton ship (official no. 9472 as successor *Takeshima Maru*) had been built in 1889. In May the *Transit* was moved to Vancouver to have passenger accommodations for 600 added after an agreement was concluded with Schubach and Hamilton of Seattle to move employees of the North American Transportation and Trading Company and over 400 gold miners with their freight to Nome, Alaska. Schubach and Hamilton had refused to accept the rates demanded by the Alaska Steamship Company. Instead the firm chartered the *Transit* at a much cheaper rate of $25 per head to Nome, via Victoria, for passage, berth, and meals. When the *Transit* returned from Nome, it was placed in service to/from Prince Rupert to carry passengers and freight.

During 1903, Mackenzie Brothers expanded its activities when it accepted two contracts involving traffic in the North. One contract was to haul copper ore from mines on Prince of Wales Island and the other was to haul livestock north to Alaska. To fulfill these contracts,

A forward three-quarter view of the modified *Victorian*. It appears that the ferry contained only one track and could haul, at most, four freight cars. Special arrangements must have been in place to unload and load cars from the bow. Unless necessitated by the location of the engine room, one wonders why it was not modified to unload and load from the stern. The risk of heavy seas flooding the car compartment and sinking the ferry in the absence of a moveable fore seagate was great, indeed. The photograph is likely from a newspaper and is of marginal quality; however, it is the only one available of the modified *Victorian*. (D.E. Muralt, *The Victoria and Sidney Railway: 1892–1919*.)

the firm purchased two vessels: the former French schooner *Henriette* and the Port Townsend (Washington) tow/tugboat *Escort No. 2*. The *Henriette* (official no. 112254) was built in northwestern France in 1874 as a schooner. After being wrecked on the Columbia River Bar in 1901, the vessel was bought as a hulk by Mackenzie Brothers

and converted into an iron barge in May 1903. The vessel's dimensions were 160 feet long, 30 feet wide, and 19 feet deep (for details, see table 2.1). The tow/tugboat *Escort No. 2* (official no. 116424) was built in Coos Bay, Oregon, in 1882. The 192-/131-ton (gross/net) vessel was 95 feet long, 24 feet wide, and 14 feet deep (for details, see table 2.2).

The ore-hauling contract was with the Northwest Smelting and Refining Company at its Crofton location to which the brothers had been delivering coke from Union Bay since the beginning of its operation in 1902. At first, ore came from nearby mines on Vancouver Island. After adding a second furnace in 1903, ores were accepted from mines all along the coast. Mackenzie Brothers also continued to haul coke to Crofton, not only from Union Bay but also from Seattle from the Great Northern rail yard as previously described.

The second contract was with Pacific Cold Storage of Tacoma, Washington, and called for the transportation of livestock from Vancouver to Yukon Territory/Alaska via Skagway. This firm also had a large cold storage plant at Dawson City, Yukon Territory, as well as at several locations in Alaska. Shipping live animals was an experiment that was necessitated by the unsatisfactory results of shipping frozen meat north. At Skagway livestock was loaded onto stock cars of the White Pass and Yukon Railway for the trip to Whitehorse where they were loaded onto barges for the trip down the Yukon River to Dawson City and beyond.

The first shipment was made on June 9, 1903, wherein 175 cattle, 250 sheep, 50 pigs, and five horses made the trip north. Homebound cargo included ore, canned salmon, and general freight. In 1904, 3,500 head of

From left to right are the tow/tugboats *Escort No. 2*, *Ivanhoe*, and *Queen* followed by the steamers RMS *Oanfa* and *Britannia*. The Johnson wharf is to the left and the Evans, Coleman, and Evans wharf is to the right. The photograph was taken in Vancouver's harbour in 1909. (Vancouver Public Library 5926.)

Smelter wharf at Crofton with the steamers *Henriette* to the left and *Capilano* to the right. Note that the wharf featured a three-track railcar barge slip and moveable overhead ore bunkers. (British Columbia Archives E-02664.)

The *Henriette* soon after conversion from a schooner barge to a twin-screw steamer by the Mackenzie Brothers Steamship Company. Here it is leaving Vancouver for Skagway in 1905. (British Columbia Archives C-07445.)

livestock from Burns of Calgary were shipped north, again by the Mackenzie Brothers, in the *Henriette*. Since there had been a steady increase in northbound general cargo, the brothers had to charter another vessel, the passenger freighter *Venture* (official no. 111776), from its Victoria owners. The *Venture* was chartered for five months beginning at the end of May, a few weeks before northbound traffic usually commenced. Owned by the Boscowitz Steamship Company, the *Venture* displaced 812 tons and was 153 feet long, 36 feet wide, and 10 feet deep. Built by N.P. Shaw in Victoria in 1902, the vessel

was powered by a steam engine with eight- and 18-inch piston diameters and a 12-inch stroke. The *Venture* was destined to be, in part, a livestock carrier.

Early in 1905, Mackenzie Brothers began the conversion of the *Henriette* from an iron barge into a twin-screw steam passenger freighter. A wheelhouse, crew quarters, and accommodations for 50 passengers in 25 staterooms were added. This work was performed at the firm's False Creek yard. On trials in late April, the vessel managed a respectable speed of nine knots. Steam was raised in two eight-foot-diameter, nine-foot-long Scotch boilers at a

Advertisement for Mackenzie Brothers' coal and steamship businesses. The date is between 1895 and 1906, based on the presence of the coasters *Fingal* and *Staffa*. (British Columbia Archives C-00596.)

pressure of 160 pounds per square inch, while power was provided by two fore and aft condensing compound engines. The engines were the product of N. Thompson and Company of Vancouver. The cargo capacity was 1,500 tons.

The "new" *Henriette* entered service on May 5, 1905, at which time in conjunction with the ore trade a northbound freight run to Skagway commenced. Because of the reduced livestock-carrying capacity of the *Henriette* due to its conversion, the barge *Georgian* had to be modified, strengthening it by the addition of trusses and arching of the deck, which was planked over to cover the rails used when it served as a railbarge.

The barge *Georgian* was lost on March 22, 1905, during a gale while in the tow of tow/tugboat *Escort No. 2*. At the time the vessels were bound from Vancouver to Union Bay with 12 railcars, three loaded with machinery, for the Esquimalt and Nanaimo Railway. The tow line broke and the *Georgian* grounded off Brown Point, Hornby Island,

and sank. Luckily, the three-man crew was rescued. Only portions of the machinery and the railcars could be salvaged. Soon, a contract was awarded for a replacement barge named *Georgian II* (official no. 117113), which was launched before mid-May. It was 187 feet long, 39 feet wide, and 10 feet deep, displacing 649 tons.

The first trip north for the season was made starting on June 3 in the tow of the *Escort No. 2*, carrying 175 cattle, 200 hogs, and 500 sheep. Meanwhile, at Britannia Creek on Howe Sound, construction began on a copper mine and concentrator for the Britannia Copper and Gold Company. By August 1905, the mine was ready to ship its first load of ore. Since the Tacoma, Washington, smelter was working at full capacity and would not agree to take Britannia ore, Britannia Copper and Gold bought an interest in the Crofton smelter. Mackenzie Brothers handled transportation of the ore. At first, since the barge *Georgian II* was engaged in the livestock trade, ore was

The Prince Rupert Grand Trunk Pacific yard in 1910 with the barge *Georgian II* docked at the ferry ramp. (British Columbia Archives E-06457.)

moved in scows towed by the chartered *Capilano* of the Union Steamship Company of British Columbia. The *Capilano* (official no. 100203), a 120-foot, 231-ton steamer, was built in 1891.

At about this time Mackenzie Brothers contracted to haul 200,000 tons of copper ore and matte (a partially refined mix of copper and iron) over a two-year period from the Hadley and Mount Andrews mines on Prince of Wales Island to Crofton. The first ore arriving at Crofton on January 15, 1906, came from the Alaska Smelting and Refining Company's Hadley location. For a while the steamer *Henriette* and the barge *Georgian II* were adequate for the task.

It did not take long for the brothers to see that larger-capacity vessels were needed. The first chartered ship, *Duneric* (official no. 106050), from Weir and Company, did not arrive on time. In fact, the vessel would only be chartered for two trips north. The second vessel, *Themis*, from the Wilhelmsen Line, was chartered for six months with an option to purchase. The *Themis* was an 1897 product of Osbourne, Graham, and Company of Sunderland, England. A 270-foot, 1,921-ton vessel, the *Themis* was powered by a triple-expansion engine (20.5-, 33-, and 54-inch piston diameters and 39-inch stroke).

Arriving in May 1906, the vessel began its northbound carriage of freight and southbound transport of

The freighter *Spratt's Ark* on Dominion Day, July 1, 1890. The vessel was rebuilt as the tow barge *Canada* in 1901 by James Hunter. (British Columbia Archives A-01619.)

copper ore and matte. Under the contract, on each northbound trip, 700 to 1,000 tons of Britannia ore were delivered to the Hadley smelter. This was done because each smelter needed the other's ore for purposes of fluxing. Due to the demands of the increased ore/coke contractual commitments, the brothers purchased the 145-foot, 800-ton-capacity barge *Canada*, which entered service in September 1906, towed by the tow/tugboat *Mystery*.

The barge *Canada* had an interesting history. It began as a self-propelled floating cannery owned by Joseph Spratt and was named *Spratt's Ark* (built in 1883, official no. 83452). Powered at first by one and later two horizontal condensing single-cylinder engines (12-inch-diameter cylinder, 18-inch stroke) by Albion Iron Works, the *Spratt's Ark* was rebuilt as a self-propelled freight barge in 1886 and hauled a wide array of goods (coal for the CPR's trans-Pacific steamers, building stone/rock, supplies for the Klondike Gold Rush, and railway equipment, including rolling stock and motive power for the Victoria and Sidney and Esquimalt and Nanaimo Railways). On June 13, 1886, the vessel was a haven to Vancouverites trying to escape a forest fire that destroyed the vast majority of the city's buildings and killed 50 people. One interesting cargo of the *Spratt's Ark* was rolling stock and one locomotive for the Tanana Railway near Fairbanks, Alaska.

The tow/tugboat *J.E. Boyden* is the front vessel followed by the tow/tugboat *Dola* docked at the Johnson Wharf in May 1909. (Vancouver Public Library 2924A.)

In November 1901, the vessel was rebuilt as a tow barge and renamed *Canada* (official no. 111772). The barge would have 14 owners over its approximate 27-year lifespan. The *Canada* was destined to experience only three reported mishaps at sea, although the last would lead to its demise. On April 11, 1898, still called *Spratt's Ark*, the vessel ran over a log in Grenville Channel, which rendered both propellers useless and required a tow to Victoria for repairs. On September 29, 1909, the tow/tugboat *Mystery* and the barge *Canada* ran onto Gossip Reef. The tow/tugboat sank while the barge, only lightly damaged, was towed

to Murchison Bay (at the south end of Whaler Bay, Galiano Island) where the tow/tugboat *Bermuda* picked it up and towed it to Vancouver for repairs. Lastly, the *Canada* capsized during a gale on November 26, 1909, while moored to Kitsilano Buoy in English Bay, Vancouver. Righted and towed to the Wallace Shipyard in North Vancouver, the barge would leave the wharf only to be sunk off Lonsdale Avenue at an undetermined date.

In 1905 the Seattle tow/tugboat *J. E. Boyden* was purchased for towing barges *Georgian II* and *Canada*. When not engaged in the ore trade, the barges were used to ship lumber and coal between ports on Vancouver Island and the mainland. In addition, the *J.E. Boyden* (official no. 122161), an 85-foot tow/tugboat built in 1888 by T.W. Lake of Seattle, was frequently chartered by the CPR to move its railbarges from Ladysmith to Vancouver. The brothers also found work for the vessel towing log booms from Vancouver Island and logging camps up the coast to the Lower Mainland sawmills along the Fraser River. In all, the *J.E. Boyden* remained on the property for two years.

With the direction of the company's business clearly leaning toward the ore trade and northern business, the brothers decided to sell their small coasters. In July 1906, the *Fingal* and *Clansman* were sold to the Coast Steamship Company, followed a few months later by the sale of *Staffa* to three Vancouverites. Up to the time of the sale, the three vessels had been employed in the transportation of farm produce from the Fraser River to Vancouver/Victoria. They had also made trips to other points in the Gulf of Georgia and on Puget Sound, carrying diverse cargoes. At other times these coasters for local trade conveyed bricks from Victoria, cement from Tod Inlet (near Victoria), limestone from Texada Island, and coal and coke from Nanaimo, Ladysmith, and Union Bay on Vancouver Island. They also transported canned salmon from canneries on the Fraser River or salted herring from plants on the Gulf of Georgia to deep-sea freighters loading in Vancouver, Seattle, or Tacoma.

After selling the three ships, the Mackenzie Brothers office was moved from Main Street in Vancouver to 330 Seymour Street. The company also retained ownership of its yard on False Creek.

In October 1906, the *Themis* was re-chartered, this time for one year. Shortly thereafter, the vessel was dry-docked to repair damage caused by grounding on its first trip north in May. On December 14, while southbound in a violent gale, the *Themis* struck a reef off Balaclava Island near Scarlet Point in the Queen Charlotte Islands. The vessel was declared a total loss and was purchased for only $500 by the B.C. Salvage Company in Esquimalt.

To replace the *Themis*, a nine-month charter was arranged for the Norwegian steamer *Haldis* (official no. 151436). At 275 feet long and 1,700 tons displacement, the *Haldis* was built in 1902 by Priestman and Company of Sunderland, England, for Brunsgaard, Kiosterud and Company of Norway. Arriving in February 1907, the vessel was immediately entered into the ore trade, which required the brothers to move 15,000 tons per month from several Prince of Wales Island mines as well as from Treadwell near Juneau and at Carter Bay to smelters in British Columbia and Tacoma, Washington.

On May 24, 1907, the *Henriette* collided with the Hudson's Bay Company river sternwheeler *Hazelton* at the wharf in Port Essington, British Columbia. The latter suffered most from the collision, being left with several hundreds of dollars in damages.

Later in 1907 an additional contract was signed, involving the movement of 3,000 tons of ore from Kassam Bay, Prince of Wales Island. The American barges *Haydn Brown* (official no. 95434) and *Melanope* (official no. 74550) were chartered to keep up with the demands of the ore trade.

At that time Mackenzie Brothers negotiated a joint freight tariff agreement with the White Pass and Yukon

Railway for all points on its line between Skagway and Dawson. Similar agreements were negotiated by the Alaska Steamship, Pacific Coast Steamship, and British Columbia Coastal Steamship (CPR) Companies with the White Pass and Yukon. A condition of the agreement with Mackenzie Brothers called for the Mackenzies to place another freighter in service to handle the movement of hydraulic pipe destined for the Guggenheim gold workings in the Yukon. The pipe was delivered by the Great Northern Railway to New Westminster where it was loaded onto Mackenzie Brothers' vessels. The *Halvard* (official no. 151440), sister ship to the *Haldis*, was chartered for eight months to handle this task. With the arrival of the *Halvard*, an eight-day freight service to Skagway commenced. The first trip began on May 16, 1907, with the *Haldis*. The *Henriette* was also employed in this service.

At about the same time an arrangement similar to that made with the White Pass and Yukon was signed with the Inland Navigation Company, a subsidiary of the Puget Sound Navigation Company of Seattle. Passengers/goods moving from Seattle to Prince Rupert or Skagway would be transferred from the U.S. firm's ships (*Iroquois* or *Chippewa*) to Mackenzie Brothers' vessels in Vancouver. Union Steamships of British Columbia were also included in the same agreement. The agreement was initiated by the Seattle firm in response to its rate war with the CPR, which was seriously eroding Inland's profitable Seattle to/from Bellingham, Washington, to/from Vancouver service. Vancouver to/from Seattle fares had fallen from $3 one way to 25 cents one way!

As early as October 1907, complaints had been expressed by Canadian coastal ship owners on both coasts about the practice of shipping companies chartering foreign-flagged ships and engaging them in Canadian coastal trade. Under Canadian law, ships of 11 countries enjoyed the same privileges as Canadian-owned ships and could operate between Canadian ports. At that time there were about 40 Norwegian ships in such use, most being on the East Coast.

Through the use of foreign-owned ships, charter parties could take advantage of their lower operating costs, often only one-third those of comparable Canadian-owned ships. For example, the charter rates for the Norwegian steamers *Transit*, *Thordis*, *Haldis*, and *Halvard* were $3,500, $3,400, $2,915, and $2,915 per month, respectively, as compared with $3,890 per month for the small British steamer *Duneric*. Monthly wages (Norwegian/American) were $30/$100–$150 for a chief engineer and $22/$80–$100 for a chief officer. Canadian deckhands received double the wages received by their Norwegian counterparts. A Dominion of Canada order-in-council dated January 13, 1908, brought this practice to an end, effective January 1, 1909, on the West Coast and December 11, 1911, on the East Coast.

Fortunately for the brothers, the end of the charter periods of the Wilhelmsen ships *Haldis* and *Halvard* in November 1907 was fast approaching when the bottom fell out of the copper market, at which time the metal's price fell 34 percent. Due to this, the Britannia Mining Group closed down the Crofton smelter and concentrator. For a while the *Henriette* continued to move ore to Ladysmith.

On January 26, 1908, the *Transit* lost its tail shaft and propeller on a voyage from Guaymas, Mexico, to Vancouver. Two vessels saw the *Transit*'s distress signal and responded: the tow/tugboat *Columbia* and the ferry or cargo ship *Tamalpais*. The former was going to charge $1,000 and the latter $6,000 for a tow to Coos Bay, Oregon. Subsequently, the *Columbia* performed the tow. The crew was able to accomplish a very difficult repair with a spare tail shaft and propeller. Although they did not have the proper tools to do the job, the ship was able to limp home from Coos Bay, arriving in Esquimalt on February 5.

In April 1908, on a trip to Steamer Bay, Alaska, Captain Simon Mackenzie captured a large horned owl with an injured wing to provide a mascot for the *Henriette*. The bird was given the run of 'tween decks between ports. It was not a friendly bird (to be expected!), since several crewmen bore the injuries caused by its beak and talons. How long the bird remained a ship's mascot is unknown. In May 1908, Mackenzie Brothers again received the coal contract for Juneau, Alaska, and in June 1908, the *Henriette* added Victoria as a port of call.

Mackenzie Brothers saw an obvious means of expanding the business by moving men, freight, and equipment north from Vancouver for construction of the Grand Trunk Pacific Railway, since the intention was to build the line from both termini (Winnipeg and Prince Rupert). The brothers entered into an agreement with Foley, Welch and Stewart, the primary contractors, to do this. On May 3, 1908, the *Henriette* delivered the first load of explosives and equipment, while on May 9, construction commenced on the roadbed east out of Prince Rupert.

In July 1908, the *Transit*, under a sub-charter to Schubach and Hamilton, was damaged by ice and two plates were broken, requiring temporary repairs before proceeding. In October 1908, Mackenzie Brothers

The waterfront Grand Trunk Pacific office in Prince Rupert in 1908. (Vancouver Public Library 49921.)

reduced its salmon freight rates to make inroads into the trade. Rates from the Skeena River and River's Inlet were lowered by 25 and 30 percent, respectively.

To replace the *Transit* and to continue its contractual obligations within Canada, Mackenzie Brothers chartered the British ship *Powhatan* from Watts and Watts. The vessel arrived on December 4, 1908. On December 6, refitting began at the brothers' yard on False Creek. A two-storey deck house was added from the bridge aft. The lower portion featured a 150-seat dining room with accompanying galley and lounges while the upper part had staterooms. There were 80 first-class staterooms, each having

The *Rupert City* docked in Vancouver, circa 1913. (British Columbia Archives B-01255.)

a single and double berth as well as hot and cold running water. Much of this work had been prefabricated prior to the ship's arrival. There was also accommodation for 250 third-class passengers. The *Powhatan* was also equipped with electric lighting and wireless telegraphy equipment. The ship was 310 feet long, 38 feet wide, and 26.7 feet deep and displaced 2,599 tons (for details, see table 2.3).

Rechristened the *Rupert City* (official no. 93691) and under the command of Captain Duncan Mackenzie, the vessel began its maiden voyage on January 5, 1909, despite the fact that the ship's alterations were not quite

completed. In May the brothers offered two low-priced excursions to Prince Rupert for prospective landowners to see the new city. Both were huge successes, with more than 400 passengers on each trip. Weekend excursions were also made to Ladysmith and Howe Sound.

Shortly after the *Rupert City* was commissioned, the brothers announced their intention to run weekend Vancouver to/from Seattle excursions with the new vessel during the months of the Alaska-Yukon-Pacific Exposition (June 1 to October 16). For the Seattle trip the ship left Vancouver on Saturdays and returned early Monday morning. The excursions would follow the vessel's return from the north. These excursions were run in direct competition with the *Princess Victoria*, *Princess May*, and *Princess Royal* of the CPR's British Columbia Coastal Steamship Service (BCCSS). The general manager of BCCSS warned Mackenzie Brothers against cutting fares on any competing routes. The threat did not deter the brothers. There was ample business for all companies moving passengers to the exposition, despite the reduced fares initiated by several firms, Mackenzie Brothers among them.

Early in 1909, Mackenzie Brothers had made arrangements with the Inland Navigation Company to sell through tickets between Seattle and Prince Rupert. Passengers brought to Seattle by the steamer *Iroquois* would connect with the *Rupert City* for the voyage to Prince Rupert for a fare of $15, a $5 discount from fares of other companies.

The *Transit* was chartered in 1909 to connect directly with Skagway where freight for Yukon Territory and Atlin in British Columbia would continue to be delivered. Southbound, the ship carried copper ore from Alaska to the smelter at Ladysmith. Effective June 30, the *Transit* was sub-chartered to an Austrian industrialist for up to four months for a trip to the Kamchatka Peninsula in Russia and Nome in Alaska. The purpose of the trip was big-game hunting. The *Henriette* took its place in the Skagway service, and Mackenzie Brothers did not re-charter the *Transit*. Upon the *Transit*'s return on October 8, 1909, it left the service of the company.

As mentioned previously, routine service to Prince Rupert began in 1908 when the *Henriette* carried the first of the Grand Trunk Pacific railway construction material

The first visit of the *Rupert City* to Prince Rupert on January 8, 1909. The steamer is docked at the Grand Trunk Pacific dock. (Prince Rupert City and Regional Archives P990-26-5261.)

and equipment. The barge *Georgian II* towed by the *Escort No. 2* also made trips for Foley, Welch and Stewart. In December the barge *Georgian II* arrived in Prince Rupert with two steam shovels, four Davenport tank construction locomotives, and 30 dump cars, all loaded aboard Northern Pacific flat cars. Northern Pacific flat car number 64067 had the distinction of being the first standard-gauge rolling stock landed on Canada's West Coast to supply the Pacific Division of the Grand Trunk Pacific. When the steam shovels, locomotives, dump cars, and loaded flat cars were to be unloaded, this was done at high tide about a half mile south of the Prince Rupert wharf where temporary landing docks had been built. Rails were laid across these docks so that locomotives and rolling stock could be run directly onto sidings on grade prepared for them.

In 1909, as the pace of construction rose, increasing amounts of material had to be hauled. The company purchased the American triple-masted lumber schooner *North Bend* (official no. 130106), which was converted into a barge for carrying construction equipment, explosives, coal, and railway ties to Prince Rupert. Coal was generally loaded at Union Bay. Built at Coos Bay, Oregon, in 1877, the dimensions of the schooner predecessor were 153 feet in length, 32 feet in breadth, and 11 feet in depth (392 net tons, 192 net tons after barge conversion).

On December 2, 1909, the barge *Georgian II* delivered the first "train" for the Pacific Division of the Grand Trunk Pacific when a locomotive, tender, caboose, and 24 flat cars were landed at Prince Rupert. These were all carried in one trip, which was done by rolling flat cars onto other flat cars that had had rails placed on them, thus forming a "double deck." During the construction phase of the Grand Trunk Pacific, more than 400 pieces of railway equipment were moved to Prince Rupert via the barge *Georgian II.*

It was announced that on October 30, 1909, Mackenzie Brothers had purchased the 260-foot, 936-ton twin-screw steamer *Puri* (official no. 98340) after seven months of negotiations with the East Indian owner. The vessel was an 1895 product of Gourlay Brothers and Company in Dundee, Scotland (yard no. 165). On January 22, 1910, it was announced that the *Puri* had stopped in Colombo, Ceylon, on its way to Canada to undergo repairs for damage caused by a monsoon. It does not appear that the sale was finalized, since the vessel was scrapped in July 1910.

In the fall of 1909, with the approach of winter and a reduction in construction work on the Grand Trunk Pacific, there was a drop in northbound traffic. Due to higher operating costs, the *Rupert City* was laid up in November as was the barge *North Bend*. The *Escort No. 2* was chartered out to others and continued in the northern ore-hauling trade from which, by this time, Mackenzie Brothers had gradually withdrawn as American firms became more successful at obtaining contracts.

The Grand Trunk Pacific Railway received a federal government subsidy to provide steamship and mail service to the Queen Charlotte Islands and to Stewart in northern British Columbia. Terms included no fewer than two round trips per month during November through March and no fewer than four round trips per month during the remainder of the year. Calls were to be made at Port Simpson, Naas Bay, Stewart, Masset, Skidegate, Queen Charlotte City, Lockeport, Ikeda Bay, Jedway, Collinson Bay, and Porcher Island. The subsidy was $200 per round trip and would expire on March 31, 1915. The Grand Trunk Pacific Railway chartered the *Henriette* to inaugurate the service. The term of the charter was until the arrival of a steamer that the Grand Trunk Pacific had purchased in the United Kingdom for the service. This was in keeping with a September 1907 press release by the railway that told of the company's intention to operate its own fleet of ships on the West Coast to serve as a feeder for the railway. The Grand Trunk Pacific's first ship was the *Bruno* (official no. 99584), which arrived in Victoria on May 31, 1910. The vessel would be rechristened *Prince Albert* (for details, see chapter 3).

The steamers *Rupert City* and *Henriette* might have cancelled mail as Travelling Post Offices (TPOs) during 1909 and 1910, respectively. The *Rupert City* cancellation (listing S-22) was of type 3D (see images in table 3.4 in chapter 3) with the text VAN. & PRINCE RUPERT, R.P.O./STR. RUPERT CITY. The designation "R.P.O." or Railway Post Office was technically incorrect since all postal cancellations performed on marine vessels were, by definition, performed by TPOs and this latter abbreviation should have been used. The *Henriette* cancellation (listing S-241) was a single one-line use of the ship's name in capital letters (type 22, see images in table 3.4 in chapter 3). It should be noted that these cancellations might have been simply pursers' stamps and had nothing to do with the Canadian postal service. There is still controversy in this regard.

In what was a surprise to many, Mackenzie Brothers Limited was sold to the Grand Trunk Pacific Railway on May 11, 1910. Included in the sale were the *Henriette* and *Escort No. 2*, as well as the barges *Georgian II* and *North Bend*. Under the terms of the sale, Mackenzie Brothers had to turn over contracts held with Foley, Welch and Stewart and withdraw all ships from service. The brothers also agreed not to compete with the Grand Trunk Pacific service to Prince Rupert. On May 26, 1910, Grand Trunk Pacific Coast Steamships Limited was incorporated.

The *Rupert City* was not included in the agreement, since it was under charter and not owned by Mackenzie Brothers Limited. That meant the brothers could continue to find work for the ship. In July 1910, two trips were made to Unalaska in the Aleutian Islands with coal. After that, several voyages from Vancouver to Prince Rupert occurred on behalf of the Grand Trunk Pacific to carry rails, lumber,

and coal. The *Rupert City* sailed to Portland, Oregon, to pick up 1,200 tons of cement for railway construction use and also travelled to Powell River, British Columbia, with machinery for a paper mill being built there. At the end of Mackenzie Brothers' charter in December 1910, the vessel was laid up in Burrard Inlet until sold in 1912 to the Marine Transportation Company.

While records exist to show what the Grand Trunk Pacific paid for the vessels — *Henriette* ($30,000), *Escort No. 2* ($25,000), *Georgian II* ($15,000), and *North Bend* ($2,750) — there is no record of what was paid for the company's goodwill, if anything. No details of the sale were ever made public, and the Grand Trunk Pacific would not comment on a figure of $250,000 that trade journal editors suggested.

Neither Duncan nor William had any knowledge that Simon was negotiating the sale of Mackenzie Brothers to the Grand Trunk Pacific. Based on the share distribution of 50 percent for Simon (through his wife Annie) and 25 percent each for Duncan and William in the incorporation papers for Mackenzie Brothers, this was probably the basis for the distribution of the sale proceeds. The Grand Trunk Pacific offered Simon the job of port captain, which he declined. After the end of the *Rupert City* charter, Simon and his family moved back to Scotland. Four years later the family returned to British Columbia. During those four years, Duncan and William came to realize they had not fared as well as Simon, not only from the company's sale but throughout the years of its operation.

Soon after arriving in Scotland in early 1911, Simon bought the steamer *Amethyst* (official no. 129472) on behalf of the Grand Trunk Pacific for the Queen Charlotte

Islands service. He supervised its conversion from a well-decked coastal freighter into a passenger freighter. Christened *Prince John* by his youngest daughter, the ship reached Vancouver in July 1911 (for details, see chapter 3).

Simon and his family settled in Victoria at the end of 1913. Three years later he moved to Vancouver where he established a ship brokerage and steamship agency, remaining in that business until his death in 1924. In the business world, when it came to publicity, Simon Mackenzie made certain his company was well represented. However, it is known that he often made exaggerated claims and frequently skirted the truth with respect to his company's plans and his own accomplishments. For example, his claims regarding the charters of the steamers *Tottenham* (1907), *Leelanaw* (1909), and *Greenwich* (1909) were clearly false. The *Victoria Daily Colonist* was at fault for presuming the *Braemont* (1908) was under charter to the Mackenzie Brothers. The false rumour that the *Rupert City* would be placed on the Seattle-Vancouver run in competition with the *Iroquois* of Puget Sound Navigation in November 1909 was likely initiated by Simon. The truth about the *Puri*, especially when examined in the context of proximity to the Grand Trunk Pacific negotiations (late 1909–early 1910) as reported, is suspect. The announcement of the brothers regarding the construction of two barges (each being 165 feet long, 36 feet wide, 10 feet deep, and 100 tons capacity) and a tow/tugboat (100 feet long, 20 feet wide, and 11 feet deep) for summer use in 1903 was similarly untrue.

Duncan Mackenzie commanded the *Rupert City* until the end of the charter period and then joined Grand Trunk Pacific Coast Steamships as master of the *Escort No. 2*. Over the years he commanded virtually all of the vessels in the fleet, rising to commodore. However, his record as a master was not spotless. When he was master of the *Prince Albert* in 1914, he was severely reprimanded in Admiralty Court after the wreck at Butterworth Rocks. As master of the *Prince Rupert* in 1920, he had his master's certificate suspended for four months after the wreck at Swanson Bay (for details of both incidents, see chapter 3). In 1922 he became a pilot for the Canadian Government Merchant Marine Limited on the Pacific coast, and in 1929, he joined the recently created Pilotage District of British Columbia. Duncan also served for several years as a director of the Canadian Merchant Service Guild. He retired in 1933 and died in 1943.

William Mackenzie remained as master of the *Escort No. 2* until 1911. He then joined others as a shareholder and built the wooden freighter *Matsqui* on which he served as master. William sold his interest in the ship in 1918 but continued as master until the late 1920s when he left the sea. He and his wife invested in rental properties, which he pursued until his death in 1948.

Although the maritime business affairs of Mackenzie Brothers ceased in December 1910 with the end of the *Rupert City* charter, the company was not voluntarily liquidated until August 6, 1934. By that time all outstanding mortgage agreements and monies due to survivors (principals/heirs) and creditors had been finalized.

Table 2.1

Henriette (official Canadian no. 112254, U.S. no. 219133)

Builder:	Built in France in 1874 by Forges et Chantiers de la Méditerranée (La Seyne et Le Havre).
Engines:	Two fore and aft compound added in 1906 (32 nhp) and removed, circa 1916.
Boiler:	Added in 1906 and removed, circa 1916.
Dimensions:	160 feet long x 30 feet wide x 19 feet deep (as restored schooner).
Funnel:	One.
Masts:	Two (as steamer), four (as schooner).
Propulsion:	Sail, 1874 to 1901; none, 1901 to 1906; twin screws, 1906 to circa 1916; sail, circa 1916 to 1922.
Tonnage:	713 (gross)/588 (net) (as original schooner); 762 (gross)/677 (net) (as restored schooner).
Speed:	10 knots (1906).
Passenger Capacity:	25 (1906).
Freight Capacity:	1,500 tons (1906).
Miscellaneous:	Built 1874 as a four-masted iron schooner. After wrecking on the Columbia River Bar in 1901, the vessel was bought as a hulk by Mackenzie Brothers for $6,000 and converted into an iron barge for the Skagway freight/livestock trade. Converted in 1906 into a twin-screw iron steamer at a cost of $50,000. Rebuilt into a four-masted iron schooner, circa 1916, for use in the Anyox trade.

Owners	Dates
H. Bergasse and Company	1874–87
C. and F. Brunneliere Brothers	1887–circa 1901
Hale and Kern	circa 1901–02
Mackenzie Brothers Steamship Company	1902–10
Grand Trunk Pacific Coast Steamship Co.	1910–circa 1916
Coastwise Steamship and Barge Company (James Griffiths and Sons, managers)	circa 1916–20
Captain Woodside (San Francisco)	1920–22

Incidents

- Wrecked on rocks in Astoria, Oregon, harbour in 1901 in a gale. Raised in 1902.
- In June 1907, lost the blades of its port propeller off Juneau, Alaska, but was able to limp along and slowly complete its voyage on the starboard propeller.
- On March 23, 1908, while loading cattle for Yukon Territory, a loading gangway broke, sending two steers into the water between the ship and the wharf. One was captured quite easily, but the other evaded capture for hours, since it was among the pilings where no boat could go. Eventually, the steer came around and was hauled aboard. Captain S.F. Mackenzie apparently launched into a tirade in Gaelic, the translation of which could not be printed in the newspaper.
- Loaded with horses and explosives for the Grand Trunk Pacific, ran aground on Protection Island off Nanaimo on July 11, 1908. Was later salvaged. Three horses drowned while trying to get them to shore.

Disposition

- Lost on Nukalaila Island in the Ellice group (Fiji area) on August 16, 1922, carrying copra bound for San Francisco. Crew was rescued by British motorship *Hauraki*.

Table 2.2

Escort No. 2 (official Canadian no. 116424, U.S. no. 135572)

Builder:	In Coos Bay, Oregon, in 1882.
Engine:	Condensing two-cylinder (20- and 38-inch piston diameters and 30-inch stroke), 61 rhp; built by Union Iron Works, San Francisco, California.
Boiler:	Received new boiler at Wallace Shipyard, North Vancouver, in May 1910.
Dimensions:	95 feet long x 24 feet wide x 14 feet deep.
Propulsion:	Steam screw.
Tonnage:	146/73 (gross/net) (1882); 192/131 (gross/net) (1907).

Owners	Dates
E. McNeil	1897
Oregon Railroad and Navigation Company	1898–1900
Pacific Cold Storage Company	1903
Mackenzie Brothers Steamships	1903–10
Grand Trunk Pacific Railway Company	1910–18

Disposition

- Converted to fish barge without power in 1917–18. Ultimate fate unknown. Ship registration cancelled in 1917.

Incidents

- On November 8, 1903, vessel was towing the barges *Kerr* and *Georgian* when a storm was encountered in Sabine Pass. Barges got "out of hand," with the *Kerr* crossing vessel's bow and being rammed and the hawser to the *Georgian* breaking. The *Georgian* drifted onto rocks off Texada Island, causing $5,000 in damage.
- On March 22, 1905, in a sou'wester gale, hawser connecting vessel with the barge *Georgian* broke off Hornby Island and barge piled up on rocks a short distance inside Norris Rock. Had nine railcars aboard, three loaded with machinery for Union Bay (Vancouver Island). Barge was a total loss.
- Vessel and the barge *Georgian II* came to the rescue of the steamer *Alaskan* at Cape Mudge where latter had grounded on the rocks at Shelter Point in Discovery Passage on December 9, 1907. Rescuers did not arrive until December 19. The *Alaskan*, in the tow of vessel, arrived in Seattle on December 22, 1907.
- On November 27, 1909, vessel and the barge *Georgian II*, latter carrying the first "train" of the Pacific Division of the Grand Trunk Pacific, had to seek shelter from a gale at Port Alexander at the northern end of Vancouver Island.
- Shortly before February 20, 1910, the coal hulk *Oregon*, under tow of the vessel, grounded at Tantallon Point near Juneau, Alaska. However, was released shortly thereafter.
- On November 21, 1913, the barge *Georgian II* broke away from vessel in Queen Charlotte Sound and drifted ashore where it was pounded to pieces. Vessel, while searching for the lost barge, suffered a broken propeller and was rescued by the SS *Humboldt*.

Table 2.3
Rupert City (official no. 93691)

Builder:	Barrow Shipbuilding Company, Barrow-in-Furness, England, in 1886 (yard no. 141) (as *Powhatan*).
Engine:	Quadruple-cylinder, triple-crankshaft (18-, 18-, 38-, and 60-inch piston diameters and 42-inch stroke).
Boiler:	No data.
Dimensions:	310 feet long x 38 feet wide x 25 feet deep.
Funnel:	One.
Masts:	Two.
Propulsion:	One screw.
Tonnage:	2,536 (gross)/1,640 (net).
Speed:	12 knots.
Passenger Capacity:	150 saloon and 250 steerage passengers after 1908 refit. None after sale to Marine Transportation Company.
Freight Capacity:	3,500 tons (four cargo hatches).
Miscellaneous:	Ship was in B.C. waters from 1908 to 1914. One of the first ships on the B.C. coast with Marconi wireless telegraph installed. Said to be the first passenger vessel to serve Prince Rupert. The Grand Trunk Pacific Coast Steamship Company contracted with the Mackenzie Brothers Steamship Company to provide a Seattle to/from Vancouver to/from Prince Rupert service with this vessel in 1909 and 1910. In 1912 the Marine Transportation Company took over the vessel and placed it on the B.C.-Australia coal trade. Dodwell and Company (N. Hardie, agent) bought the vessel at auction and placed it on the trans-Pacific trade route with Japan.

Owners	Dates
Mediterranean and New York Steamship Company (Phelps Brothers) (as *Powhatan*)	1886–1905
Watts, Watts, and Company (Britain Steamship Company) (name changed to *Rupert City* in 1909)	1905–12
Marine Transportation Company	1912–13
N. Hardie (Dodwell and Company)	1913–14
S. Tsunaakira, Suda T., Dairen (name changed to *Chinto Maru*)	1914–17

Incidents

- Alaska Steamship Company's SS *Ohio* struck a reef in Millbank Sound 250 miles southeast of Ketchikan, Alaska (in B.C. waters) in August 1909. Vessel sent out SOS immediately and the *Rupert City* was one of two vessels to respond. Only five of 213 on board the *Ohio* were lost.
- As he stepped off the *Rupert City* on September 29, 1909, in Vancouver, John Wade, alias Harry Wade, was arrested for defrauding his Prince Rupert partners out of a large sum of money. A miner with a criminal record, Wade had been arrested previously in Vancouver for an incident in Nanaimo. A Prince Rupert officer came down to Vancouver to return Wade to Prince Rupert. Not exactly in the same league as the incident with Dr. Crippen on the CPR steamer *Montrose*!

Disposition

- Sunk by German submarine *U-79* in waters southeast of Cabo de São Vicente, Portugal, on January 4, 1917.

3

"PRINCE" SHIPS (AND OTHER VESSELS) OF GRAND TRUNK PACIFIC COAST STEAMSHIPS

As far back as 1904, the Allan Line had contemplated initiating a trans-Pacific steamship service to China and Japan in connection with the Grand Trunk Pacific Railway. However, nothing further developed in this regard. The Grand Trunk Pacific Railway, through its subsidiary the Grand Trunk Pacific Coast Steamship Company, launched its north Pacific coast steamer service before the completion of the transcontinental line to Prince Rupert. In fact, as discussed previously, the Grand Trunk Pacific Railway contracted with the Mackenzie Brothers Steamship Company to use the *Rupert City* to provide passenger and freight service between Vancouver and Prince Rupert in 1909 and 1910. This was before and concurrent with the beginning of the Grand Trunk Pacific Coast Steamship Company whose letters patent of incorporation were approved on May 26, 1910. After

the arrival of the *Prince Rupert* (see below), the *Rupert City* became a freight-only vessel. Its charter with the company expired on December 15, 1910, and was not renewed. The *Rupert City* (built as the *Powhatan* by the Barrow Shipbuilding Company, Barrow-in-Furness, England, in 1886) was a 310-foot, 2,536-ton, single-screw vessel (official no. 93691). As the *Chinto Maru*, it was a victim of the First World War when it was torpedoed by the German submarine *U-79* on January 4, 1917, off the coast of Portugal (for details, see chapter 2, table 2.3).

The Grand Trunk Pacific Coast Steamship Company leased the propeller freighter *Henriette* from Mackenzie Brothers in 1909, purchasing it in 1910 and using it until 1916 when it was sold to the Coastwise Steamship and Barge Company (James Griffiths and Sons, managers). The *Henriette* had a very interesting history. The vessel

The *Henriette* after restoration to a sailing vessel in 1918. (British Columbia Archives C-07443.)

was built in 1874 near Le Havre, France, as a four-masted schooner. After being wrecked on the Columbia River Bar in 1901, Mackenzie Brothers purchased it as a hulk and rebuilt it in 1902 as an iron barge and in 1906 as a twin-screw, 160-foot-long propeller steamer. This was the vessel leased, then purchased by the Grand Trunk Pacific Coast Steamship Company. In 1916 the ship was converted by its new owners back to a four-masted schooner for the Anyox/Britannia ore trade. On August 16, 1922, it was lost on Nukalaila Island (in the Ellice group) near Fiji, carrying cargo to San Francisco (official Canada no. 112254, U.S. no. 219133; for details, see chapter 2, table 2.1).

In late 1909, Grand Trunk Pacific's engineering staff deposited plans with the Dominion Public Works Department for a wharf to be reconstructed in Victoria on lots 7–13, including and on the southerly portion of lot 14, block 70, having a frontage on Wharf Street of approximately 390 feet, together with the foreshore and water lots in front of the above-cited lots. In early 1910, bids were requested for the Victoria wharf project, which had an estimated cost of $100,000. It was also reported that the company had leased the *Flyer* dock in Seattle and would erect a large wharf complex there at an estimated cost of $250,000.

Grand Trunk Pacific Coast Steamships was capitalized at $100,000, with its head office located in Montreal. Provisional directors included C.M. Hays, W. Wainwright, W.H. Biggar, E.J. Chamberlin, and C.H. Nicholson. Captain C.H. Nicholson, former traffic manager of Northern Navigation in Sarnia, Ontario, was named manager. Officers in 1910 included C.M. Hays, president; E.J. Chamberlin, vice-president; H. Philips, secretary; F. Scott, treasurer; and W.H. Ardley, auditor.

In 1910 the newly built sister ships *Prince Rupert* and *Prince George* arrived from their British builder and began providing express services between Vancouver, Victoria, Prince Rupert, Seattle, and northern ports such as Stewart and Anyox, British Columbia, as well as the Queen Charlotte Islands. These ships were virtually identical products of Swan Hunter & Wigham Richardson of Wallsend, England, in 1910 (respective official nos. 129743 and 129748). The darlings of the company, they were well-appointed vessels, each 307 feet long and displacing 3,380 tons. With pale grey hulls, white

China badging with the "flag-and-leaf" crest of Grand Trunk Pacific Coast Steamships. (Manufacturer: Maddock & Sons. Jacques Marc Collection.)

The *Prince Rupert* docked at the Grand Trunk Pacific pier in Vancouver in 1912. (Vancouver Public Library 13661.)

superstructures, and black funnels, these "greyhounds of the sea" had a service speed of 19 knots. It was very rare at that time for coastwise ships to bear three funnels. Since the competition (Canadian Pacific Railway BCCSS) had broken this unspoken rule with the *Princess Victoria* and *Princess Charlotte*, the Grand Trunk Pacific felt obligated to do so, as well. In addition, the company would have "Prince" ships, not "Princess" ships. With a freight capacity of only 350 tons, it was clear that the upscale passenger trade was the target for these two vessels. Their passenger capacities were 220 (first class) and 36 (second class) (for details, see table 3.1).

In the same year the *Prince Albert* (the former *Bruno*) took over from the *Henriette* on the mail contract between Vancouver, Prince Rupert, and the Queen Charlotte Islands. This had been the contract held previously by the Canadian Pacific Navigation Company and serviced by the steamer *Amur*. The Canadian Pacific Navigation Company had been an important independent coastal shipping line between its founding in 1883 and its purchase by the CPR in 1901. The *Prince Albert* (official no. 99584) was an 1892 product of the Earles Shipbuilding and Engineering Company of Hull, England. Purchased from Thomas Wilson and Sons Company circa 1909, the vessel faithfully served the company until 1923. At that time the ship was sold to Western Freighters Limited to be used in the "Mexican ore trade" (a euphemism for "rum-running" during Prohibition). It ended its days on May 19, 1950, foundering on Vancouver Island (for details, see table 3.2).

In 1911 the *Prince John* was purchased for use on the Queen Charlotte Islands route. The *John*, as it was

Grand Trunk Pacific Coast Steamship Company docks in Prince Rupert in 1913. One company ship lies at anchor (in the right side; note the funnel) next to a non-company ship. (Vancouver Public Library 49919.)

nicknamed, was a beloved ship as evidenced by the following anonymous tribute made in 1930 by an old-timer:

> To the scattered people of the islands, the *John* is more than a ship. She is an institution, a parent, a friend. Often they swear at her; more often they swear by her. She is as steady and as perennially welcome as the rising sun. She crawls into holes with her belly barely clear of the mangling rocks.

She pounds for days into southeast seas, with chairs charging adrift in her dining room, all to bring the mail and provisions and the grace of contact with the outside world to a score of lonely camps and settlements.

Purchased second-hand (although only a year old!), the *Prince John* was a 1910 product of Scott of Bowling, Scotland (as the *Amethyst*). The vessel was 185 feet long,

Grand Trunk Pacific and Canadian National ticket office at 527 Granville Street, Vancouver in 1920. (Vancouver Public Library 10902.)

displaced 905 tons, and was rebuilt into a passenger freighter before entering Grand Trunk Pacific service. Prior to this, the *Prince John* had functioned solely as a cargo-only vessel. This ship was destined to have a quiet, productive life until scrapped in 1951 (official no. 129472; for details, see table 3.3). The *Prince John* arrived in Vancouver in early July 1911. Also received in 1911 at the head office in Vancouver were two magnificent seven-foot-long scale models of the *Prince Rupert* and *Prince George*.

In addition to the "Prince" ships, Grand Trunk Pacific Coast Steamships continued to operate a tow/tugboat-barge service with the tow/tugboat *Escort No. 2* and the barges *Georgian II* and *North Bend* as previously established by Mackenzie Brothers. When not needed for railway purposes, the *Escort No. 2* and its barges were chartered out to carry a wide variety of loads. Examples included ore/matte copper from Anyox to Tacoma, lumber/machinery to Prince Rupert to build a cold storage plant and a sub-agency of the Dominion Marine and Fisheries Department, cross-ties to Prince Rupert for telephone poles, and lumber to Naden Harbour on Graham Island to build a new whaling station. In the latter case the vessels were chartered to a subsidiary of competitor Canadian Northern Railway (Canadian Northern Pacific Fisheries Company). Details of subsequent tow/tugboat–barge services are provided later in this chapter.

It should be recalled that this tow/tugboat–barge service involved much greater distances than similar services on the East Coast or Great Lakes. For example, in late 1912–early 1913, the *Escort No. 2* completed a 2,000-mile towing trip involving three barges. Three barges loaded

Prince George postcard. Date unknown. (British Columbia Archives D-06450.)

The *Prince Rupert* at the Grand Trunk Pacific Coast Steamship Company dock in Victoria, circa 1911. (British Columbia Archives D-08394.)

Grand Trunk Pacific freight sheds and dock in Prince Rupert in 1910. (British Columbia Archives H-01037.)

with lumber were towed from Vancouver, one being dropped at Prince Rupert and the other two at Granby Bay. After unloading, two of these barges were immediately towed back to Vancouver.

In 1912 the *Prince George* and *Prince Rupert* were converted from coal- to oil-burners by the B.C. Marine Railway Company in Esquimalt, using Dahl products. It was also decided to convert the *Prince Albert* and *Prince John* to oil-burners, this being done in 1913.

By 1913 the *Prince Rupert* and *Prince George* had proven very successful in the express service between Vancouver and Prince Rupert and the triangle run between Vancouver, Victoria, and Seattle, which required an average speed of 16.8 knots. The *Prince Rupert* would leave its namesake city at 0900 hours on a Monday,

The *Prince John* in Vancouver's harbour in June 1925. (British Columbia Archives A-07590.)

The *Prince Albert* wrecked at Tipple Island. (British Columbia Archives B-04022.)

arriving at Vancouver at 1630 hours Tuesday; sail at 1800 hours for Victoria, arriving at 2230 hours; and sail at 0000 hours to Seattle, arriving at 0600 hours Wednesday. On Wednesday it would sail at 0900 hours for Victoria, arriving at 1330 hours; sail at 1600 hours for Vancouver, arriving at 2030 hours; and sail at 0000 hours for Prince Rupert, arriving at 0900 hours Friday. The *Prince George* ran the same route on a staggered schedule, leaving Prince Rupert on Friday at 0900 hours and Seattle on Sunday at

0000 hours. Thus, each ship made a complete round trip every five days with only one clear day layover. This was an arduous schedule considering the navigational hazards throughout the tortuous Inside Passage. In addition, six-day "Northern Cruises" were offered using the two ships, running from Victoria and Vancouver to the Alaskan coast across from Stewart and Observatory Inlet (Granby Bay) and returning. Departures occurred on Mondays (*Prince George*) and Thursdays (*Prince Rupert*) in late August

The *Prince Albert* wrecked on Butterworth Rocks on August 18, 1914. (British Columbia Archives B-04025.)

and early September. Other offerings included weekend sailings to Seattle and Thanksgiving Day specials. At the same time, the *Prince John* and *Prince Albert* serviced B.C. outposts north of Prince Rupert, becoming the lifelines for these scattered communities, lumber camps, and mining locations. Later this would be followed by an extension of service to Alaskan ports.

Also in 1913 the first of the Mackenzie Brothers vessels sold to Grand Trunk Pacific Coast Steamships in 1910 would be lost. The barge *Georgian II* broke away from the tow/tugboat *Escort No. 2* in Queen Charlotte Sound on November 21, 1913. The tow/tugboat, while performing a search for the lost barge, suffered a broken propeller and had to be rescued by the steamer SS *Humboldt*. In the meantime the *Georgian II* had been

driven ashore and was pounded to pieces. Fortunately, the vessel's two-man crew was rescued.

In 1915 the Dominion of Canada subsidy to service the Queen Charlotte Islands was ended. As a result, the *Prince John* was taken off the route and one or more tow/tugboats substituted. In the same year the company's mail contract to township 4, Graham Island, was terminated because, in the view of the postal authorities, the one or more tow/tugboats used to provide this service was or were not suitable for the carriage of mail, passengers, and/or freight. The authorities were possibly referring to the tow/tugboat *Escort No. 2*, since this was the only vessel of this type in the possession of the company at that time. The tow/tugboat *Lorne* would not arrive until 1917 (see below). Obviously, they could have also been referring to

Grand Trunk Pacific Coast Steamships uniform button. "Grand Trunk Pacific Steamships" appears on a stippled band around a rippled flag with "GTP" on a maple leaf at its centre. (Author's Collection.)

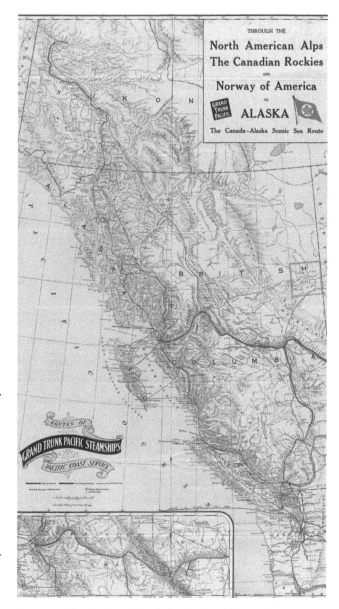

Route map for the Grand Trunk Pacific Coast Steamship Company, 1910 edition, by Poole Brothers, Chicago, Illinois. (University of Alaska-Fairbanks UAF-G3511 P53 1910 P6.)

one or more chartered vessels, the identity or identities of which has or have been lost to time.

The 1915 season mileages of the *Prince Rupert* and *Prince George* were impressive for vessels confined to the coastwise trade of British Columbia. From June 8 through October 30, the *Prince Rupert* logged 40,898 miles. From June 10 through November 2, the *Prince George* logged 40,840 miles. Mean (average) speed was 16.5 knots. On average these vessels arrived six and 10 minutes ahead of schedule on the longest non-stop run of 482 miles when northbound and southbound, respectively.

The inauguration of service to Alaskan territory occurred on March 27, 1916, when the *Prince John* began a Prince

Rupert to/from Skagway service. Other Alaskan ports such as Juneau and Ketchikan were soon added. Business was so good that the propeller vessel *Chelohsin* of the Union Steamship Company of British Columbia was chartered for the summer of 1916. Built in Dublin, Ireland, in 1911, the *Chelohsin* was 175 feet long and displaced 1,134 tons. The ship had a long service life until wrecked in April 1949 (official no. 130805). It was in 1916, too, that the former Mackenzie Brothers vessel *Henriette* was sold to the Coastwise Steamship and Barge Company of Vancouver. In the summer of 1916, as well, limited staterooms for second-class passengers were provided on the *Prince George* and *Prince Rupert*. Each vessel had six four-berth and one two-berth second-class staterooms.

In 1917 the Grand Trunk Pacific Railway Company purchased the most famous of British Columbia's wooden coastal tow/tugboats, the *Lorne* (official no. 94809). This well-known and beloved vessel toiled for the company until 1921 when it was sold to the Hecate Straits Towing Company (for details, see chapter 4). The purchase of the *Lorne* clearly made the ancient tow/tugboat *Escort No. 2* redundant, and in 1918 the latter was laid up. It was dismantled in Seattle and its machinery was transferred into the steam schooner *H.B. Lovejoy* (official U.S. no. 216542). Since its hull was still sound, it found a new use as a fisheries barge for the Columbia Salmon Company. In early 1918, the Grand Trunk Pacific purchased the barges *C.C. Co. No. 7* and *C.C. Co. No. 8* from U.S. owners (official U.S. nos. 167033 and 167055, respectively) and renamed them the *G.T.P. No. 1* and *G.T.P. No. 2*, respectively. Displacing 445 and 459 tons each, they were built in Portland, Oregon, in

1915 and 1917, respectively. After they were purchased, the two vessels were converted into railbarges.

Grand Trunk Pacific railbarge services using the tow/tugboat *Lorne* and the barges *G.T.P. No. 1* and *G.T.P. No. 2* were announced in October 1917. It was planned to service the Whalen Pulp and Paper Company's pulp, lumber, and shingle mills at Swanson Bay from Prince Rupert and, hopefully, other coastal mills. However, initiation of railbarge services was delayed until 1920.

This delay was due to the First World War and the great demand for high-quality spruce wood for aircraft construction. Early in November 1917, the Aeronautical Supply Department of the Imperial Munitions Board ordered huge quantities of spruce logs/lumber from the Queen Charlotte Islands. These had to be hauled across Hecate Strait to the mainland for transportation/use. The *Lorne* and other tow/tugboats towed barges of lumber and Davis rafts of logs for months thereafter.

The Swanson Bay service began in 1917, but utilized Grand Trunk Pacific Coast propeller steamers to haul pulp bales to Prince Rupert that were then loaded into boxcars for transport east. Electric derricks had been installed at Prince Rupert to facilitate the transfer of goods from barges/scows/vessels directly into freight cars. The *Prince John* was the first Grand Trunk Pacific Coast vessel to load pulp bales at the Whalen mills at Swanson Bay. The work of building barge slips at Swanson Bay and Prince Rupert commenced in 1919 as did efforts to strengthen the barges in light of the heavy carloads to be carried. Railbarge service finally started on February 14, 1920, with the *Lorne* towing nine empty boxcars aboard the *G.T.P. No. 1* 110 miles one way to Swanson Bay. Due to the tidal range of

Prince Rupert Grand Trunk Pacific railcar ferry slip in action in 1910. (Prince Rupert City and Regional Archives LP984-29-1759-464.)

24 feet, barge loading was limited to eight hours daily. The mills shipped 27 box/flat cars weekly. The *Lorne* participated only briefly, since it was replaced by the chartered tow/tugboat *Queen* on February 24, 1920.

The *Lorne* was then delegated to tow Davis rafts of logs from the Queen Charlotte Islands. The *Queen* was built in 1914 in New Westminster, British Columbia (official no. 134285), and was 83 or 85 feet long (sources differ), 21 feet wide, and eight feet deep, displacing 106 or 115 tons (sources differ). In 1972 it was moved to the United States to become a yacht. Owners included the Queen

City Towboat Company, International Towing of Victoria, Dominion Tug/Barge, M.R. Cliff Towboat Company (twice), Hendry Cliff Towing, and H.R. Crossley.

The charter of the *Queen* ended on March 21, 1921. After that date and for the next three years, Grand Trunk Pacific Coast Steamships chartered the tow/tugboats *Earl*, *Point Hope*, and *Francis L. Cutting*. The *Earl* (official no. 94906) was built by P.S. Wescott of Vancouver in 1890. It was 72 feet long, 16 feet wide, and seven feet deep; displaced 75 tons; and possessed a twin-cylinder engine (12- and 22-inch piston diameters with a

16-inch stroke) built by Doty Engine Works. During its lifetime, it transitioned from a quarantine steamer to a tow/tugboat. Owners included Victoria Terminal Railway and Ferry, D. McGillivray, the Canadian government, Pacific Tug and Barge, and Pacific (Coyle) Navigation. The *Point Hope* (official no. 130310) was built in Vancouver in 1910 or 1912 (sources differ) as the *Protective*. It was a diminutive 63 feet long, 11 feet wide, and eight feet deep, displacing 66 tons. The vessel was dieselized in 1912 (250-horsepower, six-cylinder Union diesel) and rebuilt in 1923. It was moved to the United States in 1964 to become a yacht and met a violent end in March 1979 when it burned and sank in Juan de Fuca Strait. Owners included A.R. Bissett, the Canadian government, C. Stannard, Northern Tug and Barge, Service Towing, Hillside Sand and Gravel, West Coast Salvage and Contracting, and D. Chilcott of Newport Beach, California. The *Francis L. Cutting* (official no. 126897) was built in San Francisco in 1889. It was 81 feet long, 21 feet wide, and eight feet deep, displacing 91 tons. Owners included D.G. McDonnell and Whalen Pulp and Paper Mills. The vessel was doomed to founder on January 12, 1924, in Grenville Channel (see below).

The mills at Swanson Bay lived a fitful existence. Bankruptcies and six ownership changes occurred during the 16 years that the mill complex survived (1909–24). The most stable period was under Whalen Pulp and Paper Mills ownership from 1917 to 1923. Unfortunately, the Whalen mills closed for good in 1923 and the last carloads of pulp were moved on January 12, 1924. As luck would have it, the tow/tugboat *Francis L. Cutting* and its Grand Trunk Pacific Coast barge grounded on Watson Rock off Gibson Island in Grenville Channel on the way to Prince Rupert. Although the barge and railcars were salvaged, a storm moved the tow/tugboat off its grounding and into deep water, making it a total loss. Little of the lumber produced by the mill's lessee was moved by railbarge, and by mid-1925 the mills were shuttered forever.

Grand Trunk Pacific Coast Steamships was unsuccessful in attracting other industries to use its railbarge service, and it was left to Canadian National Railways to reinvigorate this service. The parent Grand Trunk Pacific Railway became insolvent in March 1919 when it defaulted on repayment of its construction loans to the Canadian government. Management of the railway was taken over by a Board of Management operating under the Department of Railways and Canals while legalities were resolved in the process of the federal government assuming the company's liabilities and assets. On July 12, 1920, the railway was placed under the management of Canadian National Railways, a Crown corporation, and in 1923 was completely absorbed. The subsidiaries Grand Trunk Pacific Coast Steamships and Grand Trunk Pacific Dock Company continued operating throughout this period and in much the same manner as previously until they were absorbed into the Canadian National Steamship Company in 1925.

In 1920 company offices were located in Seattle (917 Second Avenue), Victoria (Grand Trunk Pacific Steamship Dock), and Vancouver (527 Granville Street). Chief personnel included Manager Captain C.H. Nicholson of Vancouver, Assistant General Freight and

Passenger Agent G.A. McNicholl of Prince Rupert, and General Agent (Passenger Department) C.E. Jenney of Vancouver. Routes at that time included the *Prince Rupert* and *Prince George* leaving Seattle on Sunday and Wednesday nights, respectively, for Victoria, Vancouver, Ocean Falls, Swanson Bay, Prince Rupert, Anyox, and Stewart, while the *Prince John* and *Prince Albert* left Prince Rupert for the Queen Charlotte Islands and Stewart.

The "Prince" ships might have cancelled mail as Travelling Post Offices (TPOs) during the period in which they were owned by the Grand Trunk Pacific Coast Steamship Company. Table 3.4 and the accompanying images illustrate the formats of the cancellations known to exist up to and including 1919. It should be noted that there is controversy as to whether these were true postal cancellations or just pursers' stamps with no postal service affiliation.

GRAND TRUNK PACIFIC VESSELS IN THE FIRST WORLD WAR

Perhaps fortunately for Grand Trunk Pacific Coast Steamships, its small fleet in the Pacific Ocean did not attract the attention of the British Admiralty. As a result, no ships entered harm's way and all survived the First World War. The *Prince George* was "drafted" into the Royal Canadian Navy (RCN) on August 8, 1914. The usual daily rental fee, which included the ship and its crew, was $500. It was under RCN command, as well. Due to a mistake, the ship received a commission instead of becoming a fleet auxiliary vessel (i.e., a troopship or armed merchant cruiser). It was sent to Esquimalt

for an intensive four-day refit and conversion into a 200-bed hospital ship.

On August 20, 1914, Lieutenant Commander A.M. Kinnersley Saul, the captain of HMCHS (His Majesty's Canadian Hospital Ship) *Prince George*, ordered a red cross painted on the centre funnel prior to departure for Vancouver. Unfortunately, he was unaware of the regulations that stated that red crosses were to be painted on both sides of the ship fore and aft. During painting, rumours surfaced regarding the possible presence of one or two enemy cruisers in Queen Charlotte Sound. The *Prince George* was immediately ordered to proceed to Prince Rupert and load sufficient *matériel* for a 21-day sail to Hong Kong. This departure occurred so quickly that more than 20 crew members were abandoned there and, due to rain, only the port side had been painted in hospital ship colours (white with a green stripe) as mandated by international law. On August 25, the ship left Prince Rupert and proceeded to Juneau, Alaska, to refuel. Orders were then received to sail to the nearest British port, which was Prince Rupert. At that point it headed for Esquimalt Naval Base to undergo a thorough Admiralty inspection.

On September 1, health-care personnel left the ship, and on September 4, the vessel was paid off, followed by reconditioning and return to its owners. Officially, the *Prince George* had been in the navy for less than 30 days. However, it had been hired out to the RCN for 47 days, and that figure is the one most frequently quoted by authors. Regardless, the *Prince George* probably enjoyed one of the shortest commissions of any vessel in the history of the Royal Canadian Navy!

ANYOX AND GRANBY CONSOLIDATED: A UNIQUE RAILWAY UNDERTAKING

Anyox on Granby Bay in Observatory Inlet was the site of a copper mine and smelter, with a unique narrow-gauge railway owned by the Granby Consolidated Mining, Smelting, and Power Company. This firm controlled the exploitation of the copper reserves found two miles from the coast in the shadow of 5,800-foot Mount Brown. The area was located up Observatory Inlet, readily accessible to ships of the era.

To develop the mine and smelter, the company had to create a townsite called Anyox, which is the Tsimpsean word for "Hidden Water," build facilities for the generation of power, and construct a railway to convey ore to the smelter on the coast.

In order to clear the way for ships in the inlet, a small island obstructing navigation had to be removed. During blasting, gold was discovered and the quantity was sufficient to pay for the townsite, smelter, and railway.

The railway was composed of a three-foot-gauge surface line and two-foot-gauge underground electric line. The grades were certainly substantial. Upon completion of the surface line from the docks to the highline junction, the grade measured a hefty 2.7 percent. Altogether the railway was about six miles long (3.5 miles on the main line and 2.5 miles of yards).

When copper production began in 1914, the railway was performing three major functions: transportation of supplies from coastal freighters, hauling of ore from the Hidden Creek mine site to the smelter at Anyox, and movement of blister (matte) copper to the docks for shipment to Tacoma, Washington, for further refining.

Overview of the property of the Granby Consolidated Mining, Smelting, and Power Company in Anyox, British Columbia, in 1913. (Vancouver Public Library 762).

Crew proudly posing with their brand-new Granby Company 0-6-0 tank locomotive No. 5 in Anyox, British Columbia, in 1913. (Vancouver Public Library 764.)

Granby Consolidated smelter complex in Anyox, British Columbia, with nearby residences illustrated toward the top of the photograph. The close proximity of dwellings to the smelter made for an unhealthy place to raise a family. A portion of the three-foot-gauge surface railway is illustrated in the foreground. (Vancouver Public Library 8368.)

On a usual day, Porter 0-4-0 tank locomotives on duty at the three major sites (mine, smelter, and docks) switched continuously around the clock. Upon arrival of a supply vessel, during the off-loading of coke, quartz, limestone, and ores from outside vendors, the assigned locomotive arrived then backed down to the pier and coupled onto the loaded cars. This train then proceeded up to the main line, adjacent to spur trackage. From that point, 42-ton Baldwin-Westinghouse (B-W) 500-volt DC electric locomotives transferred the loads to the scale house and onto the smelter bins. After processing of the ore, the finished product of 500-pound slabs of blister (matte) copper were placed on flat cars for transport to the docks and then transferred to outbound ships.

In terms of the mining operation, before 1919 there were two-foot-gauge lines operating on three levels in the

An example of the "Granby car" developed by Granby Consolidated. This display was photographed in Phoenix, British Columbia, near Greenwood in 1907. (Vancouver Public Library 34090.)

A variety of narrow-gauge locomotives are present in front of the Anyox, British Columbia, engine house in 1917: 0-4-0 tank steam locomotives and Baldwin-Westinghouse 500-volt DC box-cab electric locomotives. (Vancouver Public Library 14408.)

mine. A six-ton B-W 500-volt DC bar-frame electric locomotive was used to haul ore to the main pockets and transport out mine waste on the 530-foot level. On the 385-foot level, the main shipping point, the ore made the three-quarter-mile journey to the crushers via additional six-ton B-W electrics. On the 150-foot level, there were two lines and yet another six-ton B-W electric was used to haul away waste material from new tunnel explorations and development within the mine. Eight- to 10-car trains carrying ore were assembled in the mine and single three-foot-gauge, 42-ton B-W electrics hauled loaded trains weighing 200 tons to the smelter storage bins. At peak times as much as 6,000 tons of ore in 30 trains were hauled over a 24-hour period.

Granby Consolidated generated its own power for both the smelter and the railway. All six miles of rail line were supplied with 500-volt DC current via overhead trolley, the wire being suspended 18 feet above the rails. Wire was fixed to cedar poles placed seven and a half feet back from the centre of the line and 55 feet apart. The wire was 0000 suspended from a mast arm. Due to the congested operating conditions on the rail lines, a block signal system was in operation by 1919. Although simple, it was remarkably effective.

With increasing copper prices and a strong market (due, in large part, to the First World War raging several thousand miles away), improvements were made. In 1919 locomotives, cars, and trackage were changed to

Mouth of Falls Creek in Anyox, British Columbia, in 1917. Note the mine buildings and trestle carrying the narrow-gauge railway line. (Vancouver Public Library 14405.)

better coordinate with the mine's output and the smelter's growing capacity. The previous system of using 54 75-cubic-foot, two-foot-gauge Granby-type ore cars pulled by five six-ton, two-foot-gauge B-W electrics was replaced by 30 140-cubic-foot, three-foot-gauge ore cars pulled by a pair of 12-ton, three-foot-gauge B-W electrics. Two of the six-ton, two-foot-gauge B-W electrics were rebuilt to

operate on three-foot-gauge trackage. The 12-ton electrics were used for pulling main-line trains on the surface while the rebuilt locomotives were relegated to the underground.

As with all non-renewable resources, a day came when the copper supply was depleted. This also coincided with slumping copper prices and soft markets due to the Great Depression. On November 27, 1934, 2,600 boxes of

An example of the Baldwin-Westinghouse 500-volt DC box-cab electric locomotives used for main-line hauling in Anyox, British Columbia. (British Columbia Archives C-05445.)

blasting powder (100 tons) were detonated in a fruitless attempt to locate new reserves at Hidden Creek, but luck had run out. With no end in sight for a poor market, mining operations were suspended on July 31, 1935. The mill remained open until the stockpiled ore was processed. Then on August 31, 1935, Anyox died.

Unlike most mining ventures, a monumental gamble at Hidden Creek paid off handsomely for its investors. For an expenditure of $14 million, the return was 140,000 ounces of gold, eight million ounces of silver, and 760 million pounds of copper. One should not forget about a narrow-gauge railway that operated tank steam

locomotives and 500-volt DC electric locomotives in one of the remotest areas in British Columbia up and down 2.7 percent grades for 21 years, hauling over 50 billion pounds of ore. The like of this will never be seen again.

GRAND TRUNK PACIFIC DOCK FACILITIES

Early in 1910, the Grand Trunk Pacific Dock Company was formed for the purposes of leasing, constructing, and/ or operating dock facilities in Prince Rupert, Victoria, Vancouver, et cetera. Officers included C.M. Hays as

Postcard illustrating the Grand Trunk Pacific Coast dock in Seattle, with a company ship dockside. The word *potlatch* is from the Chinook trade language of the North Pacific Coast Natives. It means "a gift" or "to give." In a larger sense, Natives applied the term to large festivals where gifting was done. Seattle's "Golden Potlatch," held from July 17–22, 1911, was a great festival in celebration of the gift of gold from Alaska to the world through Seattle. The first day of the festival, July 17, was the anniversary of the arrival of the first "treasure ship" from Alaska. (University of Washington 36737.)

president, J.S. Gibson as vice-president, H. Philips as secretary-treasurer, and S.H. Smith as assistant secretary. Trustees included C.M. Hays, E.J. Chamberlin, J.S. Gibson, S.H. Smith, and L.V. Druce.

The Grand Trunk Pacific Coast Steamship docks in Victoria in 1914 were small compared with those of the CPR or R.P. Rithet and Company. For example, the capacities (in tons) of the three sets of docks were, respectively, 1,350, 10,000, and 30,000.

In contrast, the Vancouver dock facilities were massive. The main pier was 870 feet long and for the first 350 feet from shore was 280 feet wide. From this latter section, a 100-foot-wide pier extended to the outer harbour line, giving on the west side a slip of 515 feet by 60 feet and on the east side a slip of 550 feet by 130 feet. Electricity was provided at each slip to allow the use of electric conveyors. Two fuel tanks (diameter by height, 76 feet by 40 feet and 16 feet by 24 feet) plus a pumphouse illustrated

From left to right, the Colman Dock, Grand Trunk Pacific Coast Steamship Company dock, and Alaska Steamship Company's Pier 2 on the Seattle waterfront. The photograph was taken from Elliott Bay sometime between 1910 and 1914. (University of Washington 30471, A. Curtis Collection.)

that coal as a fuel for Grand Trunk Pacific Coast steamers was doomed. Carpenter and machine shops (34 feet by 140 feet) were located on the west side of the approach to the pier. The CPR spur track to the dock was depressed so that the car floors were level with the dock surface.

The Grand Trunk Pacific Dock Company of Seattle was incorporated on December 9, 1909, for the purposes of leasing, constructing, and/or operating dock facilities in Seattle on behalf of the Grand Trunk Pacific Coast Steamship Company. The dock, office tower, warehouse, and terminal building were built in 1910 at the foot of Madison Street. This area had previously been used to dock the Puget Sound ferry *Flyer*. It was located immediately to the north of the Colman Dock (the base for the Puget Sound Navigation Company)

with the small U-shaped dock for the West Seattle ferry in between. Immediately to the north of the Grand Trunk Pacific dock was the base for the Seattle fire department fireboat *Duwamish*. The next dock north was Pier 3 or the Galbraith dock.

This 625-foot-long, 120-foot-wide pier was the largest wooden pier on the West Coast, requiring 5,000 timber pilings and 3.7 million board feet of lumber. It had a capacity of 9,000 tons. The complex had three buildings:

- A large three-storey warehouse with a deck area for freight 440 feet long by 104 feet wide. Sixty-nine office spaces were located on the second and third floors. The width of the apron to the dock edge was eight feet (south side), while it was 16.5 feet on the north side where the rail spur was located. The spur was depressed so that the car floors were even with the dock surface.

- An office tower building at the end of the pier that was 20 feet square and 104 feet tall.
- Closest to the street was the terminal building, which was three storeys tall on the street side with commercial space on the first floor, ticket offices and 45 rental suites on the second floor, and a large waiting room with overhead roof garden on the third floor.

The dock/building complex opened to the public on December 3, 1910. In 1912 local management of the dock complex was transferred to F. Waterhouse and Company, whose offices were subsequently relocated there.

On the afternoon of July 13, 1914, the Seattle dock was destroyed by fire, allegedly started by a cigarette or cigar landing on a sawdust pile. When fire broke out, two vessels were moored alongside the pier: the wooden inland steamer *Athlon* and the coastal steamship *Admiral Farragut*. According to one source, the engineer on the *Athlon* first noticed the fire at 1500 hours and alerted the fire department. Another source claims that C.B. Hicock, a wharfinger (i.e., warehouseman on a commercial dock/wharf), spotted the fire at 1540 hours and raised the alarm.

The *Athlon* and *Admiral Farragut* were rescued from this precarious situation despite the rapidity with which the fire spread throughout the creosote-laden piers/timbers of the dock. Engine Company No. 5 of the Seattle Fire Department arrived and proceeded onto the dock. The fire engine's fuel tank holding 50 gallons of gasoline exploded, injuring many firemen. Two firemen, Patrick Cooper and John Stokes, were trapped by the fire and

Firemen fighting a spectacular blaze at the Grand Trunk Pacific Coast Steamship Company all-wood dock on July 30, 1914. Two ship- and land-based steam-powered engines maintained water pressure in the hoses. An estimated 50,000 spectators viewed the event. (University of Washington 30744 and 30747, A. Curtis Collection.)

had to jump off the dock to save themselves. Cooper died three days later, and Stokes was never able to return to full-time duty as a fireman.

Fire companies from throughout the city responded as did the fireboats *Duwamish* and *Snoqualmie*. The latter vessels, with assistance from the revenue cutter *Unalga*, were able to prevent destruction of the Colman Dock.

Five people died and 29 more (10 being firemen) were injured in the blaze. Burning for two hours, the fire attracted an estimated 50,000 spectators. Unfortunately, some individuals took advantage of the tragedy by looting nearby businesses. The loss to the Grand Trunk Pacific was more than $410,000.

In late November 1914, tenders were opened for construction of the replacement pier and, in mid-December, for construction of the building complex. The pier would be 680 feet long and 116 feet wide. A hardwood driveway would extend along the entire length of the pier and use Australian ironwood. The warehouse would again be three storeys tall, with six, 26, and 20 rental suites located on the first, second, and third storeys, respectively. The terminal building would also be as before, i.e., 60 feet square with a massive waiting room, ticket offices, baggage rooms, and ladies' restroom within. This time the ceiling would be domed and extend the entire ceiling width. There would be liberal use of fire-resistant materials such as galvanized iron siding and asbestos shingles on the monitor roof of the warehouse. In one deviation from the previous complex, passengers would be under cover at all times and embarking/disembarking would occur much closer to the street. On December 8, 1914, the contract for the dock was awarded to the Nettleton-Bruce-Eschbach Company

of Seattle. Construction of the dock was estimated to take only three months and cost $75,000. Construction was not completed until July 1915. Details are unavailable regarding the construction of the building components.

With the collapse of the Grand Trunk and Grand Trunk Pacific Railways and their subsidiaries followed by the federal government takeover as Canadian National Railways, the dock became rundown after several years. In 1927 the Kitsap County Transportation Company and Puget Sound Freight Lines formed a joint venture called the Ferry Dock Company, which took out a long-term lease of the dock facilities. Stockholders of both companies were poised to sell out to Wilbur B. Foshay until the October 1929 stock market crash ruined the latter financially.

In August 1930, the Canadian Pacific BCCSS began using the dock as its Seattle terminal. The last Canadian National steamship service via the dock occurred on September 15, 1931. The Grand Trunk Pacific Dock Company of Seattle was dissolved on March 1, 1945, and the dock itself was dismantled in 1964.

GRAND TRUNK PACIFIC ALASKA STEAMSHIP COMPANY

This company was an American subsidiary wholly owned by the Grand Trunk Pacific Dock Company and was incorporated in Olympia, Washington, on May 4, 1917. Its board of directors included Captain J.S. Gibson of Seattle (vice-president, Grand Trunk Pacific Dock Company), J.H. Burgis of Seattle (general agent, Passenger Department, Grand Trunk Pacific Coast Steamships), F.L. Norman of Seattle (commercial agent, Grand Trunk Pacific

Coast Steamships), Carl E. Croson, and Karl F. Hass. It was organized to own American-flagged vessels and compete against American shipping companies operating in the Alaskan port-to-port system.

The interest of Grand Trunk Pacific in this trade was the need to generate eastbound traffic on the railway from Prince Rupert. The proximity of Prince Rupert to the North Pacific fishing grounds would give the railway a competitive advantage with respect to hauling fresh fish to eastern markets at a much reduced cost, despite the longer rail distance from the Pacific coast to Winnipeg compared with that of the CPR's line. Securing the Alaskan fish market required an expansion of the intermittent bonding privileges for American fishermen in Canadian ports established in 1897. At the end of 1914 the railway and merchants in Prince Rupert lobbied the Canadian government to extend these privileges to small American operators who could pool their catches into carload freight. The Canadian government extended these privileges to American operators for 1915 and 1916.

However, this proved to be only the beginning of the railway's foray into the Alaskan sea-based trade. In 1911 Grand Trunk Pacific Coast Steamships' vessels had started service to Stewart, British Columbia, while in 1916 company vessels began to compete in the Seattle to/from Skagway route via the "foreign" ports of Victoria, Vancouver, and Prince Rupert. Almost immediately the company cut its fares/rates compared with American lines. Grand Trunk Pacific Coast Steamships was alleged by its many U.S. detractors to have contravened American law prohibiting foreign vessels from engaging in U.S. port-to-port trade. The company was accused of employing British (i.e., Canadian)

vessels chartered or owned by the firm to convey passengers/freight (baggage) between Seattle and Skagway. Grand Trunk Pacific was able to technically circumvent the law, in terms of freight transport, by billing for transportation from Seattle to Vancouver, paying the duty, and rebilling for transportation from Vancouver to Alaskan points in bond. In terms of the passenger trade, it was alleged that agents issued railway tickets from Seattle to Vancouver via the Great Northern Railway, at which point passengers boarded company ships for Skagway.

A close working relationship had existed between the Grand Trunk and Great Northern Railways since 1903 when a traffic agreement was signed with the Great Northern Steamship Company, authorizing the latter to carry all Grand Trunk cargo to/from the Far East until the latter had its own trans-Pacific steamships (which never happened). In many cases, tickets were issued from Seattle to Skagway on the same ship, which showed blatant disregard for the law. Such passages were only legal if two different Canadian ships were involved, i.e., the first from Seattle to a Canadian port and the second from that Canadian port to Skagway. To comply with the law a layover of several days was required at the intermediate Canadian port due to the vagaries of the ships' schedules. This would clearly not be a selling point to prospective passengers.

Grand Trunk Pacific applied in 1916 to the secretary of the U.S. Treasury for a carriers' bond to enable it as an initial carrier to compete further with American vessels for transportation of U.S. freight. However, the application was denied by Assistant Secretary Peters. This confirmed the illegal nature of the methods used by the company, as described above.

The coaster *Tillamook* as originally built. Undated. (Puget Sound Maritime Historical Society 2892.)

Via other channels, the American government was asked to temporarily suspend the prohibition of foreign vessels from American port-to-port trade due to wartime conditions. Although the prohibition had existed since 1898, the request for temporary suspension was approved by the U.S. Shipping Board under a special permit and was not officially repealed until 1920.

Of interest, even before the temporary lifting of the ban due to the war, agents for foreign carriers had persisted and, as a result, entered the trade carrying domestic goods from Alaska via Prince Rupert and the Grand Trunk Pacific to points in the United States as if they were in bond from Alaska. In fact, the U.S. Treasury Department in Juneau allowed the railway to handle

Alaskan domestic goods intended for delivery to the continental United States in bond via Prince Rupert. U.S. customs officials bonded the shipments through Canada, despite the ruling of Assistant Secretary Peters!

The Alaskan subsidiary owned a single vessel, the motor (gas) schooner *Tillamook* (official no. 208718) (for details, see table 3.5). Purchased in 1917, the *Tillamook* was engaged in the cannery trade in southeastern Alaska with its only regular port of call being Ketchikan, Alaska. Initially after being purchased, it had been placed on the Prince Rupert to/from canneries route. Carrying only cannery crews and no regular passengers, the *Tillamook* appears only to have had the sole purpose of creating business for the Grand Trunk Pacific. It did so by means of a verbal understanding (nothing was conveyed in writing) that, in return for handling supplies from Seattle to Alaskan canneries, these canneries would ship their products east via Prince Rupert and the Grand Trunk Pacific Railway.

Dissenters continued to hound the U.S. federal government even after incorporation of the Alaskan subsidiary in 1917, claiming that it was really only a "dummy corporation" with a board of directors and officials largely drawn from the Grand Trunk Pacific Dock and Coast Steamship Companies. Both of these latter companies were wholly owned Grand Trunk Pacific Railway subsidiaries (see elsewhere in this chapter). The sole purpose of the Grand Trunk Pacific Coast Steamship Company was to divert American Alaskan business to Canadian ports, especially the Grand Trunk Pacific terminus at Prince Rupert.

In the end, admissions to the U.S. Shipping Board in 1918 that the stock of the Grand Trunk Pacific Alaska Steamship Company was wholly owned by the Grand Trunk Pacific Dock Company led to the end of the former company. The U.S. Bureau of Navigation held that the citizenship requirement for owners under section 38 of the Merchant Marine Act had been violated and the *Tillamook* was laid up. In 1925 the *Tillamook* was sold.

China badging with the "Prince Rupert" crest of Grand Trunk Pacific Coast Steamships. (Manufacturer: Maddock & Sons. Author's Collection.)

Table 3.1

Prince Rupert (official no. 129743) (No. 1) *Prince George* (official no. 129748) (No. 2)

Builder:	Swan Hunter & Wigham Richardson, Wallsend, England, in 1910. No. 1 launched on December 19, 1909, and No. 2 launched on March 10, 1910.
Engines:	Two four-cylinder, triple-crankshaft (23.5-, 37-, 41-, and 41-inch piston diameters, 33-inch stroke); 6,500 ihp at full speed.
Boilers:	Two double-ended and two single-ended (180 psi).
Dimensions:	307 feet long x 42 feet wide x 24 feet deep.
Funnels:	Three.
Masts:	Two.
Propulsion:	Steam screw (twin).
Tonnage:	3,380/1,626 (gross/net).
Speed:	18.5 knots.
Passenger Capacity:	220 (first class), 36 (second class) (1,500 excursionists on promenade deck).
Freight Capacity:	350 tons.
Miscellaneous:	Had large bilge keels to reduce rolling in heavy seas. The *Prince Rupert* first arrived in its namesake city on June 15, 1910. The *Prince George* arrived in Victoria on July 12, 1910. Burning coal initially, both were converted to oil-burning in 1912.

Owners	Dates
Grand Trunk Pacific Steamship Company	1910–25
Canadian National Steamship Company	1925–56 (No. 1) 1925–49 (No. 2)

Incidents

No. 1 (an "unlucky ship").

- On December 28, 1916, the tugboat *Cleeve* collided with the *Prince Rupert* in Vancouver's harbour.
- On March 23, 1917, while steaming out of Anyox in a gale with poor visibility, vessel ploughed into Genn Island. Low tide left ship high and dry on rocks only 30 feet from trees. No casualties. Two months in dry dock to repair.
- On May 1, 1918, propeller blades were stripped and vessel docked at Victoria for repairs.
- On January 14, 1919, struck by lightning in Vancouver's harbour, fracturing vessel's mast and necessitating moving up the time of annual refit.
- In October 1919, fire broke out in cargo hold and forced to return to Vancouver for repairs costing $25,000.
- On September 20, 1920, struck a reef in Swanson Bay and was beached with a 12-foot tear in its bottom. Due to enormous complexities of salvage (including construction of 120,000+ board foot cofferdam!), was underwater for two months. Out of service until May 1921.
- On August 22, 1927, struck notorious Ripple Rock twice. Rescued by the SS *Cardena*, which pulled vessel off sharp pinnacle before disaster ensued. The SS *Cardena* and the *Princess Beatrice* took all passengers, baggage, cargo, and mail aboard and two tugs towed disabled vessel to Prince Rupert dry dock.
- On March 6, 1931, sank at Yarrows yard at Esquimalt while undergoing annual refit. Caused by crew opening a porthole to accelerate paint drying in a compartment close to the waterline. When tide rose, water rushed in and ship heeled over 45 degrees. Luckily, the salvager *Salvage King* was docked alongside same dock and, with powerful pumps, ship was righted. Its departure was delayed one month. (Author's note: one wonders what happened to the paint crew.)
- On August 20, 1951, collided with the *Princess Kathleen* just north of Prince Rupert in heavy fog. Vessel crashed into the port bow of the *Princess Kathleen*, cutting halfway into the main deck and creating a V-shaped, 28-foot gash close to the waterline. Damages were $250,000 to the *Princess Kathleen* and $100,000 to the *Prince Rupert*. Both ships were at fault (per Admiralty inquiry).

Table 3.1 Cont'd

Incidents	Disposition
No. 2 (a "lucky ship with an unlucky end"). • In July 1910, a disruption in the bridge to the engine room telegraph caused the ship to crash into the new company wharf at Victoria. Fortunately, the ship was not damaged. • Grounded in the First Narrows on December 19, 1910, but was refloated by the tow/tugboat *Lorne* without serious damage. • Had a serious collision on October 14, 1912, in Puget Sound when the small halibut steamer *Lief E.*, loaded with 15 tons of fish, struck it in heavy fog. Captain Duncan Mackenzie lowered boats to rescue the eight-man crew and skillfully manoeuvred his ship in the act of passing steel cables under the sinking vessel and towing it to Harbor Island, Seattle, where it was beached. • On July 23, 1920, struck North Bluff in Seymour Narrows but was able to continue to Prince Rupert dry dock. Returned to service on August 1. • On December 30, 1933, vessel was briefly stranded on Vadso Rock near Anyox. • On December 20, 1937, grounded briefly off Kingcome Point, Princess Royal Island, in a snowstorm.	• No. 1: Ship was laid up in April 1955. Scrapped in 1956. • No. 2: Destroyed by fire after a fuel tank exploded on September 22, 1945, at Ketchikan, Alaska. No lives lost. Scrapped in 1949.

Table 3.2
Prince Albert (official no. 99584)

Builder:	Earles Shipbuilding and Engineering Company Limited, Hull, England, in 1892 (yard no. 365) as the *Bruno*.
Engine:	One triple-expansion.
Boilers:	Two single-ended (six furnaces) (150 psi).
Dimensions:	232 feet long x 30 feet wide x 14 feet deep.
Funnels:	One.
Masts:	Two.
Propulsion:	Steam screw (single).
Tonnage:	Originally, 841 (gross); 1,015/587 (gross/net) after rebuild.
Speed:	13 knots.
Passenger Capacity:	50 (first class) plus ? (third class) (1910), total 188 (1914).
Freight Capacity:	1,200 tons.
Miscellaneous:	Operated on charter in 1915 between San Francisco and Los Angeles.

Owners	Dates
Thomas Wilson and Sons Company (as *Bruno*)	1892–1909
Grand Trunk Pacific Coast Steamship Company (name changed to *Prince Albert*)	1909–23
Western Freighters Ltd.	1923–25
Pan American Shipping Company	1925–29
Farquhar and Company	1929–35
Badwater Towing (name changed to *J.R. Morgan*)	1935–50

Disposition

- Foundered on May 19, 1950, off Perez Rocks on Vancouver Island.

Incidents

- In leaving Vancouver's harbour in March 1912, vessel struck a rock off Shoal Island and sank. On March 26, vessel was raised and proceeded to Esquimalt for repairs.
- On May 23, 1913, vessel grounded on a shoal only a few hundred feet from the Port Simpson wharf, causing $20,000 damage and necessitating repairs that kept vessel out of service until July 10.
- In mid-September 1913, vessel collided with Canadian Fishing Company's *Flamingo* in Johnstone Strait, causing minor damage to both.
- On August 18, 1914, vessel ran up onto Butterworth Rocks off Melville Island, close to Prince Rupert. Although initially felt to be beyond repair, vessel was refloated, repaired, and sailed for another 35 years.
- In January 1920, vessel grounded at Masset Bar. Docked at Yarrow yard on February 3 for repairs and returned to service on February 10.
- Involved in "Mexican ore trade" (i.e., as a rum-runner) in 1923. Sold by Admiralty court order in 1925 after capture by government officials in the act of smuggling.

Table 3.3
Prince John (official no. 129472)

Builder:	Scott, Bowling, Scotland, in 1910 as *Amethyst*.
Engine:	Triple-expansion (17-, 28-, and 45-inch piston diameters, 33-inch stroke).
Boilers:	Two Scotch.
Dimensions:	185 feet long x 30 feet wide x 11 feet deep.
Funnels:	One.
Masts:	Three.
Propulsion:	Steam screw (single).
Tonnage:	905/540 (gross/net).
Speed:	12 knots.
Passenger Capacity:	None until 1911 rebuild, 44 (first class) in 1911, and 225 in 1914.
Freight Capacity:	1,000 tons.
Miscellaneous:	In 1911 the vessel was rebuilt into a passenger freighter. Was the primary passenger freighter between Prince Rupert, Queen Charlotte Islands, and Stewart.

Owners	Dates
Williams Robertson and Company (as *Amethyst*)	1910–11
Grand Trunk Pacific Development Company (name changed to *Prince John*)	1911–25
Prince John Limited (Canadian National Steamships Company)	1925–40
Union Steamships (name changed to *Cassiar*)	1940–51

Disposition

- Scrapped in 1951 (Stockton, California).

Incidents

- On May 19, 1912, the *Prince John* grounded on the bar at Old Masset harbour. After beaching to do temporary repairs, it proceeded to Esquimalt for full repairs.
- On March 3, 1914, vessel collided with Dominion Government fisheries protection vessel *Newington* in Queen Charlotte Sound, resulting in considerable damage above the waterline to the latter vessel, which proceeded to Esquimalt for repairs.
- When leaving Ikeda in mid-1914, vessel struck a log and broke off two of its propeller blades. Repairs were done in Victoria.
- On January 26, 1917, vessel grounded in Wrangell Narrows and required dry-dock repair.
- On May 1, 1918, vessel struck an unknown object (perhaps an uncharted rock) in Masset Inlet on the east side of the Queen Charlotte Islands but was able to make Vancouver.
- On March 30, 1920, the *Prince John* and *Prince Albert* collided near the entrance to Skidegate Harbour off Dead Tree Point in a blinding snowstorm that obliterated all aids to navigation. The *Prince John* was holed in her side 24 feet from the stern, and after passengers were transferred to the *Prince Albert*, an attempt was made to beach the vessel. Unfortunately, it sank in 27 feet of water and required five days of work by the salvage steamer *Algerine* to raise the vessel for transfer to the Prince Rupert Dry Dock and Steamboat Works for repairs. Although considerably damaged, the *Prince Albert* could still proceed on to Vancouver. During the Admiralty inquiry, both captains were exonerated of any blame and commended for their coolness and resourcefulness. Vessel returned to service on June 4.

Table 3.4

Possible Travelling Post Office Cancellations Used on Grand Trunk Pacific Coast Steamship Vessels Prior to 1920

Listing	Text	Type[a]	Years in Use
S-6	PRINCE RUPERT-Q.C.ISLDS. R.P.O.[b]/STR. PRINCE ALBERT	3D	1912
S-19	VANCOUVER-PRINCE RUPERT R.P.O.[b]/ [steamer name]	3D	
	a. STR. PRINCE GEORGE		1911–12
	b. STR. PRINCE RUPERT		1911–17
S-21	VANCOUVER-PRINCE RUPERT/ T.P.O./S.S. PRINCE RUPERT	3C	1917–19
S-22	VAN. & PRINCE RUPERT, R.P.O./ STR. RUPERT CITY	3D	1909
S-23	VAN.-P.R., R.P.O./steamer name	3C	
	a. STR. PRINCE GEORGE		1912–14
	b. STR. PRINCE RUPERT		1913–14
S-166	GRAND TRUNK PACIFIC/COASTSS. CO.LTD./PURSER'S OFFICE/S.S. PRINCE RUPERT	?	1911
S-241	HENRIETTE	22	1910
S-254	S.S. PRINCE GEORGE	22	1918

[a] Examples of the format of each type are illustrated to the right.
[b] RPO or Railway Post Office is an incorrect term. For marine vessels, TPO or Travelling Post Office, should have been used.
From: L.M. Ludlow, *Catalogue of Canadian Railway Cancellations and Related Transportation Postmarks* (Tokyo: Self-Published, 1982).

Type 1E:

Type 3C:

Type 3D:

Type 7B:

Type 13B:

Type 22:

NORTHERN RAILWAY

Table 3.5
Tillamook (official U.S. no. 208718)

Builder:	Kruse and Banks, North Bend, Oregon, in 1911.
Engines:	Twin 175-hp Frisco Standard gas engines, 400 bhp. In 1926 replaced with twin 200-hp Fairbanks-Morse diesel engines.
Dimensions:	119 feet long x 28 feet wide x 11 feet deep.
Funnels:	N/A.
Masts:	Two.
Propulsion:	Gas screw (single).
Tonnage:	281/233 (gross/net).
Speed:	10 knots.
Passenger Capacity:	Berths for 21–27 passengers. Carried up to 450 tons of freight.
Miscellaneous:	Had raised decks fore and aft with a well deck and large hold amidships. Passengers/officers had quarters in the deck house aft with the engine room below. Wheelhouse occupied the forward end of the deck house. Had originally engaged in coastal trade north and south of the mouth of the Columbia River. Rebuilt in 1917 with a shelter deck, raising its tonnage to 424/283 (gross/net). Arrived in Victoria in late May 1917 after refit at Portland. In January 1918, the vessel received a new pilothouse, steam-heating plant, and two electric winches of five tons capacity each. Extensively rebuilt in 1926, with hull lengthened 32 feet and gas engines replaced by diesel engines (615/478 gross/net tons).

Owners	Dates
Nehalem and South Coast Transportation Company	1911–17
Grand Trunk Pacific Alaska Steamship Company	1917–25
Northland Transportation Company (name changed to *Norco*)	1925–29
Citizens Light, Power, and Water Company	1929–36
Ketchikan Cold Storage Company	1936–42
Nessim Alharieff	1943
Whiz Fish Products Company	1944

Incident

- On September 16, 1916, the Tillamook assisted the Pacific Coast Steamships' *Congress*, which burned to a total loss. All 253 passengers and 170 crew members were rescued from the burning hulk eight miles offshore near Coos Bay, Oregon.

Disposition

- Burned in Tongass Harbor, Annette Island, Alaska (near Ketchikan), on March 8, 1944.

4

"Working Stiffs": The Iconic Tow/Tugboat *Lorne* and the Skeena and Upper Fraser Sternwheelers of the Grand Trunk Pacific Railway

LORNE

The state of tow vessels in the 1880s on the Canadian West Coast was woeful indeed. The presence of a variegated collection of motley watercraft that serviced the large ocean-going vessels undermined the boasts of Vancouver's infant business community that it was a world-class port. The strangest, indeed, was the *Union*. This vessel was born of a partnership, with one man contributing a scow and another donating a threshing-machine engine. Attaching a paddlewheel, the partners went into business with their one-gear (ahead) wonder!

James and Alexander Dunsmuir, who had taken over the family's Vancouver Island coal empire from their father, Robert, needed a vessel to assist sailing ships taking company coal from Wellington and Comox to waiting customers on the U.S. mainland. They decided they would remedy the situation by building their own tow/tugboat.

George Middlemas, renowned San Francisco naval architect, was selected in 1888 to design the vessel. The design he created was, in its essential features, the blueprint for the next century of coastal tow/tugboats: strong hull, powerful engine(s), large screw, and deep draft. No cabins for passengers, no holds for cargo. The pilothouse was high for visibility, the aft bulwarks low so that the tow line could swing freely. The tow post was mounted low and positioned about one-third of the distance from stern to bow — the best location for manoeuvrability. This was a single-purpose vessel. Middlemas's tow/tugboat was designed to tow and nothing else.

To the Dunsmuirs' credit, they had the vessel built locally rather than at the proven boat works and machine

The tow/tugboat *Lorne* in a photograph taken sometime during the 1890s or beyond. (City of Vancouver Archives AM54-S4-:VLP70.)

shops of San Francisco. The boat contract was awarded to Scottish boat builder Robert Laing, who had moved to Victoria in 1850. This was a massive undertaking for a local firm. Close by, workers at Albion Iron Works assembled the boilers and engine. The Albion Iron Works was owned by Joseph Spratt, a San Francisco–trained engineer who had built his business by powering sternwheelers during the Fraser Canyon gold rush of 1858.

The hull was constructed of select five-inch-thick lumber and sheathed with 1,337 sheets of copper. The two massive boilers had a total heating surface area of 2,782 square feet. They provided steam to two huge engines weighing 25 tons each. Additional details of the *Lorne* are available in table 4.1.

This was the most public shipbuilding in B.C. history to date. Readers were kept informed of the ship's progress on almost a daily basis by the newspapers of the day. It was as if this vessel was a test of Victoria's shipbuilding industry. If it was successful, more work would go to local shipyards. If it was not, work would continue to go to the shipyards in San Francisco. Day after day, articles appeared attempting to convey the scope of the project. When the newspapers ran out of engine or boiler talk, they could always mention the Dunsmuir clan.

In June 1889, the *Victoria Daily Colonist* announced that the Dunsmuirs' tow/tugboat, costing $60,000, was ready to be launched. The brothers chose June 3 for the launching. Prior to the launch, the shipbuilders requested that the government dredge, stationed nearby, clear a deep channel by the ways to ensure a soft launching. The harbour engineer — a man named Gamble — replied that the job would only take two hours but first he required permission from his superiors in Ottawa. Infuriated, Alex Dunsmuir and the shipbuilders appealed to the local Canadian Member of Parliament, Lieutenant-Colonel E.G. Prior, who eventually telegraphed the minister of public works for approval. By the time that approval was secured, Gamble had left town on business. When other arrangements had to be made to get the dredge moved, it was discovered that the government tow/tugboat *Pilot* was preoccupied. Only the *Pilot* was permitted to move the dredge.

This comedy of errors was the last straw for the Dunsmuirs. The launch would go on despite the failure to get the channel dredged. The tug was christened *Lorne* after the Marquess of Lorne, Canada's fourth governor general, whose wife was Princess Louise, fourth daughter of Queen Victoria. The tug slid majestically down the ways but, instead of riding easily into the harbour, it skidded sideways on the bottom, grinding off a large area of the hull's copper plating. Obviously siding with the Dunsmuirs, the *Daily Colonist* announced that the

problem was the result of "too much red tape and too little judgement in Victoria officialdom."

By late August, repairs had been made, fitting out was completed, and the ship was ready for its sea trials. Portraits of the Dunsmuirs were hung in the ship's dining room. Captain James Christensen, former pilot and veteran seaman, was chosen to command the ship on its first runs. Arriving in British Columbia as bosun on a Norwegian vessel, he jumped ship to try his hand in the local trade. His commands read like a "who's who" or all-star list of pioneering West Coast ships: *Surprise*, *Pilot*, *Beaver*, et cetera. Pioneering the sealing industry, he was involved in the daring apprehension in 1869 of 10 Native Canadians accused in the murder of the crew of the wrecked barquentine (bark) *John Bright*.

The Dunsmuirs celebrated completion of their new vessel with a gala run. Decks were crowded with Victoria's elite as the *Lorne* sped out of the harbour to the cheers of onlookers from the shore. Captain Christensen blasted the ship's whistle, and nearby vessels answered in chorus. Alex Dunsmuir, the flamboyant and verbose brother, lobbied his business-minded brother to delay putting the ship to work until they had had a second "fun run." This time the ship carried its cargo of partiers to Race Rocks where "even in the teeth of a strong breeze, it made 14 knots." Then Alex decided that it would be fun to do an overnight trip to Comox. James registered his opposition to the jaunt by refusing to participate, claiming pressing business demands instead. After a tour of company operations in Comox, the guests enjoyed hunting, fishing, and feasting. Once returned to Victoria, the ship was finally deemed ready for work.

The unofficial job description of life aboard a tow/tugboat was epitomized by the saying "hurry up and wait." Frantic moments of activity — for example, when coming alongside a ship in heavy seas — were separated by long periods of boredom. One of the vessel's first jobs was towing the British bark *Titania* from Esquimalt to Cape Flattery. At Race Rocks the *Lorne* and its tow were hammered by a sudden squall. Soon they were ploughing through huge seas. Conditions became so bad that a nearby vessel, the steamer *Wilmington*, was forced to seek shelter in Neah Bay. Captain Christensen chose to press on. Despite such heavy seas, the *Lorne* made a steady eight knots, finally casting the *Titania* free off Cape Flattery. It then took in tow the collier *Yosemite* and delivered it to Departure Bay. Elated by his vessel's performance, Captain Christensen called the *Lorne* the "staunchest, handsomest, and best-handling boat on the Pacific Coast."

With its great, deep wedge-shaped hull, the *Lorne* was a fine sea boat, but it was not nimble enough to work well in confined harbours. Its massive wooden rudder was turned by block and tackle and a huge wooden wheel. Two strong men had to spin the wheel 18 times to bring the ship about. Recalling a trip on the *Lorne*, Charles W. Cates, a veteran seaman and towboater whose father founded a pioneer B.C. towing firm, had this to say about the ship's turning ability: "When entering Vancouver harbour near the south shore, the order was given to bring it about. Despite the Herculean effort of two men at the helm, the ship could not complete the turn. It had to go astern before it grounded on the other shore. The harbour at that point was two nautical miles wide!"

The vessel's tow line was equally cumbersome. Sixteen inches in circumference (5.1 inches in diameter) and 1,800 feet long, it was an enormous hawser made of the best Manila hemp. The tow line was usually retrieved by a steam capstan. When weather was rough, as it frequently was when the *Lorne* released outbound sailing ships, the aft decks were unsafe. The *Lorne* then would drag the line until sheltered waters were found. At that time the crew started the capstan and brought in the line.

Early in its first year of service, the *Lorne* picked up the sailing ship *Glory of the Seas* bound for Nanaimo. As Captain Christensen altered course to bring both vessels into the wind, a squall struck. Instantly, the main sails of the *Glory of the Seas* were blown clear off their bolt ropes. The gusts blew the ship nearly on its beam ends (i.e., heeled over so far on one side that its deck was almost vertical) where it remained unable to manoeuvre. Aboard the *Lorne*, all the crew could do was cast off the hawser and watch in horror. For several minutes the fate of the *Glory of the Seas* hung in the balance. Then, as the nimble crew scaled the rigging and cleared away the tattered canvas, the vessel returned to an even keel.

To the Dunsmuirs' delight, the *Lorne* was often taxed to perform all of the work offered. In a two-week period in December 1897, for example, it towed the collier *Eclipse* (from Departure Bay to Cape Flattery), returning with the bark *Columbia* (in ballast to Port Townsend, Washington); towed the German bark *Magellanes* (into Vancouver) and the *Glory of the Seas* (from Comox to sea); worked as far south as the Columbia River to fetch the lumber-laden bark *Leslie D.*; and hauled the bark *America* (from Comox) and the collier *Rufus E. Wood* (from Nanaimo) to Cape Flattery. The same month the coal-laden, 1,700-ton bark *Sterling* was towed from Nanaimo to Cape Flattery in 13 hours and 30 minutes, a record for the day.

When not towing coal or lumber ships, the *Lorne* assisted ships of the sealing fleet. Sealers referred to the ship as the "fleet mother." Since the tow/tugboat was the last sight for crews heading on long voyages, occasionally their children would be allowed to ride the *Lorne* as it towed a schooner to sea. Obviously, it was an intensely emotional time as the children watched their fathers sail away for months at a time. For some children the sight of a sailing schooner being towed behind the *Lorne* would be the last memory of their fathers.

In the days before wireless telegraphy or ship-to-shore radio, the *Lorne* often received orders via flag signals at the Cape Flattery lighthouse. Otherwise, it freelanced with the captain becoming a business agent, haggling with tight-fisted sailing ship captains over rates. When weather was foul, there was no negotiation. Sailing ships took a tow at virtually any price, and the *Lorne* would plough through heavy seas to pick up the waiting vessels. Sometimes these ships had been holding in place for weeks.

In the early 1890s, the *Lorne* was running in heavy fog between Cape Flattery and Carmanah Point when it came across a ship lost in the fog and drifting toward the beach. The vessel was out of Liverpool, bound for Burrard Inlet, and had been at sea for six months. The crew had survived on hardtack and salted horsemeat. For several days they had been on Calashee watch (i.e., all hands on deck), exhausted and afraid. The *Lorne* took the ship in tow. At Royal Roads the tow/tugboat came alongside its tow, and a deckhand hollered for the crew to step aboard. In the *Lorne*'s dining room, they found a sumptuous feast of roasts, vegetables, and fresh bread. One of the young apprentices from the rescued ship was Barney Johnson. He eventually earned his master's papers and built up Hecate Straits Towing into a powerful firm whose fleet eventually included the *Lorne*.

In fine weather the *Lorne* could not buy a tow. Proud, miserly captains took their vessels right up the strait themselves. If the weather had just broken, there would be a fleet of such ships. There was not much that the crew of the *Lorne* could do except admire the view.

Traditionally, seamen on coastal boats are less superstitious than their ocean-going brethren. Until they ran into a notorious black cat, the crew of the *Lorne* shared this skepticism. In 1906 the *Lorne* was standing by in the west entrance of Juan de Fuca Strait, waiting for a chance to tow a sailing ship. Off Barkley Sound, on a clear day, an alert crewman spotted masts in the distance. The *Lorne* went to investigate. The vessel, for some unknown reason, was derelict. Scrambling through the ship, the crew could find only a scrawny black cat, which cowered near a sea chest. A crewman picked up the cat and headed across the deserted decks for the *Lorne*. On the way he slipped and broke his leg. The *Lorne*, attempting to come alongside, crashed into the schooner and smashed several timbers. Some crew members suggested tossing the cat overboard with a boom chain for a life vest, but the captain refused. When the *Lorne* returned to Vancouver, it went ahead instead of astern and crashed into the wharf. A dispute arose between labour and management, and the crew walked away.

The tow/tugboat *Lorne* surrounded by portraits of men who had served on the vessel, circa 1892. The portrait in the upper row, far left, is that of Jim Cates, one of the *Lorne*'s future masters. (City of Vancouver Archives AM54-S4-:Bo P245.)

Somehow Captain Jim Cates (uncle of Charles W. Cates) was elected to look after the cat. Through his marine connections he traced the cat's owners to San Francisco. He put the animal in a box and placed it on the next ship bound for San Francisco. On the way south the ship ran aground. Eventually, it arrived in San Francisco. The cat was placed on the wharf on April 18 — at the very moment the great earthquake struck. The crew of the *Lorne* received the news from the lighthouse keeper at Neah Bay who conveyed news and weather reports to passing ships by megaphone. He reported "black cat delivered safely to San Francisco. City completed destroyed by earthquake and fire."

In 1903 the Dunsmuirs sold the *Lorne*. It passed through a succession of owners, including the Grand Trunk Pacific Railway, Hecate Straits Towing, and Pacific (Coyle) Navigation Company where it towed giant Davis rafts (floating bundles of logs), each containing more than a million board feet of timber.

A vessel with the reputation and power of the *Lorne* would be expected to provide rescue and salvage work in British Columbian coastal waters. From a perusal of the *Victoria Daily Colonist*, the following examples were gleaned. The *Lorne* was involved in search, rescue, and recovery missions for the steamers *Warrimoo* (1895) and *Valencia* (1906) and the schooner *Willis A. Holden* (1914). It rescued the steamers *Highland Light* (1890), *Islander* (1891), *Willamette* (1901), *Tees* (1903), *Queen City* (1904), *Tampico* (1907), and *Corona* (1907), as well as the bark *George Thompson* (1892) and schooners *Sadie Turpel* (1900 and 1903) and *Bangor* (1910) after they had run aground. The *Lorne* also towed several vessels out of danger before they could be claimed by the rocky reefs and shore of western Vancouver Island: the sailing ships *Old Kensington* (1893), *Inveramsay* (1907), *Falls of Dee* (1908), *Lord Shaftsbury* (1908), *Alice Cooke* (1910), and *Tees* (1911). Eleven Japanese fishermen were rescued during a severe storm in October 1905. Unfortunately, 25 to 30 other fishermen drowned. Two of five individuals from a capsized boat at Tatoosh were also saved when, against better judgment, they attempted to row from the Tatoosh wireless station out to the *Lorne* in February 1911. Lastly, the *Lorne* was an active salvor of the steamers *San Pedro* (1892), *Michigan* (1893), and *Cleveland* (1897), as well as the schooner *Vesta* (1898).

Careful examination of the contents of the *Victoria Daily Colonist* from 1888 to 1920 provides some interesting details regarding the *Lorne*. During this period, tows of 202 unique vessels (plus those of three unidentified vessels) were described, with the total tows being 285 (range of tows per vessel, 1 to 11). In 58 cases (28 percent), the origins of the towed vessels were provided. Most were of British (including Canadian) (25 or 43 percent), U.S. (11 or 19 percent), or German (eight or 14 percent) registration, with 10 other countries being represented in only one (2 percent) or two (3 percent) cases each. In 112 cases (55 percent), the types of vessels were provided. In 109 cases (97 percent), these were sailing vessels (one sloop, nine schooners, and 99 barks). And what a group of proud ships soon to be relegated to the boneyard of history! They had names such as *Carnedd Llewellen*, *Glory of the Seas*, *Henriette*, *Magellanes*, *Pass of Balmaha*, *Richard III*, *Thermopylae*, and *Vercingetorix*.

Only one steamer, one log raft, and two barges were identified. Tow destinations were provided for all but two tows. Destinations represented in at least 10 cases each included "out to sea" (107 or 38 percent), Vancouver (40 or 14 percent), Victoria (26 or 9 percent), Royal Roads and Esquimalt (18 or 6 percent each), Departure Bay (11 or 4 percent), and Nanaimo (10 or 4 percent). Examining only those departures "out to sea" where cargo identities were provided (103), the major cargoes were lumber/timbers (40 or 39 percent) and coal (42 or 41 percent, most frequently for San Francisco), followed by salmon (10 or 4 percent), mining props (four), wheat (three), copper ore (two), and mining supplies for the Klondike or tea (one each). These findings are likely a gross underestimate of the workload of the *Lorne* over this 32-year period. Still, it is a tribute to the vessel and its crew how the *Lorne* remained newsworthy down through the years!

The *Lorne* had at least 11 masters: J. Christensen and his son, J.A. Christensen, as well as Urquhart, T.P. Locke, Brown, Langley, Butler, H. Bilton, Cutler, Barney Johnson, and Cates.

A source of great pride to residents of Victoria, the *Lorne* participated in several important civic events. In May 1890, Captains Urquhart and Christensen, along with the lieutenant governor of the province, met the steamer *Abyssinian*, which brought the Duke and Duchess of Connaught. The duke and duchess and their attending party were conveyed to the landing in the *Lorne*. On April 27, 1891, the *Lorne* helped to welcome the CPR's new steamer, the *Empress of India*, to its home port. When the *Empress of India* was sighted off Race Rocks, a fog alarm was sounded followed by fire station bells. Twenty minutes after the beginning of the sounding of the fire station bells, the *Lorne* started off from the dock with a welcoming party to meet the *Empress of India*.

The *Lorne* was not "all work and no play." On at least one occasion after beginning its working career, the vessel was chartered for a pleasure cruise. This happened in July 1906 when Mrs. J.O. (Joan) Dunsmuir chartered the *Lorne* for a cruise among the Gulf Islands after the end of the Dunsmuirs' ownership of the tow/tugboat. The duration of the charter is not known.

Although the *Lorne* led a charmed life, considering the foul conditions in which it frequently sailed, the ship was not immune to mishap. In July 1896, the *Lorne* became beached with the bark *Melrose* at night off Beachy Head. Once freed, the *Lorne* proceeded to Esquimalt for repairs. In February 1900, the dismantled bark *Colorado* rammed the *Lorne* in Johnstone Strait on the northeastern corner of Vancouver Island. While towing the *Colorado*, which was carrying copper concentrates for the smelters in Tacoma, Washington, the tow/tugboat ran ashore and then the bark rammed it, smashing the *Colorado*'s bulwarks and creating an immense hole just above the waterline in the bark. The accident had occurred during a very heavy snowstorm. The *Lorne* was refloated at high tide and continued on to Victoria for repairs.

In May 1908, the *Lorne* was crippled by its tow, the German ship *Chile*, which was laden with wheat for Europe. The accident occurred near Marrowstone Point before daylight. In brief, the hawser had parted and an attempt was made to pass another line to the *Chile*. The *Lorne* had backed up close to the German ship, and the hawser was successfully passed to the bark when the latter was suddenly caught in a riptide that swung its bow around suddenly and its bowsprit became entangled in the mainmast of the *Lorne*. Before the gear on the mainmast could be released, the *Lorne* swung in under the bowsprit, twisting the mast timbers while the jib-boom of the *Chile* smashed into the smokestack of the tow/tugboat, destroying it. Then the hull of the *Lorne* was pulled up to the bow of the *Chile*, damaging it in several places above the waterline. The main steam pipe was severed and immediately filled the vessel with scalding steam. Miraculously, no one on either vessel was injured or killed. The U.S. tow/tugboat *Tyee* assisted the limping *Lorne* into Seattle.

In August 1914, the *Lorne* was towing the barge *America* when both vessels grounded in Kanaka Bay, San Juan Island. Both were salvaged, with the *Lorne* being towed to Victoria for repairs. In September 1930, the *Lorne* was towing the log barge *Pacific Gatherer* under the Second Narrows Rail Bridge. The tow was caught in an eddy, and the barge sheered under the bridge's centre span. It stuck fast, held tight by the current and rising tide. For an hour Captain Barney Johnson and the crew of the *Lorne* watched as the barge heaved the 8,000-ton span off its mounts. Then the bridge tumbled into the Narrows.

The details of the end of this famous vessel are somewhat uncertain. In 1936 its useful days being over, it was tied up at Terminal Dock. At low tide the tug went aground, then keeled over. A valve had been negligently left open, and the *Lorne* flooded. Most likely, it was bought by Shaeffer-Haggert and dismantled at the B.C Marine Engineers and Shipbuilders Yard, so ending the life of a marine icon of Canada's West Coast.

SKEENA RIVER STERNWHEELERS

Native Canadians called it *K-shian* or "water of the clouds." Riverboat men called it names that cannot be repeated here. It was a temperamental river, impatient and unstable, hurrying its way to the sea from the Skeena Mountains as western Canada's fastest-flowing waterway. Most sternwheeler captains thought that it was the toughest of North America's navigable rivers. Water levels can

The sternwheeler *Conveyor* at Kitsumkalum near Terrace, British Columbia, in 1909. (British Columbia Archives C-05491.)

rise 17 feet in a single day and fluctuate 60 feet between low and high water. Ships' hulls can be ripped apart in a dozen rapid-torn canyons or rock-strewn rapids.

The first sternwheelers on the river were the *Union* and *Mumford*, which battled upriver for 90 and 110 miles, respectively, before turning back. Only beginning with the *Caledonia* (official no. 97162) of the Hudson's Bay Company in May 1891 could the entire navigable distance of 180 miles to Hazelton, British Columbia, be negotiated. Captain J.H. Bonser of the *Caledonia* christened the 11 major rapids and canyons that laced these 180 miles. Generally, he chose names matching the temperament of the obstacles. Cross currents at the Whirly Gig shook a sternwheeler like "gravel in the bottom of a prospector's gold pan." At the Hornet's Nest vessels ran a

The sternwheeler *Operator* on a particularly narrow section of the Skeena River in 1910. (British Columbia Archives C-05493.)

gauntlet of boulders. Sheep Rapids was a section of white water resembling galloping sheep. At the Devil's Elbow the river flowed straight into a rock bluff, then veered abruptly right — a section unnerving to even the most seasoned river crew and passengers.

To aid vessels in their fight up the most turbulent rapids, ringbolts were anchored in the canyon walls. With steel cable and steam capstans, the vessels hauled themselves upstream in a hand-over-hand manner, a process known as lining. In sections where rapids were present but there was no rock for anchoring ringbolts, a deadman was used. This device was simply a log dug into the gravel at the head of the rapids and anchored. From the deadman downstream ran a cable buoyed by a block of wood. An upstream-bound vessel picked up the cable and lined itself up the rapids using its steam capstan. At the crest the buoyed cable was dropped overboard where it floated downstream ready for the next upstream vessel.

A quotation from C.H. French, a Hudson's Bay Company employee, provides a description of the thrilling and perilous ride:

The excitement — the thrill that one gets when passing through the canyons of the Skeena is beyond word-picturing.

Entering the Little Canyon from the lower end, one gets the impression that he is starting through a subterranean passage, because of the towering, straight walls — so high that darkness appears to be gathering.

After proceeding a little further one notes that the "boils" [whirlpools] are getting larger and if you look over the side of the ship you will note that an extra large "boil" has struck the steamer right on the stem, and has caused her to settle until the water is rushing in over the bow. Suddenly the "boil" has careened the boat to one side and has shifted to her quarter. The crew, with large rope bumper, rush to the side opposite the "boil" so that in case the captain is not able to straighten the boat up they will be able to swing the bumpers between the guard of the steamer and the rough, jagged walls of the canyon.

Now the "boil" has reached amidships just under where you are standing, and when you look down into it (they could be 20 and more feet deep) and feel the boat settling under you, you wonder if there is really any bottom to it and whether the boat will be sucked under or whether she will eventually rise.

Probably when the guard of the boat is under water and the decks are actually flooded, the "boil" will shift a trifle to one side. Then the boat will immediately float up and go along.

On the trip the paddlewheel was damaged and the boat stopped for repairs. A large Indian canoe came downstream and we endeavored both by signs and shouting to warn the crew that they should not enter the canyon, but the only reply they gave us was to paddle harder and in a flash this large war canoe with a crew of sixteen Indians shot into the canyon and out of our sight.

Neither the canoe nor any of its crew were ever found and it can only be surmised that one of those large "boils" took the craft and held it, gradually sucking it lower until at a certain point the canoe would stand straight on end and disappear, the crew either being held in the eddy or carried down and deposited underneath the large drift piles.

The onset of the Klondike gold rush led to a surge in traffic on the Skeena, especially as it was part of the "all-Canadian" route to the Yukon. In addition, the Canadian government commenced building a telegraph line from Quesnel, British Columbia, to Dawson City, Yukon Territory, with Hazelton being designated a main supply base. The sternwheelers *Caledonia*, *Strathcona* (official no. 107146), and *Monte Cristo* (official no. 107824), followed in 1901 by the *Hazelton* (official no. 109834) and in 1902 by the *Mount Royal* (official no. 111778), provided passenger and freight service from Port Essington at the mouth of the Skeena to Hazelton. In general, the upstream trip took about 40 hours while the downstream trip took about 10 hours!

The sternwheeler *Distributor* stops at an unknown location along the Skeena River in 1911 to drop off and/or take on passengers. (British Columbia Archives C-05487.)

The *Hazelton*, owned by Robert Cunningham, and the *Mount Royal*, owned by the Hudson's Bay Company, engaged in a bitter and acrimonious rivalry to best each other in round-trip and upstream elapsed times. This rapidly rose beyond a war of words and soon degenerated into a side-by-side race on a dangerous river, with the *Hazelton* deliberately ramming into the *Mount Royal* several times until the *Mount Royal* was pushed broadside to the current. At that point the *Mount Royal* was pushed downstream by the current, and the *Hazelton* blew its whistle and wagged its stern in triumph. In addition, during a formal investigation of the incident by the Dominion Department of Marine, it was discovered that the captain of the *Mount Royal* had left the helm to search for a rifle to shoot his adversary! Both captains were found at fault and disciplined. Such antics obviously put passengers and crews at grave risk. Fortunately, both parties met and "arrived at an understanding."

The sternwheelers *Omineca* and *Operator* at Kitselas Canyon on the Skeena River. (British Columbia Archives D-06808.)

According to hearsay, the Hudson's Bay Company agreed to pay Cunningham $2,500 to tie up his vessel, to haul his freight at no charge, and to purchase the *Hazelton* if traffic warranted. The Hudson's Bay Company eventually did purchase the *Hazelton*.

The river would not be deprived of its victims. On July 6, 1906, the *Mount Royal* reached Kitselas Canyon, a mile-long, rock-studded chute 93 miles downstream from Hazelton. Here the river splits into three channels, the rock outcrops acting like a dam. A one-foot rise in the river level can raise the water level five feet at the head of

the canyon, while fluctuations between low and high water in the canyon can reach 60 feet! Only two of the three channels were navigable. To maintain steering ability, vessels shot down these channels at full speed. As the *Mount Royal* approached the centre channel, a wind gust spun it into a rock pillar called Ringbolt Island. The 10-knot current swung the *Mount Royal*'s stern to the opposite bank, jamming the vessel broadside in the channel. Fortunately, the sternwheeler held fast while passengers and crew escaped to shore. Meanwhile, although creaking and buckling due to the torrent buffeting it, the vessel appeared to

A procession of four Skeena sternwheelers (from left to right, *Skeena*, *Conveyor*, *Distributor*, and *Omineca*) leaving Prince Rupert for the Skeena River. (British Columbia Archives F-04141.)

withstand the pressure. The captain and 10 crew members returned to save the *Mount Royal*. The captain decided to run a cable through a snatch block at the stern and up to the capstan on the bow in order to pull the stern back up and over against Ringbolt Island. At first all went well, but then the king post jumped off its footing in the hold and went through the bottom. The vessel subsequently buckled in the middle and rolled over bottom up and broke in the middle. Six of the 11 who had returned to the ship drowned. Wreckage floated downstream, including one large chunk of the hull that grounded on a bar.

A hand waved from a hole in the planking. Miraculously, the chief engineer, Ben Maddigan, had survived due to an air pocket in the bilge!

Only two months later the river claimed another victim: the sternwheeler *North West* (official no. 122366). After the vessel had struck a rock, passengers and crew were lucky to have big boulders in the channel over which they could scramble to safety on the shore. From the shore they witnessed the battered hulk being swept on its side with a shriek as the fires beneath the boilers were extinguished. Unfortunately for all, the cargo on the

The sternwheeler *Skeena* docked at Kitselas on the Skeena River in 1911. (British Columbia Archives C-05484.)

North West was the liquor supply for all upriver points for the coming winter. To the delight of all, the *Caledonia* freighted upstream a replacement cargo before freeze-up. Lonely inhabitants along the river would have some solace during the long winter nights.

Alexander Watson, a highly skilled sternwheeler builder from Victoria, became extensively involved in the construction of sternwheelers targeted for use on the Skeena. He had travelled widely across the province, making all arrangements, equipment orders, and purchases before packing up his tools and heading off with some skilled assistants for months at a time to build well-designed and rugged sternwheelers on riverbanks, sometimes many miles from sources of supply. Between 1897 and 1900, he designed the famous Klondike sternwheelers *Yukoner* of the John Irvine Navigation Company (later of the Canadian Development Company, followed by the British Yukon Navigation Company [BYN Company], a subsidiary of the White Pass and Yukon Railway [WP&YR]), and the *Dawson*, *Selkirk*, and *White House* of the BYN Company. He designed and built the Klondike sternwheelers *Gleaner* and *Reaper* (latter renamed the *Zealandian* — possibly for superstitious reasons — when later purchased by the Canadian Development Company) for the John Irvine Navigation Company in 1899–1900 at Lake Bennett, Yukon Territory. Both vessels carried tons of construction materials for the WP&YR between Bennett and Carcross, Yukon Territory.

The Skeena River at the end of 1907 became the focus of a new development. The Grand Trunk Pacific Railway, a subsidiary of the Grand Trunk Railway of Canada, was about to commence construction from its western

Woodshed along the Skeena River for refuelling sternwheelers.
(Prince Rupert City and Regional Archives LP 984-29-1759-513.)

terminus on a small island (Kaien Island) just north of the Skeena estuary where a port city called Prince Rupert would rise from the rocks, trees, and muskeg. The Hudson's Bay Company sold the *Caledonia* and ordered a replacement sternwheeler called the *Port Simpson* (official no. 122390) for 1908. That same year two new sternwheelers, the *Skeena* (official no. 126212) and *Distributor* (official no. 122393), were built for Foley, Welch and Stewart, the major contractors for the railway and the Grand Trunk Pacific Railway, respectively. For details on these vessels, see tables 4.2 and 4.3, respectively. Foley, Welch and Stewart also purchased the veteran sternwheeler *Omineca* (official no. not known). However, this vessel was wrecked near Port Essington, British Columbia, in the summer of 1908. Captain Alex McLean was hired in 1908 by Foley, Welch and Stewart to run cargoes of blasting powder up the Skeena River for the Grand Trunk Pacific construction work. In 1908–09 Foley, Welch and Stewart built an aerial tramway from the bottom end of the Kitselas Canyon to the top and placed a boat on the upper river so that goods could get through even when the canyon was impassible. This tramway is still extant (although inoperable) today. In the winter of 1908–09, the *Distributor* wintered in Victoria while the *Skeena* wintered in Prince Rupert. Captain S.B. Johnson was the marine superintendent for the Grand Trunk Pacific Railway's Skeena River service at that time.

By the summer of 1909, the new *Omineca* (official no. 126248) appeared with two additional new sternwheelers, the *Conveyor* (official no. 126250) and *Operator* (official no. 126501), each costing $35,000, bringing the Foley, Welch and Stewart fleet to five sternwheelers (for

Oops! The results of a tree falling on the sternwheeler *Operator* along the Skeena River, circa 1910. (British Columbia Archives A-01528.)

details on these vessels, see tables 4.4–4.6, respectively). This is because the Grand Trunk Pacific had sold the *Distributor*, *Conveyor*, and *Operator* to Foley, Welch and Stewart sometime in 1909. In the winter of 1910–11, the five-ship fleet wintered on the Foley, Welch and Stewart company ways on Digby Island.

Foley, Welch and Stewart had purchased the sternwheeler *Caledonia* (official no. 107145) in the spring of 1908 from the Hudson's Bay Company for construction work, but it struck a rock in the Skeena River on October 15 of the same year, sank, and was deemed non-repairable (for details, see table 4.7). However, its machinery was reused in the rebuilding of the *Omineca*. In addition, the sternwheelers *Strathcona* and *Craigflower* (official no. 126233) were considered for the Grand Trunk Pacific construction work but were rejected. In fact, the *Craigflower* was so underpowered, with two engines of only 2.4 nominal horsepower each, that it was only able to reach Kitseguecla Rapids (Minskinish) on its first trip and was derisively called "Cauliflower"!

The section of railway along the Skeena River from Hazelton to Prince Rupert was the most difficult and expensive to build west of Winnipeg. One section of 60 miles was almost solid rock. To get past Kitselas Canyon (gravesite of the *Mount Royal*), three tunnels (400, 700, and 1,100 feet long) had to be hacked out of solid rock. Within 10 miles of each other, just west of Hazelton, were two bridges each over 900 feet long.

The route was so difficult that to locate 186 miles of railway line more than 12,000 miles of surveys and trial lines were run. Construction of the 80-mile section from Kitselas Canyon to Prince Rupert alone required 12 million pounds of explosives and cost $80,000 per mile!

Construction camps were established every two miles, requiring a great number of stops for the sternwheelers. These five sternwheelers were tireless workhorses, hauling tens of thousands of tons of railway construction materials as well as thousands of labourers and the materials required to house and feed them. By 1910 the Skeena section of the railway was nearing completion and the time of the sternwheelers on the Skeena River was rapidly approaching an end. Locomotive whistles quickly replaced ship whistles along the river.

The *Distributor*, *Operator*, and *Conveyor* sailed to Victoria for dismantling. Machinery from the *Distributor* was used to create a new sternwheeler of the same name at Kamloops, British Columbia, in 1912 (official no. 130619). This vessel assisted in the construction of the Canadian Northern Railway in east-central British Columbia (see chapter 5). The same machinery was used

in 1920 to create yet another sternwheeler for use on the Mackenzie River (*Distributor III*, official no. 150523) (for details of the *Distributor III*, see table 4.3). The *Skeena* plied the lower Fraser River until 1925. The *Omineca* helped to build yet another railway (U.S. Government Railroad in Alaska, completed in 1923 and reorganized as the Alaska Railroad). Purchased by the U.S. government in 1916, the vessel was assigned to the Alaskan Engineering Commission and used on the Susitna River and at Cook Inlet. Retired in 1917, the *Omineca* was gone between 1923 and 1930.

Machinery from the *Conveyor* and *Operator* was used to build two new sternwheelers with identical names. The new vessels were employed in Grand Trunk Pacific Railway construction along the upper Fraser River near Tête Jaune Cache (official nos. 130885 and 130886, respectively) (for details, see tables 4.5 and 4.6, respectively). Construction of these new sternwheelers was no easy task. Plenty of wood was available at Tête Jaune Cache; machinery was another matter. Machinery was hauled from Victoria by rail via Jasper, Alberta, to Red Pass, just inside the Alberta-B.C. border. In all, there were 10 carloads, including two 50,000-pound boilers. From Red Pass tons of parts were dragged by mules over a 25-mile, roller-coaster tote road to a shipyard hacked out of the forest on the bank of the Fraser River one mile east of Tête Jaune Cache. Moving the boilers alone took one week and the life of a worker. In addition, six scows were built for carrying freight.

Both vessels were launched on May 12, 1912, and were the largest on the upper Fraser. However, 1912 was not a good year for the two sternwheelers as the river fell to an extremely low level, exposing a host of new bars, reefs, and boulders, making travel exceptionally hazardous. Both vessels were withdrawn from service in early September.

However, the 1913 navigation season was an unqualified success. Rail construction between Fort George and Tête Jaune Cache employed 5,000 labourers, and settlers were moving in by the hundreds. Despite being safer than the Skeena River, the upper Fraser River had several challenges of its own. Among the obstacles were seven-mile-long Giscome Rapids, Goat River Rapids, and the Grand Canyon. The last named was a fearsome double slash through volcanic rock just over 100 miles upstream from Fort George. Here the river width constricts by 75 percent and the compressed water swirls through the cleft rock at such a velocity that down-bound sternwheelers with engines full astern careened through at 15 knots.

Below this was another stretch described by one traveller as a "cavernous opening scarcely fifty feet wide, presenting a specter of somber, awful grandeur. It was like peering into a huge vault…. At the mouth of the canyon the entire river becomes a whirlpool, its vortex easily swallowing complete trees in a pulsing confusion of foam." During 1913, its swirling waters drowned dozens of men — the crews of scows used for freighting supplies downstream. The scows, each averaging 40 feet long and 16 feet wide with a capacity of 25 tons, were launched at Tête Jaune Cache and allowed to drift downstream. A pole at the stern was used to control the scow's movement. The railway contractors frequently sent 100 scows downstream daily with construction supplies. In the first few weeks of the 1913 season, more than 20 men drowned in Grand Canyon alone and, by July, the value of lost goods exceeded $100,000.

Arrival of the first train to Prince George on January 27, 1914, was fatal for the upper Fraser sternwheelers, although their usefulness had not yet ended. Construction began on a new railway, the Pacific Great Eastern, to link Prince George to Vancouver. By October 1914, nearly 5,000 men were working on the roadbed with the Foley, Welch and Stewart sternwheelers again loaded to capacity. Two sternwheelers, the *Conveyor* of Foley, Welch and Stewart, and the *B.X.* (official no. 126516) of the B.C. Express Company, were considered the fastest on the river. In July 1914, when they arrived at Soda Creek and prepared to leave for Fort George the next morning, the opportunity to race presented itself. Captain Shannon of the *Conveyor* promptly suggested a one-hour race in which the lead vessel would be declared speed queen. Captain Browne of the *B.X.* agreed, despite being disadvantaged by a load of 40 tons of cargo and mail and the necessity to make his regular stops along the river. On the other hand, the *Conveyor* was empty and had no stops to make.

The "fastest show on H_2O" began at dawn, and a complete description is available in a manuscript written by Willis J. West, superintendent of the B.C. Express Company, for the July-October 1949 issue of the *British Columbia Historical Quarterly*. A condensed version follows:

B.X. steamed around a bend and there, brilliantly lighted, was *Conveyor*. As *B.X.* drew near, Browne, hearing the safety-valve of *Conveyor* blowing, realized that her boiler had a full head of steam and that she was ready for the start of the contest. When

B.X. was still some distance away, the other ship's engine-room gong and jingle could be heard ringing as Captain Shannon signaled for the big steamer to begin moving out into the stream. The compound-condensing engines of *B.X.* exhausted noiselessly into her condenser so that the only sound made by her was that of her sternwheel buckets striking the water. *Conveyor's* high-pressure engines exhausted into her smokestack with a roar that could be heard for a mile. As she steamed into the channel of the Fraser, the top of her stack appeared to be ablaze, and she resembled some great fiery monster.

Passengers on *B.X.* were soon awakened by the alarming sound of *Conveyor's* exhaust and came out on deck to investigate, and before long they became enthusiastic over the prospect of their ship winning the contest. At the end of about the first half-hour of the race the big construction steamer had not passed nor even gained on her smaller rival. *B.X.* soon arrived at a point where it was necessary to make a landing to deliver a sack of mail. The landing was made as quickly as possible and when she moved out in the channel again, she was still ahead of her opponent by a considerable margin. In the run to Twan's Landing, a distance of about 20 miles, she made four calls and was still half a mile in the lead when she docked at Twan's. Here considerable delay was caused by the checking and signing of the freight bills. This enabled *Conveyor* to overtake *B.X.* and to pass on up the river.

In about half an hour after leaving Twan's Landing *B.X.* had caught up with *Conveyor*, but when Captain Browne started to pass in the narrow channel, he was prevented from doing so by the manner in which Captain Shannon crowded his steamer over in the channel. Browne made several attempts to get by, but Shannon evidently had forgotten the conditions which he had suggested and which Browne had accepted. The former's Irish temper was gaining the ascendancy over his usual affable and level-headed disposition, and he was determined not to let *B.X.* make her way past.

Further upstream when it became obvious that *B.X.* was going to pass, Captain Shannon deliberately rammed her. It was only through great good fortune that *Conveyor* struck *B.X.* where the shear of their guards met. Had she not been in that fortunate position, the much wider guard on the Foley boat would have smashed through the side of her engine-room, damaging her port engine and probably putting her out of commission for the remainder of the season.

This race proved the climax of upper Fraser steamboating. In August 1914, the First World War began and work on the Pacific Great Eastern was halted. John W. Stewart of Foley, Welch and Stewart soon went to France to coordinate railway construction and operations along the British sector of the Western Front, leading over 20,000 Canadian Railway Troops as a brigadier-general. Machinery from the *Conveyor* and *Operator* was sold to local sawmill operators, and the hulls were hauled out of the river and allowed to rot on the riverbank.

The sternwheeler *Caledonia* at Hazelton, British Columbia, circa 1901. (British Columbia Archives B-01314.)

The *Distributor* had yet another distinction compared with its sternwheeler compatriots. It functioned as a Travelling Post Office (TPO) along the Mackenzie River as *Distributor III*. Its first postal cancellation (listing S-171) appeared only in 1937 in the form of type 3D (see images in table 3.4 in chapter 3) with the text reading HUDSON'S BAY COMPANY/S.S. "DISTRIBUTOR". Its second cancellation (listing S-172), being of the same type as the first, had the text HUDSON'S BAY COMPANY / MACKENZIE RIVER / TRANSPORT / S.S. "DISTRIBUTOR" and was used from 1937 to 1946. A third cancellation (listing S-229), in the form of type 13B (see images in table 3.4 in chapter 3), was a temporary one, only being used during Governor General Lord Tweedsmuir's visit to northern Canada via the Mackenzie River in 1937. Its text read S.S. DISTRIBUTOR/·POST OFFICE.

Table 4.1
Lorne (official no. 94809)

Builder:	Middlemas and Boole in Victoria, British Columbia, in 1889.
Engine:	Triple-expansion (18-, 28-, and 48-inch piston diameters and 36-inch stroke).
Boiler:	16 feet x 11.7 feet (Scotch type) (1909).
Dimensions:	151 feet long x 26 feet wide x 13 feet deep.
Propulsion:	Steam screw (single).
Tonnage:	288/155 (gross/net).
Speed:	14 knots.
Miscellaneous:	Rebuilt in 1917–18 and 1927. One of the most powerful tow/tugboats on the Canadian and northern U.S. West Coast. Commonly towed lumber and pulp-and-paper rafts later in its career.

Owners	Dates
J.O. Dunsmuir	1889–1904
Puget Sound Tug Boat Company (Vancouver Tug Boat Company)	1904–14
Alexander McDermott	1914–17
Grand Trunk Pacific Railway	1917–21
Hecate Strait Towing Company	1921–25+
Puget Sound Tug Boat Company (Vancouver Tug Boat Company)	?
Pacific Navigation Company	1927
Pacific (Coyle) Navigation Company	1931, 1935, 1937
Shaeffer-Haggert Company	1937

Incidents

- On November 16, 1894, the *Lorne* towed the steamer *Harold* from the vicinity of Race Rocks (reef in Juan de Fuca Strait, about five miles from Esquimalt) into Esquimalt after latter had been holed on the rocks.
- In July 1896, the *Lorne*, while towing the steamer *Melrose*, grounded near Sooke. The *Lorne* floated off at high tide and made for Victoria for repairs. The *Melrose* was a total loss.
- On January 26, 1900, the *Lorne* rescued the crew of the steamer *Miami* after the latter struck a reef between Danger Reef and White Rocks. The *Lorne* and the tow/tugboat *Pilot* tried to pull the vessel off but could not move it. As the tide dropped, the vessel fell apart.
- On August 10, 1911, the *Lorne* assisted when the barge *Big Bonanza* of the Alaska Barge Company (towed by the tow/tugboat *Pioneer*) got into trouble.
- Wrecked on August 30, 1914, in Kanaka Bay, San Juan Island. The sailing ship in tow (*America*) was a total loss. The *Lorne* was raised but was left in derelict condition in Eagle Harbor, Washington, until bought by the Grand Trunk Pacific Railway in 1917 from Alexander McDermott.
- In September 1930, the *Lorne* and the barge *Pacific Gatherer* were involved in a spectacular accident. Fast, unpredictable tides caused the two to collide side to side when the *Lorne* was slowed and both hit the Second Narrows Bridge. C.H. Cates Towing was sent out, but its strong fleet made no headway. As the tide came in, the barge slowly rose and caused the bridge span to come off its foundation. As a result, the bridge plunged into the water.
- On December 11, 1934, the *Lorne* had to drop a raft of hemlock pulp logs due to a vicious gale and unpredictable tides pulling them toward a reef. Raft could not be found later despite extensive searches being made.

Disposition

- Broken up in 1937 at British Columbia Marine Engineering and Shipbuilding Yards.

Table 4.2

Skeena (official no. 126212)

Builder:	D. McPhee in Robertson's yard in Coal Harbour, Vancouver, in 1908.
Engines:	Two high-pressure, horizontal, 11-inch cylinder diameter, 54-inch stroke, 8.3 nhp, by Albion Iron Works, Victoria (1908).
Boiler:	No data.
Dimensions:	121 feet long x 27 feet wide x 6 feet deep.
Propulsion:	Steam sternwheel.
Tonnage:	515/310 (gross/net).
Passenger Capacity:	450.
Miscellaneous:	Launched on the Skeena River in the spring of 1909. Once the Grand Trunk Pacific line from Prince Rupert to Hazelton was completed, vessel was sold to Captain Charles Seymour and taken to the lower Fraser River where it plied its trade between New Westminster and Chilliwack until Seymour's death in 1925. In 1925–29, vessel became a floating dormitory barge for Ewen's Cannery and later a barge for an unidentified oil company. Operated by Captain Magar from 1909 until sold to Captain Seymour. From 1908–11, virtually exclusively used to supply meat to construction camps every two miles along the Skeena River. Cattle were driven from the Chilcotin for slaughter at Hazelton. Meat was then loaded onto the vessel and delivered to camps. Became known as "Pat Burn's boat."

Owners	Dates
Foley, Welch and Stewart	1908–1911/1914
Captain Seymour (North Arm Steamship Company and Mainland Navigation Company)	1911/1914–1925
Ewen's Cannery	1925–?
Unidentified oil company	?–1929

Disposition
• After becoming a dormitory barge and then an oil barge, vessel's ultimate fate is not known.

Table 4.3

Distributor (official nos. 122393, 130619, 150523)

Builder:	Alexander Watson, Jr., in Victoria West in 1908 (official no. 122393). M. MacAskill in Kamloops in 1912 (official no. 130619). Unknown builder in Fort Smith, Northwest Territories, in 1920 (official no. 150523) (*Distributor III*).
Engines:	Two high-pressure, horizontal, 15-inch cylinder diameter, 72-inch stroke, 15 nhp, by Polson Iron Works, Toronto (1908) (same machinery used in all three vessels).
Boilers:	Four locomotive-like (each 27.4 feet long and 5.7 feet in diameter) at 212 psi.
Dimensions:	137 feet long x 30 feet wide x 5 feet deep (official no. 122393); 143 feet long x 35 feet wide x 5 feet deep (official no. 130619); 151 feet long x 35 feet wide x 6 feet deep (official no. 150523).
Propulsion:	Steam sternwheel.
Tonnage:	607/379 gross/net (official no. 122393); 624/393 gross/net (official no. 130619); 876 gross (official no. 150523).
Freight Capacity:	200 tons.
Miscellaneous:	In 1908 the Hudson's Bay Company chartered vessel to make several trips up the Stikine River. After completion of the Grand Trunk Pacific line from Prince Rupert to Hazelton, vessel was dismantled in 1911 and machinery was used to build a second *Distributor* in Kamloops. This vessel was used on the Thompson River in the construction of the Canadian Northern Railway and was subsequently rebuilt as a barge in 1918. Its machinery was used in 1920 to build the *Distributor III* at Fort Smith for use on the Mackenzie River.

Owners	Dates
Grand Trunk Pacific Railway	1908–09
Foley, Welch and Stewart	1909–12
J.M. Mercer/Twohy Brothers (?)	1912–21
Alberta and Arctic Transportation Company (renamed *Distributor III*)	1921–30
Hudson's Bay Company	1930–46

Incidents

- While escorting the *Omineca* in November 1909, vessel grounded and was hauled onto sandbar and overwintered on Skeena River. Repaired in Prince Rupert in the spring of 1910 before resuming work.

Disposition

- *Distributor* (no. 1) was dismantled in 1911–12.
- *Distributor* (no. 2) was beached and scrapped in 1927. Machinery previously removed in 1911–12 had been reused to create this vessel.
- *Distributor III* was abandoned in 1946. Machinery previously removed in 1918 had been reused to create this vessel.

Table 4.4

Omineca (official no. 126248)

Builder:	Original builder and official number not known. Builder in rebuilding of original wrecked vessel was Alexander Watson, Jr., of Victoria West in 1909 (official no. 126248).
Engines:	Two high-pressure, horizontal, 16-inch piston diameter, 72-inch stroke by Albion Iron Works, Victoria (1891/1892). Came from the *Caledonia* (official no. 107145).
Boiler:	No data.
Dimensions:	138 feet long x 31 feet wide x 5 feet deep.
Propulsion:	Steam sternwheel.
Tonnage:	583/380 (gross/net).
Miscellaneous:	The original *Omineca* was purchased in 1908 (seller unknown). It was wrecked in the same year near Port Essington, British Columbia. Its machinery was reused by Alexander Watson, Jr., to build another sternwheeler, rechristened in 1909 with the same name (official no. 126248). Worked for the Grand Trunk Pacific until the Prince Rupert–Hazelton line was completed. Sold to the U.S. government in 1916 for use in railway construction in Alaska Territory (U.S. Government Railroad/Alaska Railroad). Was assigned to the Alaskan Engineering Commission and located on the Susitna River and in Cook Inlet. Retired in 1917.

Owners	Dates
Grand Trunk Pacific Railway	1908–09
Foley, Welch and Stewart	1909–16
U.S. federal government	1916–1923/1930

Incidents

- Struck Beaverdam Rock in the Skeena River 15 miles below Hazelton on November 8, 1909. Was refloated and was being escorted by the *Distributor* when both grounded. Both were hauled onto sandbars and overwintered on the Skeena River. Proceeding to Prince Rupert in the spring of 1910, both were repaired before starting the 1910 freighting season.
- Grounded in the Skeena River in August 1910. Pulled off by the *Distributor* with no serious damage from the grounding.

Disposition

- After being retired in 1917, vessel was gone sometime between 1923 and 1930 (destination and fate unknown).

Table 4.5

Conveyor (official nos. 126250, 130885)

Builder:	Alexander Watson, Jr./G.A. MacNicholl in Victoria West in 1909 (official no. 126250). G. Askew in Tête Jaune Cache in 1912 (official no. 130885).
Engines:	Two high-pressure, horizontal, 15-inch cylinder diameter, 72-inch stroke, 15 nhp, by Polson Iron Works, Toronto (1909) (used in both vessels).
Boiler:	No data.
Dimensions:	138 feet long x 31 feet wide x 5 feet deep (official no. 126250); 142 feet long x 35 feet wide x 5 feet deep (official no. 130885).
Propulsion:	Steam sternwheel.
Tonnage:	583/380 gross/net (official no. 126250); 725/457 gross/net (official no. 130885).
Passenger Capacity:	200.
Freight Capacity:	200 tons.
Miscellaneous:	*Conveyor* (no. 1) was launched on the Skeena River in 1909. Once the Grand Trunk Pacific line from Prince Rupert to Hazelton was completed, vessel was dismantled in 1911 and its machinery was used to build *Conveyor* (no. 2) at Tête Jaune Cache in 1912. Vessel was then used to assist in building the Grand Trunk Pacific line from Tête Jaune Cache to Fort George. Made occasional trips between South Fort George and Soda Creek. Vessel was retired once this line was completed. Machinery was sold to nearby sawmills, etc., and hull was hauled out and left to rot. Operated by Captain Jack Shannon. Could, with itself fully loaded, push a scow carrying 90 tons against the current. In 1912, due to a light snowfall, could only be used for three weeks due to the shallowness of the river!

Owners	Dates
Grand Trunk Pacific Railway	1909
Foley, Welch and Stewart	1909–15

Table 4.6

Operator (official nos. 126501, 130886)

Details are identical to those under *Conveyor* (table 4.5), with the exceptions of the official numbers and its captain (Captain "Con" Meyers, aka "Flying Dutchman" and "Terrible Swede").

Table 4.7

Caledonia (official no. 107145)

Builder:	Unknown builder in New Westminster, British Columbia, in 1898.
Engines:	Two high-pressure, horizontal, 16-inch piston diameter, 72-inch stroke, 17 nhp, by Albion Iron Works, Victoria (1892). Original engines were from the first *Caledonia* (official no. 97162).
Boiler:	No data.
Dimensions:	142 feet long x 30 feet wide x 4 feet deep.
Propulsion:	Steam sternwheel.
Tonnage:	569/359 (gross/net).
Miscellaneous:	This is the second *Caledonia*. Made six trips up the Stikine River to Glenora in 1898. Last trip in 1898 up the Skeena River took one month and vessel did not get within 50 miles of Hazelton due to low water. Engines were used in the *Omineca* (official no. 126248) after the *Caledonia* (no. 2) was wrecked.

Owners	Dates
Hudson's Bay Company	1898–?
Columbia Trading	?–1907
Alexander McDermott et al. (name changed to *Northwestern*)	1907–08
Foley, Welch and Stewart (name changed to *Caledonia*)	1908

Disposition
• Wrecked on a rock in the Skeena River on October 15, 1908, at mile 44 and scrapped.

5

"ROYAL" AND "DUKE" SHIPS (AND OTHER VESSELS) OF CANADIAN NORTHERN RAILWAY PASSENGER/FREIGHT SHIPPING INITIATIVES ON SALT WATER

The Canadian Northern Steamship Company was a late entry into the transatlantic passenger and freight trade, being incorporated under Dominion letters patent on October 21, 1909. However, its origins and timeline actually involve three other shipping lines: New York and Continental Line (1907–08), Northwest Transport Line (1909–10), and Uranium Steamship Company (1910–16). This chapter will describe, in brief, all four shipping lines as well as their contributions to the Entente war effort during the First World War, which will be followed by a discussion of

- Sternwheelers in the construction of the Canadian Northern Railway.
- Coastal B.C. passenger and freight services of the Canadian Northern Steamship Company.

- Coastal B.C. Canadian Northern barge, railbarge, and railferry services.
- Log boom towing by the Canadian Tugboat Company, a subsidiary of the Canadian Western Lumber Company (in which Mackenzie, Mann and Company were major shareholders).

NEW YORK AND CONTINENTAL LINE

This firm was established by Robertson, Shankland, and Company in 1907 to carry grain/flour to Europe (capitalized at $500,000). The company also wished to break into the lucrative immigrant trade to fill its ships on their westward sailings to North America. Routes included Hamburg, Germany to/from Rotterdam, Holland to/from Halifax to/from New York City. Ships left every two weeks from

Hamburg (loaded only with freight), proceeded to Rotterdam where passengers were embarked, then sailed to Halifax, followed by New York City. The company had three vessels: the 5,183-ton *Avoca* (official no. 98663), 5,186-ton *Jelunga* (official no. 98596), and 3,586-ton *Volturno* (official no. 123737). The *Avoca* and *Jelunga* were owned by the company, while the *Volturno* was chartered from the Volturno Steamship Company for two round trips in 1908.

Unfortunately, for the company, there were four shipping lines competing for passengers/freight on the Rotterdam to/from New York route. In addition, financial difficulties worsened after the *Avoca* collided with an anchored German steamer (*Lordsee*) at the Hook of Holland in July 1908. When the company declared bankruptcy in 1908, Northwest Transport Line assumed its routes, effective in 1909. The *Jelunga* was sold back to its former owner, the British India Steam Navigation Company. The *Avoca* was auctioned off and purchased by C.G. Ashdown for £15,000. Ashdown, in turn, sold the vessel to the Northwest Transport Line for £35,000, earning a healthy profit. Details about the *Avoca*, *Jelunga*, and *Volturno* are provided in tables 5.1 to 5.3, respectively.

NORTHWEST TRANSPORT LINE

The Northwest Transport Line was founded in 1909 by Peterson and Company of London, England, and was largely a revival of the New York and Continental Line with the injection of new capital. Ports of call included those of the defunct New York and Continental Line.

The steamer *Jelunga*. (Ian Lawler Collection.)

The steamer *Volturno* burning in the North Atlantic. Note that the lifeboat in the foreground was a "later addition" to the photograph, as evidenced by the unnatural appearance of the sea near the boat plus the absence of sea spray at the bow or from the oars. (Fotocollectie Het Leven SFA022806644.)

The Steamer *Uranium* disembarking passengers on Ellis Island in New York City in 1913. Note the Uranium Steamship Company "colours" on the funnel. (Fotocollectie Het Leven SFA022818943.)

The Canadian Northern Steamship Company acquired the line in 1910 and changed the firm's name to the Uranium Steamship Company. Six vessels sailed on behalf of the Northwest Transport Line: the 9,001-ton *Campania*, later renamed the *Campanello* (official no. 115224, table 5.4), the 5,183-ton *Uranium*, previously the *Avoca* and then the *Atlanta* (table 5.1), the 3,586-ton *Volturno* (table 5.3), the 2,900-ton *Napolitan Prince* (official no. 114432, table 5.5), the 4,342-ton *Raglan Castle* (official no. 108181, table 5.6), and the 2,964-ton *Sicilian Prince* (official no. 115845, table 5.7). The latter three vessels were chartered from their owners for limited periods of time, while the former three vessels were all transferred to the successor Uranium Steamship Company. For example, the *Napolitan Prince* and *Sicilian Prince* were chartered from the Prince Line for four round trips each in 1909–10. The *Raglan Castle* was chartered from Barclay, Curle and Company in 1909 for the entire summer season. The *Campania* was chartered from Navigazione Generale Italiana for two round trips in 1910, while the *Volturno* was chartered for 10 round trips in 1909–10. Both vessels were then transferred to the Uranium Steamship Company, which purchased them. The *Uranium* had already been bought by the company at its inception.

URANIUM STEAMSHIP COMPANY

The Uranium Steamship Company was a continuation of the Northwest Transport Line from 1910 onward, owned by the Canadian Northern Steamship Company. In January 1911, it was announced that the Uranium Steamship Company agent in Halifax had been charged with attempting to land 15 passengers with trachoma,

The steamer *Napolitan Prince* shown as *Manouba*, the latter becoming the former's successor in 1911. (Author's Collection.)

The steamer *Sicilian Prince*. (Peabody Museum of Salem.)

Cigar tin from the Uranium Steamship Company. (Alf van Beem Collection.)

Advertising card for the Uranium Steamship Line, featuring the *Campanello*. (Ian Lawler Collection.)

the case being subsequently dismissed. Trachoma is a highly contagious eye infection caused by the sexually transmitted bacterium *Chlamydia trachomatis*, which left untreated causes blindness. Its presence in immigrants resulted in an automatic refusal of entry into Canada and the United States. In May 1911, a London, England, press dispatch announced that the Uranium Steamship Company had been "banished" from trade in Holland for infringement of regulations pertaining to the landing of third-class passengers bound for Eastern Europe. This case was eventually amicably settled such that Rotterdam would still be a port of call for the Uranium Line.

Until 1914 the passenger route of Rotterdam to/from Halifax to/from New York City was maintained. Beginning in 1914, the route was changed to Avonmouth (Bristol, England) to/from Quebec City to/from Montreal. The three ships in the fleet (the 9,291-ton *Campanello* [table 5.4], 6,705-ton *Principello* [official no. 136640, table 5.8], and 5,183-ton *Uranium* [table 5.1]) were sold to the Cunard Steamship Company in 1916, becoming the *Flavia*, *Folia*, and *Feltria*, respectively. The 3,581-ton *Volturno* had been destroyed by fire at sea in 1913 with the loss of 136 persons (for details, see "Canadian Northern Ship Disasters" later in this chapter). The three vessels had been purchased by the Canadian Northern Steamship Company and chartered by the Uranium Steamship Company. All three vessels sold to Cunard were victims of German submarines, thus wiping out the former Uranium Steamship Company.

The two predecessors of the Uranium Steamship Company were driven out of business by the predatory activities of the Atlantic Steamship Conference. Using

The steamer *Campanello*.
(Ian Lawler Collection.)

The steamer *Principello*. (Author's Collection.)

tactics such as withdrawing Conference business from agents selling tickets on an independent line, the use of "fighting ships," or withholding of railway commissions from agents selling tickets on an independent line, independent lines were crippled, gaining just two percent of the westbound immigrant trade. The term *fighting ships* refers to the use of one or more Conference ships placed on the same route with the same ports of call as the target independent line. By continually undercutting the independent line's fares, it would not be long before the independent was driven out of business. The losses incurred by the fighting ships were then spread across all of the conference members. Even the Uranium Line was crippled by these tactics, leading in 1910 to its sale to the Canadian Northern Steamship Company.

CANADIAN NORTHERN STEAMSHIP COMPANY

The Canadian Northern Steamship Company was incorporated in Toronto on October 21, 1909, and capitalized at $2 million. Provisional directors included F.H. Phippen, G.G. Reid, G.F. MacDonnell, R.H.M. Temple, and A.J. Reid (all with Canadian Northern affiliations). The appointed directors included W. Mackenzie, D. Mann, Z.A. Lash, D.B. Hanna, A.D. Davidson and, beginning late in 1912, R.M. Horne-Payne. The initial Atlantic fleet comprised four vessels: the *Cairo* (subsequently renamed the *Royal Edward*, official no. 125656, table 5.9), the *Heliopolis* (subsequently renamed *Royal George*, official no. 125643, table 5.9), the *Volturno* (chartered by Canadian Northern

Hollowware badging of Canadian Northern Steamships. From a silver plated egg cup with no manufacturer identification. (Author's Collection.)

to the Uranium Steamship Company with a planned name change to the *Royal Sovereign*, table 5.3), and one steamer to be determined (which was never added). Avonmouth (Bristol) would be the U.K. port of call with Quebec City and Montreal being the Canadian ports of call, at least during the spring, summer, and fall seasons.

By April 1910, company personnel had already been assigned. Captains Roberts and Harrison were to be masters of the *Royal Edward* and *Royal George*, respectively. H.J. Cowle, W.J. Cartmel, and W.F. Haydon were to be European traffic manager, general passenger agent, and publicity manager, respectively. Lastly, Captain Gregory was to be acting marine superintendent. All of the preceding personnel would be headquartered in Bristol. On the Canadian West Coast, until the Canadian Northern Steamship Company passenger business became established there, the Canadian Mexican Steamship Company would act as the agent for Canadian Northern Steamships. At some point Halvor Jacobsen and Company of San Francisco became Pacific coast agents for Canadian Northern Steamships.

THE ROYAL LINE   T.T.S.S. "ROYAL GEORGE".

DINNER.

HORS D'ŒUVRES VARIES

CONSOMMÉ SULLESTINE

BOILED COD—OYSTER SAUCE

SALMI OF BLACK GAME
FRENCH BEANS—LYONNAISE

RIBS of BEEF, YORKSHIRE PUDDING
HIND-QUARTER of LAMB—MINT SAUCE
ROAST CAPON—BREAD SAUCE

SPRING CABBAGE   JULIENNE ROOTS
BOILED & BAKED POTATOES

CHEESE RINGS

CHANCELLOR PUDDING   WINE JELLY
SMALL PASTRY   ICES

CHEESE   FRUIT   COFFEE

September 22, 1910.

Dinner menu, 1910, from the *Royal George*. (Author's Collection.)

Canadian Northern Steamships uniform button. "Canadian Northern Steamship Co." appears on a stippled band around the sun. A queen's (illustrated) or king's crown on a stippled circle appears in the centre. The border is cable. (Author's Collection.)

Early in 1910, the three Canadian Northern steamships entered dry dock for renovations. The *Volturno* was refitted with accommodations for 1,000 third-class passengers and saloon accommodations for "a few." The "Royals" were refitted on the River Clyde in Scotland, since their alterations were much more extensive. A considerable portion of what had been second-class accommodations were converted to third-class accommodations. A third-class dining room was built near the third-class cabins. All public rooms for first and second class remained unchanged. Coal bunkers were enlarged due to the greater distances to be travelled, bows were strengthened to withstand the effects of ice, and the funnels were shortened. The colour scheme was an attractive lead (or grey) on the lower superstructure, white on the upper superstructure, and yellow on the funnels, which were topped with blue bands.

It did not take long for the "Royals" to make their marks with respect to speed across the Atlantic. Even early in 1910, the *Royal Edward* had set a record for the Bristol–Quebec City crossing of five days, 20 hours, eclipsing the old record by six and a half hours.

Starting on May 1, 1913, the *Royal Edward* became one of 15 ships (from a total of four companies) engaged in the Canadian mail contract to/from the United Kingdom. In the same month, Canadian Northern Steamships joined the Canadian North Atlantic Westbound Freight Conference. In late 1913, Canadian Northern Steamships purchased the *Principe di Piemonte* (name subsequently changed to the *Principello*) and leased it to the Uranium Steamship Company to take the place of the sunken *Volturno*

The "Royal Edward" Entering Avonmouth Dock.

Postcard view of the *Royal Edward* in Avonmouth, England. Date unknown. (Author's Collection.)

(see "Canadian Northern Ship Disasters" later in this chapter). The *Principe di Piemonte* was purchased for the princely sum of £135,000, costing only £120,000 when brand-new in 1907. Ownership of the *Principello* was actually vested in Principello Steamship Limited, organized in May 1914, capitalized at $150,000, and possessing a board of directors strongly affiliated with Canadian Northern. In August 1914, ownership of the *Campanello* was vested in another Canadian Northern subsidiary, Campanello Steamship Limited, capitalized at $100,000 with a similar composition of the board of directors.

After the British declaration of war, Canadian Northern Steamships operated the *Uranium* and *Principello*, while the two "Royals" were taken over by the British Admiralty as troopships (see "Canadian Northern Steamship Company Vessels and the First World War"

Postcard view of the *Royal George* at Avonmouth, England. (Author's Collection.)

Will's 1914 cigarette card of RMS *Royal Edward*. (Author's Collection.)

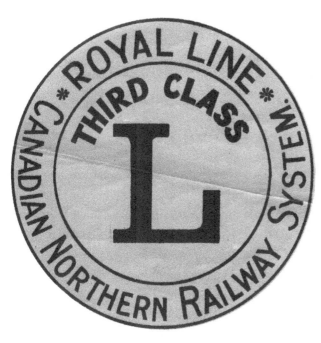

Royal Line (Canadian Northern Railway System) third-class "L" baggage label. (Author's Collection.)

later in this chapter). At this point the *Uranium* became one of the first single-fare vessels, with a fixed transatlantic one-way fare of $55 for all passengers.

The Cunard Steamship Company purchased the entire assets of the Canadian Northern and Uranium Steamship Companies early in 1916. This was probably based on two factors. One, the Cunard Line had been especially hard hit by the German submarine offensive and the British Admiralty felt that Cunard needed an infusion of shipping to keep going. Second, the financial difficulties of the parent Canadian Northern Railway, due to a lack of British investment capital secondary to

the war, were becoming extreme and the sales of these assets would bring some relief, albeit temporary. The two firms had had a close working relationship, the various Canadian services having become, in effect, one transportation company between the British Isles and Canada.

Table 5.10 illustrates in graphic form the timeline of ownership/chartership of the 10 vessels involved in the transatlantic freight and passenger services of the Canadian Northern Steamship Company.

CANADIAN NORTHERN SHIP DISASTERS

On Thursday, October 2, 1913, the *Volturno* sailed from Rotterdam with 562 passengers (22 cabin, 540 third class) and 93 crew, for a total of 655 on board. Early on October 9, during a strong northwest gale that created 30-foot waves, a cry of "Fire" was heard on board. The No. 1 cargo hold in the fore of the ship was fully engulfed by a fire of unknown origin.

The initial surge of fire killed four crewmen sleeping in the forecastle. Captain Francis Inch began to oversee firefighting efforts while other crew members hustled passengers to the aft area of the ship. Shortly after beginning efforts to control the blaze, an explosion in the other cargo hold killed, perhaps, dozens of passengers and/or crew. Fearing a further explosion that could send the ship to the bottom, Captain Inch ordered the lifeboats to be filled and lowered. Six launches were attempted into the towering seas. Four boats, full of women and children, smashed into the heaving ship, killing all aboard. Only two boats got away with anyone on board and one of these had to be righted after capsizing and spilling its cargo of women and children into the sea.

Meanwhile, the two wireless operators had sent out distress calls to nearby ships, asking for assistance. Knowing that help was on its way, the captain suspended further lifeboat launches and focused on "buying time" with effective firefighting. Several passengers despaired of rescue and chose the sea over the fire. By mid-afternoon the fire had reached the ship's coal bunkers, consuming precious fuel for the engines that was needed to keep the firehose pumps, electric lights, and wireless running. When power ceased, the wireless operators switched over to batteries and kept sending/receiving messages until the antenna was destroyed in another explosion.

A total of 10 ships arrived to render assistance. The *Carmania* had been the closest vessel to respond, at 80 miles away, and took four hours to arrive. It immediately launched a lifeboat that tried for hours to reach the stricken vessel, only to return without a single person. As other ships arrived, they likewise launched lifeboats and made for the *Volturno*. Although several boats did get close, the rolling ship and towering waves prevented all rescue attempts.

Early on October 10 at 0700 hours, to help calm the seas, the *Narragansett* sprayed 50 tons of oil on the surface of the water, converting crashing waves into gentle swells. This, plus the lessening of the gale itself, enabled nearly all of the ships to swarm around the *Volturno* and remove all remaining passengers and crew. Captain Inch was the last to leave. All 10 ships left in different directions to search for the *Volturno*'s two lost lifeboats (which were never found) before resuming their transatlantic journeys (four proceeding to North America and six to Europe).

The North German Lloyd *Grosser Kurfurst* and the Russian-American *Czar* rescued the largest number of people, with 208 between them. The other ships rescued one (*Carmania*) to 86 (Red Star Line *Kroonland*) people. In all, 520 of 655 (79 percent) embarking were rescued (457 passengers and 63 crew).

All but 20 of those landing on European soil did set out again for the New World. Those landing in the United States were assisted by the American Red Cross, Hebrew Sheltering Home, Clara De Hirsch Home, and Settlement House. Those with an intended destination in Canada were helped financially by the Red Cross.

Other disasters for which fewer details are available include the sinking by German submarines of the *Royal Edward* (see "Canadian Northern Steamship Company Vessels and the First World War" below), *Uranium / Feltria*, *Campanello / Flavia*, and *Principello / Folia*. With the exception of the *Royal George*, the entire ocean-going fleet of Canadian Northern Steamships was destroyed during the First World War. Even the *Royal George* did not contribute to Canadian National Steamships after the war. Instead, it remained in Europe and was scrapped in 1922.

CANADIAN NORTHERN STEAMSHIP COMPANY VESSELS AND THE FIRST WORLD WAR

The following Canadian Northern vessels were requisitioned by the British Admiralty as troopships in 1914: the *Royal Edward* and *Royal George* (which were taken over) and the *Campanello / Flavia* and *Uranium / Feltria* (which were chartered). Overnight the "Royals" were transformed from luxurious Royal Mail Steamers (RMS) to His Majesty's Transports (HMT). By the end of hostilities, only the *Royal George* was left afloat to convey troops home, since the other three vessels were all victims of German U-boats.

At a meeting with the minister of militia, Sir Sam Hughes, on August 15, 1914, it was announced that 20 ships were needed to carry some 20,000 men across the North Atlantic, sailing about mid-September. On September 11, contracts were signed for 30 ships after it was decided to send the entire force already assembled at Valcartier camp. Troopship conversion occurred in Montreal after which ships proceeded to Quebec City to embark their troops. After an embarkation period lasting from September 23 to October 1, which could only be described as "chaos reigning supreme," the First Contingent proceeded to Gaspé Bay to form the first of many Canadian convoys, setting out on October 3.

The *Royal Edward* was assigned to column Y (White Squadron) and the *Royal George* to column X (Red Squadron). Column Y was led by the cruiser HMS *Eclipse*, while column X was led by the cruiser HMS *Charybdis*. Five other warships also accompanied the convoy, which reached Devonport, England, on October 14. The *Uranium* sailed separately with First Contingent troops on board, setting out on August 24, 1914, with HMS *Glory* as an escort. It was subsequently used as an accommodation ship for German prisoners of war from September 1914 through March 1915. The cost to the British government for use of the two "Royals" as troopships in 1914 added up to nearly $100,000 ($45,080 for the *Royal Edward* and $54,243 for the *Royal George*). These monies paid for vessel refit and lease, food, supplies, and crew.

For several months the *Royal Edward* was employed as an internment ship for enemy aliens. When John B. Jackson of the American embassy in Berlin visited Britain to report on the treatment of German prisoners of war in England, he inspected the *Royal Edward* during its time as an internment vessel. In his report he stated:

> Of the ships, the *Royal Edward* was obviously the show ship. On board, the interned were separated into three classes dependent to a certain extent upon their social standing, but to a greater extent to their ability to meet extra expenses. Prisoners were permitted to avail themselves of the regular first-class cabins upon payment in advance of from 5s (shillings) to 2s 6d (2 shillings, 6 pence) a week, according to the number of persons occupying a cabin. At that time, the ship was lying off Southend, and Mr. Jackson reported that all the prisoners were locked below decks at night, which caused some nervousness among them owing to the apprehension of danger from Zeppelin attack.

Early in 1915, the *Campanello* and *Principello* served as troopships of a different sort. They were chartered to carry horses from Newport News, Virginia, to Saint-Nazaire, France. Horse transport was vital to the war effort, especially in the movement of artillery pieces.

Reinforcements for the Dardanelles campaign at Gallipoli boarded the *Royal Edward* on July 28, 1915, at Avonmouth, the former peacetime embarkation point for Canadian Northern Steamships. The ship was bound for Mudros on the Greek island of Lemnos via Malta and Alexandria, with a cargo of government stores, soldiers from a number of regiments, and medical personnel. The *Royal Edward* set sail on July 28, 1915, at approximately 2000 hours.

On the same day, the *Royal George* set sail with Dardanelles reinforcements from Devonport. Of interest, the *Royal Edward* followed the *Royal George* in the Mediterranean about a day behind. Even in wartime the sister ships were inseparable. On this voyage the *Royal Edward* had a crew of 220 and 1,366 military personnel (31 officers, 1,335 other ranks) for a total of 1,586 individuals.

On Friday, August 13, 1915, German submarine UB-14 sighted the unescorted *Royal Edward* making for Mudros. A single torpedo was fired from less than one mile away, hitting the ship stern portside. After a huge explosion, the ship began to sink and did so very quickly in only six minutes. Its final position was six miles west of Kardeliusa (Kandhelioussa), 36°31′N, 26°51′E. Although initial reports suggested that only 132 were lost, this figure is clearly inaccurate, even though it has been repeated in many publications up to the 1980s. The loss of life was more likely from 985 to 1,500 individuals.

One relevant question is why was the death toll so high? This can be explained as follows. Just before the attack there had been a lifeboat drill so that when the torpedo struck many men were beneath decks stowing their life vests. Another account states that the men, who had undertaken a route march prior to leaving Alexandria, were waiting on deck for foot inspection at about 0920 hours when the torpedo hit. Their lifebelts were below deck, so most of the men ran there to fetch them and never saw daylight again.

Survivors were picked up by the hospital ship *Soudom*, two French destroyers, and some Greek trawlers, most likely from Nisyros or Kos. Another, the *Achilles*, managed to rescue 21 survivors. The UB-14 did not harass the rescue ships. The submarine's compass had become defective, so it returned immediately to its home port of Bodrum in what is now Turkey for repairs. The defenceless *Royal Edward* holds the dubious distinction of being the first conscripted ocean-going troopship to be destroyed by enemy fire in the 20th century.

The *Royal George* went about its transport work quietly and with no fanfare. However, in March 1916, it became indirectly involved in two circumstances: one possibly being the most dishonourable act ever perpetrated by a British government and one that would unmask a most unlikely hero whose legendary tales would be the inspiration for many books and movies.

On the morning of March 22, 1916, the *Royal George* quietly slipped from its moorings at Port Suez in Egypt, turning south into the Red Sea on a 14-day journey around the Arabian Peninsula to southern Mesopotamia (today's Iraq). On board was Captain T.E. Lawrence from British military intelligence in Cairo, bearing a letter of introduction from High Commissioner Henry McMahon to Sir Percy Cox, British India's chief political officer in Mesopotamia.

Captain Lawrence bore from War Secretary Lord Kitchener himself an offer to bribe the Ottoman commander of the siege at Kut on the Tigris River into letting go an encircled and starving British army in return for gold equivalent to £1 million. This mission was so clandestine and so against the British notion of honour that its true nature was largely expunged from the history books. In a nice touch of irony, it was a mission necessitated by a catastrophe of British India's creation.

To back up briefly, after the Ottoman Empire's entrance into the First World War on the side of the Central Powers of Germany and the Austro-Hungarian Empire, Britain was justifiably concerned about the safety of its petroleum supplies in Persia (today's Iran). A decision was made to undertake a military campaign in Mesopotamia (today's Iraq) against the Ottomans to safeguard these assets. In addition, at the same time, the landings on the Gallipoli Peninsula were under intense pressure from Ottoman forces entrenched in advantageous positions at all of the landing areas. Thus, another justification for the Mesopotamian campaign emerged: to relieve pressure on the Gallipoli landings by drawing Ottoman forces away from the Gallipoli theatre. Major-General Charles Townshend's Indian forces enjoyed a series of impressive victories over larger Ottoman armies on the way up the Tigris River toward Baghdad until defeat at Ctesiphon. As a result of this defeat, the Indian army retreated downstream until making its stand at Kut. Ottoman forces laid siege to Kut beginning in November 1915.

In three long and bloody campaigns to relieve Townshend's embattled army at Kut, thousands of infantry troops were slaughtered in a series of frontal assaults on well-entrenched Ottoman positions. It appears that local commanders had learned nothing from the butchery of the Western Front and Gallipoli. During the second rescue attempt at Dujaila, just eight miles from Kut,

the 36th Indian Infantry Brigade had come upon "the Citadel," a 40-foot-high earthen fortress commanding the plain, after it had lost its way at night. Rather than being the prelude to destruction, after reconnoitre, the fortress was judged to be either deserted or held by only a tiny skeleton guard force.

Instead of taking immediate advantage of the situation, Lieutenant-General Fenton Aylmer had the brigade withdraw so that he could continue to engage in his farcical attack strategy of bombardment followed by frontal assault. Aylmer lost 14,000 men over the course of a campaign to rescue 12,000. In addition, he attempted to cover up the report of the 36th Indian Infantry Brigade to no avail. These three failed rescue attempts left Kitchener with only one desperate alternative: attempt to "buy off" the Ottomans. As it turned out, the offer was extended, unbeknownst to the British, after the garrison had formally surrendered to the Ottomans in April 1916.

The second momentous event was the launching of the much-admired legendary exploits of "Lawrence of Arabia." Yes, Captain T.E. Lawrence, intelligence master in Cairo, would emerge on the world stage after this mission. No longer would he be confined to a desk at the Savoy Hotel in Cairo. The subject of a multitude of books, films, television programs, and theatrical plays up to the present day, Lawrence would begin his public career in the weeks following the arrival of the *Royal George* in Basra, Mesopotamia, on the morning of April 5, 1916. As was usual, the docking facilities of this port city could not accommodate a ship with the draft of the *Royal George*, so a Royal Navy launch was sent to collect this most valuable passenger.

STERNWHEELERS FOR THE CANADIAN NORTHERN RAILWAY

One of the Skeena River sternwheelers detailed in chapter 4 was also involved in the construction of the Canadian Northern Railway. The second *Distributor* (official no. 130619), built in 1912 at Kamloops using machinery from the first *Distributor* (official no. 122393), was the last sternwheeler to appear in the Kamloops area. This vessel carried explosives, rails, supplies, and labourers for construction crews working on the line along the Thompson and North Thompson Rivers. It could travel 110 miles upstream on the North Thompson to supply work gangs. When this section of the line was completed, the *Distributor*'s machinery was removed and its hull was abandoned near Sicamous. This machinery was used yet again in the third reincarnation of the vessel (*Distributor III*, official no. 150523), built in 1920 for use by the Hudson's Bay Company along the Mackenzie River.

COASTAL SERVICES OF CANADIAN NORTHERN STEAMSHIPS

Early in August 1910, Canadian Northern officials announced that a contract had been awarded for the construction of two 20-knot, triple-funnelled steamers larger than those of the Grand Trunk Pacific and Canadian Pacific British Columbia Coastal Steamship lines. The coastal service would be known as the "Duke" Line and the vessels as the *Duke of Connaught* and *Duke of Clarence*. At the end of December 1910 an announcement was made that the *Duke of Connaught* was nearing completion in a Middlesborough shipyard and was scheduled to leave the United Kingdom in April 1911 to enter the Victoria to/from Vancouver to/from Stewart service. The *Duke of Clarence* was to follow a few weeks later. In January 1911, it was publicized that the two vessels would also serve the ports of Prince Rupert and Skagway. As late as November 1913, a press release declared that a contract had been awarded to Fairfield Shipbuilders to build two 20-knot steam turbine ships to serve all of the aforementioned ports. In addition, it was revealed that they would visit San Francisco during the Panama-Pacific International Exposition in 1915 as well as other Californian and Mexican ports.

In the end, none of the above was true. In addition, Canadian Northern ships for the planned Far Eastern and Australian trades did not materialize. With the financial exigencies of the parent company culminating in bankruptcy and asset transfer to the Canadian government, all of these plans were shelved.

CANADIAN NORTHERN BARGE, RAIL-BARGE, AND RAILFERRY SERVICES

Barge Service (Stewart)

Mackenzie and Mann acquired mining claims in 1909 in the Stewart district of northwestern British Columbia. To develop these claims, the company began building a railway (Portland Canal Short Line) to provide service between the Red Cliff mine and the ore concentrator in Stewart. In addition, due to extensive tidal flats, the firm had to build a 5,960-foot-long dock at the head of the Portland Canal in order to create a 22-foot water depth for ocean-going ships. To carry rails, ties, and other necessary materials, Mackenzie and Mann bought the former American schooner *Ivy* to use as a barge (official no. 100190, 184.3 feet long, 37.2 feet wide, and 23.8 feet deep, 1,243/1,181 tons [gross/net], built in 1876). It was towed by chartered tow/tugboats such as the *British Columbia* (official no. 119063).

In August 1910, the *Ivy* delivered a load of rails, ties, and other materials but unloading was delayed, since the dock was not yet completed. The *Ivy* remained in Stewart until March 1911 when the first load of iron concentrates (400 tons) was ready for transfer to the Ladysmith smelter. After the concentrates had been delivered to Ladysmith, the *Ivy* was brought to the B.C. Marine Railway yard in Esquimalt for repairs and overhauling. Ready on April 4, the *Ivy* took on a load of lumber for Stewart. By August 1911, the line to Red Cliff had been completed, and by early October, the spur to the Red Cliff mine was finished (milepost 13.5).

Unfortunately, the yield from the ore was disappointing, and by April 1915, the line had shut down and the two 2-6-0 locomotives and rolling stock of the Canadian North-Eastern Railway (the name had been changed in 1911) were on a barge heading south to the Canadian Northern terminus in Port Mann, British Columbia. Although Mackenzie and Mann considered extending this short line to its Edmonton, Yukon, and Pacific Railway property or the Grand Trunk Pacific, this was not pursued. The date on which the *Ivy* became the *Donald D* (official no. 126941, named for Donald D. Mann) is not precisely known. However, by 1916 the *Donald D* was the property of the Canadian Fish and Cold Storage Company, and in November of that year, it foundered.

Glenbow Museum Poster-16.

THE UNSINKABLE SCHOONER *IVY*

The schooner *Ivy*, owned by Morris Marcus of San Francisco, came ashore at Point Barrow, Alaska, on September 1, 1908. It would also be wrecked again in 1909, adding another chapter to the interesting life story of Captain Klengenberg, the old-time Arctic whaler who was acquitted in San Francisco in 1908 of the only murder charge among several upon which he was tried. The following tale was related by Captain John Backland of the schooner *Volante* after he had returned to Puget Sound in September 1909.

In 1908 Captain Klengenberg was on his way to San Francisco from Point Barrow when, after a hard chase by the revenue cutter *Thetis*, he was apprehended and taken to San Francisco. There he was to stand trial for the cold-blooded murder of his engineer while on board his auxiliary whaling schooner. It was alleged that the captain had shot the engineer while he was asleep in his berth. At the trial, evidence was produced to the effect that the engineer had threatened to shoot the captain and that the killing was "more or less in self-defence."

Exonerated, Klengenberg rushed back to Point Barrow to rejoin his Inuit wife and their children after taking charge of the *Ivy* as master. Caught in a storm, the schooner was driven high onto the beach to a point so close to Klengenberg's home that it was stated he could almost step from the bowsprit of the *Ivy* into his doorway. When the vessel was given up by the insurance underwriters and ordered sold, Klengenberg bought it for $50, having obtained the money by selling some of the cargo of the ship that he had, with great foresight, removed previously from its hold. Hauling the *Ivy* up on the beach for the winter, he set about repairing it.

The spring of 1909 arrived and Klengenberg wished to set off on a trading voyage. Unable to obtain a crew (obviously unwelcomed by his neighbours, for all had a deadly fear of him), he took aboard his wife and children and set sail in the teeth of a strong wind. His wife was at the helm and he tended the sails. Before covering 30 miles, the *Ivy* crashed head-on at full speed into a large iceberg, crumpling its bow and creating an immense hole through which the sea poured. With superhuman strength and immense skill, the captain managed to tack the vessel and succeeded in beaching it at Point Barrow to the great annoyance of his neighbours in that Arctic outpost.

Railbarge Service (Vancouver Island)

The actual physical western terminus of the Canadian Northern Railway was at Port Mann, several miles above New Westminster, on the south bank of the Fraser River. To provide a link between the company's new Victoria to Patricia Bay line on Vancouver Island and the mainland, the railway transferred two whaling vessels from the Canadian Northern Pacific Fisheries fleet (*Sebastian*, official no. 117323, and *Germania*, official no. 131310) to Canadian Northern Steamships and built two wooden railbarges at their Port Mann yard (*Canadian Northern Pacific No. 1* and *Canadian Northern Pacific No. 2*). These barges, designed by A. Angstrom, were 158 feet long,

48 feet wide, and 11.5 feet deep. The first was launched in July and the second in early October 1916. The railbarges were also registered with Canadian Northern Steamships and each had three tracks (eight-car capacity). The two whalers were sister ships and were built at the Akers shipyard in Oslo, Norway, in 1904 and 1903, respectively. The *Sebastian* had been purchased in Newfoundland and arrived in Victoria in the spring of 1910. The *Germania* arrived the same year from the Chilean whaling grounds (for details, see tables 5.11 and 5.12, respectively).

When all units were ready for operation, they had to be used elsewhere, since the line into Patricia Bay and the railbarge slip there had not yet been completed. On September

The whaler *Germania* in the harbour of Victoria, British Columbia, circa 1912. (British Columbia Archives A-00915.)

26, 1916, the first of what were to be many such trips was made from Port Mann to the Imperial Oil refinery at Ioco in upper Burrard Inlet to pick up tank cars for the mainland.

In an interesting twist, the *Germania* with the *Canadian Northern Pacific No. 1* called on the Victoria Whaling Company's dock in Victoria's inner harbour. Whale oil was being loaded into tank cars owned by the whaling company! The tow/tugboat and barge were left in port for four days while loading occurred. The barge, laden with tank cars, then proceeded to Port Mann where the tank cars were loaded onto a Canadian Northern train headed east. Earlier shipments of whale oil had been made via the Esquimalt and Nanaimo line, which barged the tank cars from Ladysmith to the Canadian Pacific Railway on the mainland or via the Victoria and Sidney line, which barged the tank cars from Sidney to the Great Northern Railway on the mainland.

The arrival of the *Germania* in Victoria was hailed as the start of the Canadian Northern Pacific's transfer service to Victoria. Alas, it was not! No further transfers occurred until 1918. In the 1918 transfer, nine Victoria Whaling Company tank cars were barged to Port Mann for shipment east, after what would prove to be the last visit to the whaling company wharf.

To develop traffic for railbarge services, Canadian Northern Pacific laid roadbed at several island industrial sites that did not have access to the railway's trackage on the island. Industrial products could be loaded directly into/onto railcars without the need to break bulk as required previously. In the past, goods had to be loaded onto barges/scows, towed to the mainland, and then loaded into/onto railcars, an extra and costly step. Barge slips were built at Britannia Beach (ore concentrates), Woodfibre (pulp), Ladysmith (coal), and Chemainus and Genoa Bay (lumber). In addition, slips were built on James Island near Victoria to serve a dynamite plant, and later at Rocky Point west of Victoria to supply a naval ammunition dump.

The *Germania* made its first trip to Patricia Bay on April 6, 1917, with the barge *Canadian Northern Pacific No. 1*, which carried rails and other supplies for the Canadian Northern Pacific line under construction between Victoria and Barkley Sound (which opened on October 26, 1917). The year 1917 also saw a request by the Sidney Board of Trade that the Canadian Northern Pacific Saanich line be connected to the Victoria and Sidney line so that railcars from Sidney could be accessible to the Patricia Bay barge slip and Canadian Northern railbarge service. This was approved and a 1.7-mile connector line was laid, which allowed access to Sidney Lumber, Sidney Roofing, Sidney Canning, and Saanich Canning. The Victoria and Sidney line performed all switching duties. The first railcars were transferred to the Canadian Northern Pacific in January 1918, and the latter assumed switching responsibilities on June 26, 1919, after the Victoria and Sidney line ceased operations. Sidney Lumber and Sidney Roofing provided 700 and 60 carloads of traffic annually, respectively.

The tow/tugboat *Sebastian* was renamed the *Saanich* in 1922 and plied its trade until sold by Canadian National in 1929. The *Germania* was renamed the *Fraser* in 1924 and became a fixture, serving Canadian National until sold in 1940. It is unexplained how the latter vessel retained its German name during the First World War when so many other German names were obliterated due to public outcry.

The whaler *Sebastian* in the harbour of Victoria, British Columbia, circa 1912. (British Columbia Archives A-00923.)

Extended Railcar Transfer Operations

Canadian Northern Pacific ordered a new passenger/railcar ferry named *Canora* from the Davie Shipbuilding and Repair Company, Lauzon, Quebec (official no. 138800), in 1916. Although designed to carry passengers, the vessel never had such accommodations completed. The *Canora* was registered in Quebec under the ownership of the Canadian Northern Steamship Company. The vessel had three tracks (20-railcar capacity). Its funnel bore the usual company colour scheme of buff, blue, and black (see Appendix 1) and, in addition, on the blue band was a black flag with the letters "C.N.R." in white placed diagonally on the flag. Since the *Canora* needed to travel astern, it was fitted with identical propellers, rudders, and steering gear on both ends and a double-ended wheelhouse. The ferry was equipped with a sea gate at the stern, operated with a steam winch to prevent following seas from swamping the vessel. Great Lakes railcar ferries had met with disaster when not equipped with sea gates, and

Railcar ferry *Canora* leaving Esquimalt, British Columbia, in April 1919. (British Columbia Archives G-07535.)

Canadian Northern/National was taking no chances on the Pacific Ocean. Below the car deck were the ship's mechanicals, crew quarters, two cargo holds, coal bunkers, and steering components (for details, see table 5.13).

A few days before leaving for the West Coast, the *Canora* was rammed on its port bow by the Canadian Pacific (Allan Line) liner *Sicilian* while it lay tied to a wharf. Repairs took several weeks to complete, delaying the *Canora*'s departure until September 29, 1918. Admiralty Court found the pilot and master of the *Sicilian* entirely at fault for the accident. With the First World War still under way, the *Canora* sailed with a four-inch gun mounted on the stern and three Royal Navy gunners. Arriving on December 7, 1918, after a 7,444-mile journey via the Panama Canal, naval supplies were unloaded at Esquimalt and the ship was then opened for public inspection.

After a refit, the *Canora* made its initial Port Mann to/from Patricia Bay run on April 30, 1919. That year the *Canora* made two round trips weekly (Port Mann to/from Patricia Bay), while the tow/tugboats and railbarges provided daily service to Chemainus, Genoa Bay, and James Island. The usual practice was to move railcars from James Island and Genoa Bay to Patricia Bay followed by transfer to Port Mann. The *Canora* also made frequent calls at Departure Bay (coal) and Imperial Oil at Ioco (fuel oil), since both were needed for their vessels and locomotives. The ferry also operated to Cowichan Bay, which was tied to the dead-end Victoria to/from Kissinger rail line by a junction at Deerholme.

In 1920 the Point Ellice (Victoria) terminal was completed. From that time forward, the *Canora* exchanged railcars only at Point Ellice, while tow/tugboats and railbarges used the Patricia Bay terminal.

Over time, Patricia Bay saw less and less marine use until 1935 when the Victoria to/from Patricia Bay line/terminal was abandoned. The *Canora* was laid up from 1932 until 1937 due to low traffic levels secondary to the Great Depression. It operated continuously thereafter for 31 years until its retirement in 1968.

Between 1917 and 1920, Victoria shipyards/shipbuilders were contracted by the Imperial Munitions Board and French government to build wooden ships. Ogden Point Pier was made into an assembly area where engines were installed and vessels were fitted out. Some components were delivered to the pier by Canadian Northern and Canadian Pacific railbarges after a barge slip was built there. Once the contracts were fulfilled, the area became inactive and railbarge traffic ceased.

LOG BOOM TOWING BY THE CANADIAN TUGBOAT COMPANY

The Canadian Western Lumber Company (CWLC), a subsidiary of Mackenzie and Mann, was incorporated on March 31, 1910, to exploit timber resources in the Fraser River Valley (as well as generate eastbound freight traffic for the Canadian Northern Railway). It acquired ownership of or an interest in other companies, including the Columbia River Lumber Company, Canadian Western Lumber Yards, Comox Logging and Railway Company, Canadian Tugboat Company, Crown Lumber Company Limited, Lumber Manufacturers' Yards Limited, Security Lumber Company Limited, Western Canada Sawmill Yards Limited, Coast Lumber Yards Limited, and Coast Lumber and Fuel Company Limited.

As a new entity, CWLC purchased the long-shuttered Ross-McLaren sawmill on the lower Fraser River at Millside in 1903 and slowly reopened it in 1906. The town was subsequently renamed Fraser Mills. At the time of incorporation CWLC owned 75,000 acres and held Crown and provincial leases/licences on a further 60,460 acres, all within the Comox district on Vancouver Island. The company owned approximately four billion board feet of timber. These holdings had been sold by the Fraser River Lumber Company to CWLC early in 1910 for a reported sum ranging between $17 million and $20 million. Fraser River Lumber had also owned the mill complex on the lower Fraser River comprising 4,000 feet of frontage on the river, a sawmill with a daily capacity of 750,000 board feet, a cedar mill with a daily capacity of 120,000 board feet, and a shingle plant producing 900,000 shingles daily.

Corporate officers in 1910 included A.D. Davidson as president, H. R. McRae as vice-president and general manager, A.R. Davidson as treasurer, and J.D. McCormick as secretary and assistant treasurer. Of eight directors, four came from the Canadian Northern camp, i.e., William Mackenzie, Donald Mann, D.B. Hanna, and R.O. Horne-Payne.

With the source of the timber and the means to process it being separated by the Strait of Georgia, it was obvious that a means of transporting logs that was under CWLC control was needed. The balance of this section will be devoted to a discussion of this entity: the Canadian Tugboat Company. Discussion will be limited to the period up to the time of sale of CWLC to Crown Zellerbach Canada.

Overview of the Fraser Mills sawmill in the 1910s. (British Columbia Archives B-08337.)

The tow/tugboat *Dreadful* approaching Active Pass, British Columbia, circa 1914. (British Columbia Archives E-00668.)

The tow/tugboat *Fearful* at the dock. Undated. (Walter E. Frost photograph, City of Vancouver Archives AM1506-S3-2-:CVA 447-2209.)

The Canadian Tugboat Company was incorporated in British Columbia by memorandum of association by CWLC on May 13, 1911. In the summer of 1912, the company took delivery of three coal-fired tow/tugboats: the *Cheerful* (official no. 130493), *Fearful* (official no. 130494), and *Joyful* (official no. 130499), all having been built locally (for details, see tables 5.14 to 5.16, respectively). The tow/tugboat *Dreadful* (official no. 131148), built at South Shields, England, also joined the company in 1912 after enduring a 15,000-mile, 72-day journey around the tip of South America to its new home (for details, see table 5.17).

In 1914 a fifth tow/tugboat was added to the fleet: the *Gleeful* (official no. 130876; for details, see table 5.18). These five tow/tugboats operated together until May 1916 when the British Admiralty commandeered the *Dreadful*

and the old wooden tow/tugboat *Active* was purchased to replace it (official no. 94894; for details of the latter, see table 5.19). In 1919 the fleet commodore, E.T. McLennan, wrote: "The *Active*, built at New Westminster in 1889, is thirty years old and cannot remain in service for any longer than seven years due to the condition of the vessel."

The Canadian government allowed double depreciation for the *Active* until 1922 when it was then reduced to 8.5 percent. The other tow/tugboats were only allowed 5 percent depreciation. Oddly enough, the *Fearful* was sold in 1920, while the *Active* remained in the fleet until 1946 and was still on the Canadian shipping register until it was wrecked off Cortes Island in the northern end of the Strait of Georgia in 1956. Not bad for a vessel given only until 1926 to be fit for use.

The tow/tugboat *Joyful* in 1912. (Vancouver Maritime Museum LM2007.1000.3262.)

From 1921 to 1926, the four remaining tow/tugboats (*Active*, *Cheerful*, *Gleeful*, and *Joyful*) continued towing log booms from Vancouver Island to the mainland. Although a company history relates that the *Cheerful* was dismantled in 1926, there is evidence that it was actually sold and survived until burning and sinking in August 1965 (see table 5.14). The *Cheerful* was replaced by the tow/tugboat *John Davidson*, named for one of the company directors (official no. 153335).

Company records are hazy from 1929 to 1943 regarding tow/tugboat operations. However, during this period, the tow/tugboat *Petrel* was acquired (official no. 121974, built in Victoria in 1905). In 1946 the *Petrel*, *Gleeful*, and *Active* were sold to Coastal Towing Limited. In their places the ex-American miki-miki type large wooden diesel-powered tugboats *Florence Filberg* (official no. 176286) and *Mary Mackin* (official no. 176287) were purchased. In 1947 the steel diesel-powered tow/

The tow/tugboat *Cheerful*. (City of Vancouver Archives AM1535-CVA 99-3209.)

The tow/tugboat *Gleeful* on June 23, 1923. (Vancouver Maritime Museum LM2006.1000.1566.)

The Canadian Tugboat Company in Fraser Mills, British Columbia, in 1914 with six vessels, including *Senator Jansen*, in a photograph commissioned by the firm. (City of Vancouver Archives AM54-S4-3:PAN N91.)

tugboat *Isabella Stewart* (official no. 177148 as the *Pacific Buoy*) was bought, and the *John Davidson* and *Joyful*, the latter being the last survivor of the originals, were sold. Tow/tugboats *Florence Filberg*, *Mary Mackin*, and *Isabella Stewart*, named after wives of company officers, comprised the entire fleet in 1955, where we leave the story of the Canadian Tugboat Company.

However, before leaving this story entirely, there is a curious vessel whose story should be told. There was a sternwheel yarding tow/tugboat that was headquartered at the CWLC sawmill with the name *Senator Jansen* (official no. 126272; for details, see table 5.20). It was named after a U.S. shareholder from Nebraska who, at one time, was the American ambassador to Russia. This vessel was used to "herd" logs for transfer into the mill after delivery by the other Canadian Tugboat Company tow/tugboats. The nature of its propulsion system must have made this quite difficult, since manoeuvrability was paramount for this task. A survivor from the Fraser River Lumber Company days, it lasted until broken up in 1921.

The tow/tugboat *Active*. (Vancouver Maritime Museum Active-12453.)

The sternwheeler *Senator Jansen*, circa 1910. (British Columbia Archives B-08356.)

Table 5.1
Avoca (official no. 98663)

Builder:	William Denny and Brothers Limited in Dumbarton, Scotland, in 1891 (yard no. 448). Launched June 9, 1891.
Engine:	Quadruple cylinder (32-, 46.5-, 64.5-, 92-inch piston diameters and 60-inch stroke); 2,650 ihp, 627 nhp.
Boilers:	Three double-ended at 180 psi.
Dimensions:	420 feet long x 48.2 feet wide x 30.6 feet deep.
Funnels:	One.
Masts:	Three.
Propulsion:	Steam screw (single).
Tonnage:	5,183/3,319 (gross/net).
Speed:	13 knots.
Passenger Capacity:	80 (first class), 1,000 (third class).
Freight Capacity:	No data.
Miscellaneous:	Between 1891 and 1907, principally ran to Australia but was chartered in 1895 (as *San Fernando*) to Cia Transatlantica. Under this 22-month charter, the vessel served as a troopship for Cuba. Under the Northwest Transport Line pennant, made only nine voyages, the last beginning on April 9, 1910. Under the Uranium Steamship Company pennant, first voyage commenced on June 4, 1910, and last voyage started on July 23, 1914. Under the Cunard pennant, Avonmouth to/from New York City sailings began in November 1916.

Owners	Dates
British India Steam Navigation Company (as *Avoca*)	1891–1907
East Asiatic Company (Copenhagen) (name changed to *Atlanta*)	1907–08
New York and Continental Line (name changed back to *Avoca*)	1908–09
Northwest Transport Line (name changed to *Uranium*)	1909–10
Uranium Steamship Company	1910–14
Canadian Northern Steamship Company	1914–16
Cunard Steamship Company (name changed to *Feltria* in 1917)	1916–17

Incidents

- Ship held liable in November 1908 after colliding with the German vessel *Lordsee* and was sold at auction to C.G. Ashdown, London, England.
- Collided with the steamer *Nordenfels* off Rotterdam in 1909, resulting in much damage to both vessels.
- Grounded January 12, 1913, near Halifax (off Shoal Point, Chebucto Head), after going to the aid of the Allan Line's *Carthaginian,* which was on fire. Vessel was subsequently salvaged on January 17 and repaired in Halifax.

Disposition

- On May 5, 1917, vessel was torpedoed by German submarine UC-48 eight miles southeast of Mine Head, Waterford, Ireland. Forty-five lives were lost, including that of the captain. Vessel had been on its way from New York to Avonmouth, England.

Table 5.2
Jelunga (official no. 98596)

Builder:	William Denny and Brothers Limited in Dumbarton, Scotland, in 1890 (yard no. 442). Launched October 30, 1890.
Engine:	Quadruple cylinders on three crankshafts (32-, 46.5-, 64.5-, and 92-inch piston diameters x 60-inch stroke), 4660 ihp.
Boilers:	Double-ended Scotch (number not specified) at 186 psi.
Dimensions:	410.5 feet long x 48.2 feet wide x 26.7 feet deep.
Funnels:	One.
Masts:	Three.
Propulsion:	Steam screw (single).
Tonnage:	5,206/3,372 (gross/net).
Speed:	16 knots.
Passenger Capacity:	No data.
Freight Capacity:	No data.
Miscellaneous:	Chartered to Cia. Transatlantica in 1893 (as *Leon XIII*) and in 1896 (as *Santiago*). Served as a troopship during the Cuban revolution and Boer War. Chartered in June 1905 by the Russian government to evacuate Russian soldiers from Shanghai to Sevastopol (Crimea). Proceeded to Odessa to load timber. While in Odessa, rioting broke out, wharves were burned, and loading ceased, since mutinous soldiers warned the ship's crew to cease work or they would be attacked.

Owners	Dates
British India Associated Steamers	1890–1903
British India Steam Navigation Company	1903–08
New York and Continental Line	1908
British India Steam Navigation Company (repossessed from New York and Continental Line)	1908–14
Bombay and Persia Steam Navigation Company (name changed to *Jehangir*)	1914–17
Lau Siu Shuen, Hong Kong (name changed to *Wing Shing* in 1920)	1917–20
Lau Wai Chun, Hong Kong	1921–23
Man Chuen Steamship Company, Hong Kong	1923

Disposition

- Wrecked in a typhoon on August 18, 1923. Grounded at Hong Kong, later salvaged and scrapped.

Table 5.3
Volturno (official no. 123737)

Builder:	Fairfield Shipbuilding and Engineering Company in Glasgow in 1906 (yard no. 448).
Engine:	Two triple expansion (19.5-, 32-, and 52-inch piston diameters and 36-inch stroke), 2,750 ihp.
Boilers:	Two single-ended at 180 psi.
Dimensions:	340 feet long x 43 feet wide x 20.7 feet deep.
Funnels:	One.
Masts:	Two.
Propulsion:	Steam screw (double).
Tonnage:	3,586/2,222 (gross/net).
Speed:	14 knots.
Passenger Capacity:	24 (first class) and 1,000 (third class).
Freight Capacity:	No data.
Miscellaneous:	When purchased by the Canadian Northern Steamship Company in 1910, it had been intended to rename the vessel *Royal Sovereign* and place it on the Avonmouth to/from Montreal route. Instead, it was chartered to the Uranium Steamship Company, a Canadian Northern subsidiary.

Owners	Dates
D.G. Pinkney and Company	1906–10
Canadian Northern Steamship Company	1910–13

Disposition

- Vessel was lost to fire on October 9, 1913. Of 564 passengers and 93 crew, 135 died (see chapter 5 text for additional details).

Table 5.4
Campanello (official no. 115224)

Builder:	Palmers Ship Building and Iron Company in Newcastle, England, in 1901 (yard no. 755). Launched August 29, 1901.
Engine:	Two triple expansion (26-, 43-, and 71-inch piston diameters and 48-inch stroke), 453 nhp.
Boilers:	Two double-ended (15.3 feet x 17.5 feet) and two single-ended (15.3 feet x 11 feet) at 190 psi.
Dimensions:	470 feet long x 56 feet wide x 32 feet deep.
Funnels:	One.
Masts:	Four.
Propulsion:	Steam screw (double).
Tonnage:	9,291/6,800 (gross/net).
Speed:	14 knots.
Passenger Capacity:	40 (first class), 50 (second class), 2,200 (third class) (from 1906 onward).
Freight Capacity:	No data.
Miscellaneous:	From 1901 to 1906, vessel was used as a cargo ship by the Phoenix Line (Antwerp, Belgium, to/from New York City). Under the ownership of the Navigazione Generale Italiana, the vessel had passenger accommodations added and its first voyage started on March 7, 1907. Its final voyage began on May 17, 1909. The two chartered voyages for the Northwest Transport Line began on February 16, 1910, and April 5, 1910. As the *Campania* under charter to the Uranium Steamship Company, the vessel started its first Rotterdam to/from Halifax to/from New York City voyage on May 21, 1910, and its third and last voyage on August 13, 1910. Renamed the *Campanello* and still under charter to the Uranium Steamship Company on the same route, the vessel recommenced service on September 22, 1910. Its last voyage began on July 9, 1914. In October 1914, vessel was transferred to the Avonmouth to/from Quebec City to/from Montreal route. Under Cunard ownership, it continued on this same route until sunk by a German submarine (see below).

Owners	Dates		Disposition
British Shipowners Limited (named *British Empire*)	1902–06		• Vessel was torpedoed by German submarine U-107 on August 24, 1918, off Tory Island, Northern Ireland (only 126 of 500+ persons on board were saved).
Navigazione Generale Italiana (name changed to *Campania*)	1906–10		
Canadian Northern Steamship Company (name changed to *Campanello*)	1910–16		
Cunard Steamship Line (name changed to *Flavia*)	1916–18		

Table 5.5
Napolitan Prince (official no. 114432)

Builder:	Scott and Company in Greenock, Scotland, in 1889 (yard no. 267). Launched July 1, 1889.
Engine:	Triple expansion (31-, 50-, and 80-inch piston diameters and 54-inch stroke), 3,250 ihp.
Boilers:	Two double-ended and one single-ended at 160 psi.
Dimensions:	363.5 feet long x 42.3 feet wide x 25.3 feet deep.
Funnels:	One.
Masts:	Two.
Propulsion:	Steam screw (single).
Tonnage:	2,900/1,757 (gross/net).
Speed:	14 knots.
Passenger Capacity:	25 (first class), 1,150 (third class).
Freight Capacity:	No data.
Miscellaneous:	Mala Real Portugueza competed for the Lisbon-Mozambique/Angola mail service and later the mail service to South America. Both times financial disaster and bankruptcy ensued. The Prince Line used vessel on the Livorno to/from Genoa to/from Naples to/from Palermo to/from New York City route. Vessel's first voyage commenced on November 24, 1902, and final voyage began on March 2, 1908. Vessel was chartered for four round trips by Northwest Transport Line in 1909–10 (first voyage started on September 6, 1909, and final one on January 8, 1910).

Owners	Dates
Mala Real Portugueza, Lisbon (as *Rei de Portugal*)	1889–1902
Prince Line (name changed to *Napolitan Prince*)	1902–11
Cie de Navigation Mixte, Marseille (name changed to *Manouba*)	1911–29

Disposition
• Scrapped on February 14, 1929.

Table 5.6
Raglan Castle (official no. 108181)

Builder:	Barclay, Curle and Company in Glasgow in 1897 (yard no. 408). Launched January 20, 1897.
Engine:	Triple expansion (26.5-, 44-, and 70-inch piston diameters and 48-inch stroke), 2,600 ihp, 419 nhp.
Boilers:	Three single-ended at 180 psi.
Dimensions:	383.5 feet long x 46.3 feet wide x 20 feet deep.
Funnels:	One.
Masts:	Two.
Propulsion:	Steam screw (single).
Tonnage:	4,324/2,743 (gross/net).
Speed:	12.5 knots.
Passenger Capacity:	No data.
Freight Capacity:	No data.
Miscellaneous:	In 1904 vessel was traded in to its builder toward the purchase of a new ship. In 1906 it was chartered by the Russian government as a troopship to evacuate soldiers from Vladivostok to Odessa in the Crimea. Chartered in 1909 to the Northwest Transport Line. Converted to a whale oil refinery (1911–20).

Owners	Dates
Castle Mail Packet Company	1897–1904
Barclay, Curle and Company	1904–1905
A/S Det Vestindiske Kompagni (name changed to *St. Domingo*)	1905–1907
Barclay, Curle and Company (name changed to *Raglan Castle*)	1907–1910
Pythia Steamship Company (Donaldson Brothers, managers)	1910–1911
A/S Dominion Whaling Company	1911–1920
A/S Odd	1920–1930
Hvalfanger A/S Africa (name changed to *Ready*)	1930–1934
Metal Industries	1934

Incidents

- On April 18, 1929, ship capsized at Sandefjord, Norway, while being repaired by Framnaes MV, which took vessel over and completed the repairs.

Disposition

- Arrived in Rosyth, Scotland, for scrapping on September 12, 1934. Scrapped in October 1934.

Table 5.7

Sicilian Prince (official no. 115845)

Builder:	Scott and Company in Greenock, Scotland, in 1889 (yard no. 269). Launched September 28, 1889.
Engine:	Triple expansion (31-, 50-, and 80-inch piston diameters and 54-inch stroke), 3,530 ihp, 570 nhp.
Boilers:	Two double-ended and one single-ended at 160 psi.
Dimensions:	363.5 feet long x 42.2 feet wide x 25.3 feet deep.
Funnels:	One.
Masts:	Two.
Propulsion:	Steam screw (single).
Tonnage:	2,964/1,830 (gross/net).
Speed:	14 knots.
Passenger Capacity:	75 (first class), 25 (second class), 120 (third class) (as built); 25 (first class), 1,100 (third class) after 1902.
Freight Capacity:	No data.
Miscellaneous:	See table 5.5 for a description of ownership by Mala Real Portugueza, Lisbon. After a brief ownership by W. MacAndrew, the Prince Line used vessel on the same route as the *Napolitan Prince* (table 5.5). Ship began its first voyage on September 30, 1902, and final voyage on March 18, 1908, for the Prince Line. It was chartered by Northwest Transport Line for four round-trip voyages in 1909. Made a troopship voyage from Mudros on the Greek island of Lemnos to the Dardanelles (Gallipoli) in 1915.

Owners	Dates
Mala Real Portugueza, Lisbon (as *Mocambique*) (name changed to *Alvarez Cabral* in 1898)	1889–1900
W. MacAndrew	1900–02
Prince Line (name changed to *Sicilian Prince*)	1902–11
Khedivial Steamship and Graving Dock Co. (name changed to *Abbassieh*)	1911–31

Incidents

- On Sunday, November 20, 1904, grounded on the southern shore of Long Island, New York, due to a misinterpretation of navigational aids.
- On April 2, 1903, collided with the steamer *Jefferson* in the Upper Bay of New York City's harbour.

Disposition

- Scrapped in Italy in 1931.

Table 5.8
Principello (official no. 136640)

Builder:	James Laing and Sons in Sunderland, England, as *Principe di Piemonte* in 1907. Launched February 26, 1907.
Engines:	Two triple expansion (24-,39-, and 64-inch piston diameters and 45-inch stroke), 869 nhp.
Boilers:	Five single-ended originally (later four) at 180 psi.
Dimensions:	430 feet long x 52.7 feet wide x 25 feet deep.
Funnels:	Two.
Masts:	Two.
Propulsion:	Steam screw (double).
Tonnage:	6,705/4,211 (gross/net).
Speed:	14 knots.
Passenger Capacity:	No data.
Freight Capacity:	No data.
Miscellaneous:	Defensively armed with a stern-mounted 1 x 12 gun but not an armed merchant cruiser. Chartered to the Uranium Steamship Company in 1914. Cunard used vessel only for cargo.

Owners	Dates
Lloyd Sabaudo Soc. Anon. Per Azioni (as *Principe di Piemonte*)	1907–13
Canadian Northern Steamship Company (name changed to *Principello*)	1913–16
Cunard Steamship Company (name changed to *Folia*)	1916–17

Disposition

- Torpedoed then sunk by surface gunfire from German submarine *U-53* on March 11, 1917, four miles off Ram Head near Youghal Island, Ireland. Seven died.

Table 5.9
Royal George (official no. 125643) (No. 1), *Royal Edward* (official no. 125656) (No. 2)

Builder:	Fairfield Company Limited in Glasgow. No. 1: 1907 (yard no. 449, as *Heliopolis*). No. 2: 1907 (yard no. 450, as *Cairo*). No. 1 launched in May 1907 and No. 2 in July 1907. Both completed in early 1908.
Engines:	Three sets of steam turbines, one high-powered turbine in the centre with one lower-powered turbine on each side of it, with a combined 18,000 ihp at 340 rpm.
Boilers:	Four double-ended and four single-ended, 48 corrugated furnaces, grate surface 989 square feet, heating surface 39,450 square feet.
Dimensions:	525.8 feet long x 60.2 feet wide x 27 feet deep.
Funnels:	Two.
Masts:	Two.
Propulsion:	Steam screw (triple).
Tonnage:	11,117/5,239 (gross/net).
Speed:	Over 19 knots (maximum of 21).
Passenger Capacity:	344 (first class), 210 (second class), 560 (third class) for a total of 1,114. Troop capacity of 1,367.
Freight Capacity:	No data.

Owners	Dates
Egyptian Mail Company (as *Heliopolis* and *Cairo*)	1907–1910
Canadian Northern Steamship Company (names changed to *Royal George* and *Royal Edward*)	1910–1916 (No. 1), 1910–1915 (No. 2)
Cunard Steamship Company	1916–1922 (No. 1)

Disposition

- No. 1: Scrapped at Wilhelmshaven, Germany, in 1922.
- No. 2: On August 13, 1915, vessel was torpedoed by German submarine UB-14 near the Dardanelles and sank with a heavy loss of life (reported to be 935–1,500). See chapter 5 text for additional details.

Miscellaneous:	Both vessels were built for the British-owned Egyptian Mail Company to run on the Marseille, France, to/from Alexandria, Egypt, route but were unprofitable, so both were laid up in 1909 in Marseille and put up for sale. After purchase by the Canadian Northern Steamship Company, vessels were refitted for North Atlantic service. The *Royal George* began the Avonmouth (Bristol) to/from Quebec City route on May 26, 1910. On October 3, 1914, it sailed from Gaspé Bay to Plymouth, England, with the first contingent of the Canadian Expeditionary Force and was then taken over as a hired military transport (HMT). The *Royal Edward* began Avonmouth to/from Quebec City route on May 13, 1910. On August 11, 1914, it sailed with 500 French reservists to join a convoy to the United Kingdom and was taken over as an HMT. The remnant of the Canadian Northern Steamship fleet was purchased by Cunard Steamship Company in 1916, but the *Royal George* remained a troopship for the rest of the war. It resumed civilian duties on February 10, 1919, starting the first of five Liverpool to/from Halifax to/from New York City round trips. The first of the Southampton, England, to/from Halifax to/from New York City voyages began on August 15, 1919. The ninth (and final) voyage on this service commenced on June 10, 1920. The retired vessel then became a depot ship to process immigrants at Cherbourg, France, followed by being laid up on the River Fal. The "Royals" were the only transatlantic ships to have Toronto as their port of registration.

Incidents

- No. 1: Grounded near Quebec City on November 6, 1912. Was refloated on November 17 and made for Halifax for repairs on December 12. Then proceeded to Liverpool. Resumed Avonmouth to/from Quebec service on June 17, 1913.
- No. 2: While eastbound, hit an iceberg 110 miles east of Cape Race toward the end of May 1914 while going dead slow in fog. Was able to continue on to Avonmouth where vessel was dry-docked for repairs, missing its next scheduled departure.

Table 5.10

Timeline of Ownership/Chartership of Vessels Affiliated with the Canadian Northern Steamship Company Atlantic Fleet (1908–18)

Vessels	1908	1909	1910	1911	1912	1913	1914	1915	1916	1917	1918
1. Avoca	!	!									
Uranium		*	* $	$	$	$	$@	@	@		
Feltria									&	&	
2. Jelunga	!										
3. Volturno[a]			@	@	@	@					
4. Campania[d]			*								
Campanello[b]			@	@	@	@	@	@	@		
Flavia									&	&	&
5. Napolitan Prince[d]		*	*								
6. Raglan Castle[d]		*									
7. Sicilian Prince[d]		*									
8. Principello[c]							@	@	@		
Folia									&	&	
9. Royal George			@	@	@	@	@	@	@ &	&	&
10. Royal Edward			@	@	@	@	@	@			

[a] Chartered to Uranium Steamship Company.
[b] Chartered to Uranium Steamship Company until August 1914.
[c] Chartered to Uranium Steamship Company in 1914.
[d] Chartered in all indicated years (either one or two years).

Abbreviations: NY&CL = New York & Continental Line; NWTL = Northwest Transport Line; CNSS = Canadian Northern Steamships; USS = Uranium Steamships; CSS = Cunard Steamships.

! = NY&CL.
* = NWTL.
@ = CNSS.
$ = USS.
& = CSS.

Table 5.11

Sebastian (official no. 117323)

Builder:	Akers Mechanske Verksted, Oslo, Norway (hull no. 229), in 1904.
Engine:	Triple expansion (10-, 17-, and 28-inch piston diameters and 14-inch stroke).
Boiler:	No data.
Dimensions:	94 feet long x 17 feet wide x 10 feet deep.
Propulsion:	Steam screw (single).
Tonnage:	103/41 (gross/net).
Miscellaneous:	In 1908 the Newfoundland government chartered the vessel to carry passengers and mail around Fortune Bay. Vessel was employed in whaling from 1910 to 1916 and in towing from 1916 to 1947. Back into whaling in 1948 for a short period. Arrived at Port Mann, British Columbia, on March 23, 1916.

Owners	Dates
Mic Mac Whaling Company	1904–07
J.W. Carmichael (name changed to *Sebastian*)	1907–?
Harvey and Company	?–1911
Pacific Whaling Company, Victoria Whaling Company (subsidiaries of Canadian Northern Pacific Fisheries Co.)	1911–16
Canadian Northern Steamships (Canadian National Steamships [?])	1916–21 (?)
Unknown owner (name changed to *Saanich* in 1924)	1921 (?)–?
G.A. Bryant	?–1945–?
Coastal Towing Co.	?–1947–?
Western Whaling Company	1948–49

Disposition

- Scrapped in 1949 after a disappointing return to whaling in 1948.

Incidents

- In early 1911, the *Sebastian* and *Germania* were chartered by the Canadian government for several weeks as fishery protection vessels, patrolling the fishing grounds for poachers violating the three-mile offshore limit.
- During the week of July 10–14, 1911, the *Sebastian* was involved in a five-day search for a physician. A Japanese employee at the Rose Harbour whaling station in the Queen Charlotte Islands stuck a needle into his left eye when, while sewing on a patch, the needle punched through the material with a jerk. He was hurried onto the *Sebastian* and proceeded to Bella Bella where the nearest physician lived. Upon arrival, there was no physician to be found, since he had gone to River Inlet. The *Sebastian* headed back to the Queen Charlotte Islands, hoping to meet the *Princess Beatrice* at Rose Harbour on its way south but missed it. The propeller on the *Sebastian* loosened and had to be repaired. Finally, after five days of searching, a physician was found at Queen Charlotte City. The patient received interim treatment and was sent south on the *Princess Beatrice* for definitive treatment. As it turned out, part of his eye had to be removed.
- The captain of the *Star of France* broke his leg on April 30, 1912, when he caught it in one of the braces. He was taken off the vessel by the *Sebastian* on May 5, 1912, and brought to Port Alberni on Vancouver Island for surgical treatment.

Table 5.12

Germania (official no. 131310)

Builder:	Akers Mechanske Verksted, Oslo, Norway (hull no. 222), in 1903.
Engine:	Triple expansion (10-, 17-, and 28-inch piston diameters and 14-inch stroke).
Boiler:	No data.
Dimensions:	94 feet long x 17 feet wide x 10 feet deep.
Propulsion:	Steam screw (single).
Tonnage:	106/41 (gross/net).
Miscellaneous:	Vessel was first steam-powered whaling ship built for a German company (Germania Walfang-und-Fischindustrie A/G of Hamburg). First in service at the Icelandic station at Faskrudfjord. Sold to a Chilean-German whaling company in 1906. Whaling station was located at Puerto de Corral near Valdivia, Chile. This company was reorganized in 1908 with Norwegian financing. Sold in early spring 1910 to the Pacific Whaling Company. Arrived at Port Mann, British Columbia, on March 23, 1916.

Owners	Dates
Germania Walfang-und-Fischindustrie A/G	1903–06
Sociedad Ballenera y Pescadora	1906–10
Pacific Whaling Company (subsidiary of Canadian Northern Pacific Fisheries)	1910–16
Canadian Northern Steamships (? Canadian National Steamships) (name changed to *Fraser* in 1924)	1916–24 (?)
Canadian National Steamships (name changed to *Canadian National No. 4* in 1928)	1924 (?)–45

Incidents

- On April 28, 1911, the *Germania* was sent to Rosedale reef off Race Rocks, British Columbia, to pick up a derelict buoy that was adrift.
- The *Germania* caught the U.S. gas auxiliary *Sophie Johnson* inside the three-mile limit and caused the latter to cut adrift $600 worth of fishing gear prior to escaping.

Disposition

- Wrecked in 1945.

Table 5.13
Canora (official no. 138800)

Builder:	Davie Shipbuilding and Repair, Lauzon, Quebec (hull no. 307). Launched June 10, 1918.
Engine:	Quadruple cylinders into three crankshafts (24-, 38-, 43-, and 43-inch piston diameters and 30-inch stroke) built by J. Inglis Foundry, Toronto (2,200 ihp). Changed from coal to oil as fuel in the 1920s.
Boiler:	Four Scotch (each 11.5 feet x 11.5 feet) at 175 psi.
Dimensions:	308 feet long x 52.1 feet wide x 18.8 feet deep.
Funnels:	Two.
Propulsion:	Steam screw (total of four: two at each end).
Tonnage:	2,383/940 (gross/net).
Speed:	12.5 knots service speed (could make 14 knots, reduced to nine knots post–Second World War to reduce fuel consumption).
Passenger Capacity:	Although planned to carry passengers, accommodations for this use were cancelled.
Freight Capacity:	Three tracks (21-car capacity in 1918); 13,000-square-foot main deck. No. 1 hold (40,000 cubic feet), No. 2 hold (30,000 cubic feet).
Miscellaneous:	Unique design (two-ended with two screws/rudder at each end, twin opposing funnels, double-ended wheelhouse). Ran Port Mann to/from Patricia Bay. Once Port Ellice (Victoria) terminal was completed in 1925, only tow/tugboats and railbarges were continued on Patricia Bay route. After 1935 abandonment of line to Patricia Bay, all marine traffic was routed through Port Ellice. Out of service from 1932 to 1937 due to Depression. Reinstated in 1937, running until 1968. Also operated to Cowichan Bay. Engine was saved and restored by Atchelitz Threshermen's Association, Chilliwack, British Columbia (to operating condition, paired with a boiler from a steam dredge). Morris Greene Industries planned for the vessel plus barges to be moored in the Inner Harbour in Victoria to form the basis of a floating convention centre (fell through). Goodwin Johnson planned to use vessel as a floating sawmill in Queen Charlotte Islands (fell through).

Owners	Dates		Disposition
Canadian Northern Railway (Canadian National Railway)	1918–68		• Scrapped in Victoria in 1972 (except engine, see above).
Morris Greene Industries	1968–72		
Goodwin Johnson	1972		

Table 5.14
Tow/tugboat *Cheerful* (official no. 130493)

Builder:	Canadian Western Lumber Company, Fraser Mills, British Columbia, in 1912.
Engine:	13- and 26-inch piston diameters and 18-inch stroke, built by J. Pollock and Sons, London, England.
Boiler:	No data.
Dimensions:	73 feet long x 18 feet wide x 8 feet deep.
Propulsion:	Steam screw (single).
Tonnage:	80 (gross).
Miscellaneous:	Steam engine was replaced by diesel motor in 1936. Became a sea cadet vessel in 1961.

Owners	Dates
Canadian Tugboat Company	1912
Straits Towing and Salvage Company (name changed to *Malaspina Straits* in 1949 and *Straits Cadet* in 1961)	1942

Incident

- In the late 1930s, several branches of two families banded together to log in Von Donop Inlet from a floating camp. They hired the *Cheerful* to tow five homes strung out on a line, each on its own float, from Seaford to Von Donop Inlet (then called Von Donop Creek).

Disposition

- Burned and sank while under tow in the San Juan Islands, Washington, in August 1965.

Table 5.15
Tow/tugboat *Fearful* (official no. 130494)

Builder:	Canadian Western Lumber Company, Fraser Mills, British Columbia, in 1912.
Engine:	13- and 26-inch piston diameters and 18-inch stroke, built by J. Pollock and Sons, London, England.
Boiler:	No data.
Dimensions:	73 feet long x 18 feet wide x 8 feet deep.
Funnels:	
Propulsion:	Steam screw (single).
Tonnage:	80 (gross).
Miscellaneous:	Steam engine replaced with diesel motor in 1936 during refit.

Owners	Dates	Disposition
Canadian Tugboat Company	1912–20	• Vessel was owned and operated by Northwestern Dredging until at least 1938. No further information on its fate is available.
Northwestern Dredging Company	1927–38	

Table 5.16
Tow/tugboat *Joyful* (official no. 130499)

Builder:	Westminster Marine Railway Company, New Westminster, British Columbia, in 1912.
Engine:	Surface-condensing, seven- and 14-inch piston diameters and 12-inch stroke, 120 ihp, built by Campbell and Calderwood, Paisley, Scotland.
Boiler:	No data.
Dimensions:	40 feet long x 14 feet wide x 5.5 feet deep (1912); 53.2 feet long x 14.6 feet wide x 6.1 feet deep (1949).
Funnels:	
Propulsion:	Steam screw (single).
Tonnage:	31/18 (gross/net).
Miscellaneous:	Rebuilt in 1949 by Star Shipyard Mercers Limited and steam engine was replaced by a 400-bhp General Motors diesel. In 1962 a new diesel motor was installed (360-bhp Caterpillar). In 1975 a new diesel motor was installed (365-bhp Caterpillar). During much of its career, the vessel was under the capable command of Captain C.E. Nordin and the watchful eye of Engineer J. Smith. In his last entry in the ship's log before the 1948 change in ownership, the captain wrote: "Thank you, *Joyful*. You done everything I ever expected of you. Goodbye." It has been estimated that when sold in 1948 the vessel had already handled four billion feet of logs (equivalent to the entire B.C. cut for an entire year).

Owners	Dates
Canadian Tugboat Company	1912–48
Westminster Charters (name changed to *Westminster Monarch* in 1949, company name changed to Westminster Tugboats in 1959)	1948–61
Bridge Towing Company (name changed to *Monarch II*, company became Marpole Towing in 1964 and name changed to Westminster Tug Boats)	1961–66
Seaway Towing	1966–69
Egmont Towing and Salvage	1969–71
Monarch Towing Limited	1971–90
Three separate private owners	1990–present

Disposition
• Still active tow/tugboat in private ownership.

Table 5.17
Tow/tugboat *Dreadful* (official no. 131148)

Builder:	Hepple and Company, South Shields, England, in 1912 (hull no. 621).
Engine:	Triple expansion (15-, 23.5-, and 38-inch piston diameters and 30-inch stroke), 74 rhp.
Boiler:	One single-ended (12 feet x 15 feet) at 180 psi.
Dimensions:	119 feet long x 25 feet wide x 14 feet deep.
Propulsion:	Steam screw (single).
Tonnage:	253/92 (gross/net).
Miscellaneous:	Converted on an unknown date to burn pulverized coal. Had exceptional accommodations for a lumber tow/tugboat: chief officer's cabin, officers' mess, stores, galley, and guests' saloon on the main deck; captain's cabin and two guest rooms on the bridge; and the engineer's quarters and a special saloon below the main deck. Crew was berthed forward. Steam radiators provided heat to all quarters, and electric lighting was employed throughout.

Owners	Dates
Canadian Tugboat Company	1912–16
British government (war service)	1916–20
William Watkins Limited (name changed to *Rumania*)	1920–23
Pacific Tug and Barge (name changed to *Pacific Monarch*)	1923–27
Pacific Navigation Company	1927–35
Pacific (Coyle) Navigation Company	1935–52

Disposition

- Foundered on December 27, 1952, en route from Vancouver to Quadra Island.

Incidents

- During a cruise off Cape Cook on Vancouver Island on the way from Quatsino in August 1912, the vessel, being painted all white, was taken to be a fishing protection vessel by three U.S. poachers inside the three-mile limit. The poachers cut their nets and beat a hasty retreat.
- In mid-May 1917, the vessel crashed into the government rock crusher *Lobnits No. 1* while the latter was docked at Yarrows wharf. This was due to an error by the engineer who put the engine ahead instead of astern as telegraphed by the captain.
- On January 1, 1918, vessel collided with the USS *Patterson* (DD36) at the entrance to Berehaven Harbour, Ireland.
- On March 4, 1922, towed SS *Thyra*, which had lost its propeller going from Newhaven, England, to Antwerp, Belgium.
- On December 13, 1925, grounded on Roscoe Point. Refloated at next tide and proceeded to Vancouver for inspection.

Table 5.18
Tow/tugboat *Gleeful* (official no. 130876)

Builder:	A. Moscrop, Vancouver, in 1913.
Engine:	Triple expansion (8-, 13-, and 21-inch piston diameters and 16-inch stroke) by McKie and Baxter, Glasgow, Scotland.
Boiler:	No data.
Dimensions:	73 feet long x 18 feet wide x 8 feet deep.
Propulsion:	Steam screw (single).
Tonnage:	88 (gross).
Miscellaneous:	Rebuilt in 1963–64, after purchased by National Fisheries Limited, into a floating fish camp.

Owners	Dates
Canadian Tugboat Company	1913–46
Coastal Towing	1946–48
National Fisheries Limited	1963/1964–?

Disposition

- After being rebuilt as a barge, vessel was taken to a fish camp on Johnstone Strait, British Columbia, in 1964. What happened to it thereafter is not known.

Incidents

- On January 21, 1923, a log boom towed by the vessel carried away an outer range navigation light. The incident was not reported to the Department of Marine and Fisheries in a timely fashion (took 10 days).
- Crew of vessel rescued three survivors of a gas boat–jetty collision at the mouth of the Fraser River at 0500 hours on May 7, 1935. They had been holding on to the jetty for three hours since the accident at 0200 hours.
- On April 22, 1936, on the north arm of the Fraser River, the log boom being towed by the *Gleeful* damaged the suction dredge *Georgia* when the barge tender (*Bug*) was inadequately powered to assist the tow/tugboat.
- On October 4, 1948, the quick-thinking master of the *Gleeful* saved the USS *Capilano* from grounding on a sandbar between the dock and barge slip in Squamish, British Columbia.
- On December 22, 1952, the crew members of the *Gleeful* were the last to sight and radio the tow/tugboat *Petrel* before the latter was sunk by the great tidal rips off Cape Mudge on Quadra Island.

Table 5.19
Tow/tugboat *Active* (official no. 94894)

Builder:	D. McNair, New Westminster, British Columbia, in 1889.
Engine:	Triple expansion (12.5-, 18.5-, and 32.5-inch piston diameters and 24-inch stroke).
Boiler:	No data.
Dimensions:	116 feet long x 21 feet wide x 10 feet deep.
Propulsion:	Steam screw (single).
Tonnage:	172 (gross).
Miscellaneous:	Vessel had a large superstructure that provided ample room for the crew but also worked against it. The master had poor visibility aft, with only small windows in aft bulkhead of the wheelhouse, and even this view was obstructed by the wide funnel. Newspaper accounts of overhauls/repairs occurring in 1892–96, 1898, and 1913 included repair/replacement of the wheel, shaft, propeller blades, caulking, and copper plating on the bottom. For vessel's first seven years, there were many newspaper accounts of the tug towing sailing ships, especially between Vancouver Island and the Lower Mainland to load lumber and fewer accounts of it towing vessels in from or out to sea. Was repowered with an 800-bhp diesel (date unknown).

Owners	Dates
B.C. Mills Timber and Trading Company	1895–1907
Canadian Tugboat Company	1916–46
Coastal Towing	1946–48

Disposition

- Grounded on reef off Cortes Island, British Columbia, on June 26, 1956, and was wrecked.

Incidents

- On August 27, 1889, had a small fire in the hold that was extinguished before any damage could be done.
- Released the grounded U.S. coast survey steamer *Gedney* off Portier Pass, British Columbia, on November 1, 1892, after one earlier unsuccessful attempt.
- In early December 1892, towed the disabled tow/tugboat *Estelle* to Vancouver after latter had its rudder smashed while coming through the Walls rapids.
- In September 1919, a boom of logs under vessel's tow struck the bow of the lightship *Bayard* and carried away part of its false keel, forcing it to undergo repairs before it could go back on station.

Table 5.20
Tow/tugboat *Senator Jansen* (official no. 126272)

Builder:	A. Weston, New Westminster, British Columbia, in 1909.
Engine:	Horizontal, 12-inch cylinder, 60-inch stroke, 9.6 nhp, by Vancouver Engineering
Boiler:	No data.
Dimensions:	112 feet long x 24 feet wide x 3 feet deep.
Propulsion:	Steam sternwheel.
Tonnage:	230/93 (gross/net).
Miscellaneous:	Licensed for 30 passengers (1914). While at mill dock, vessel provided excellent fire protection, since it could pump 1,000 gallons of water per minute.

Owners	Dates
Fraser River Lumber Company	1909
Canadian Western Lumber Company	1917, 1921

Disposition

- Broken up in 1921.

Incidents

- On July 9, 1918, vessel was towing a scow carrying 225 tons of granite blocks. Latter was lashed diagonally to vessel's port bow. The pair floated down the Fraser River with the tide. While passing through an 85-foot-wide drawbridge (between New Westminster, British Columbia, and Lulu Island), scow struck a projecting boom stick, tearing off a stern plank. Scow and cargo sank to the bottom. The crew were found at fault and paid $2,700 in damages to the owners of the scow/cargo.

6

CANADIAN NORTHERN RAILWAY PASSENGER/FREIGHT SHIPPING INITIATIVES ON FRESH WATER

NIAGARA, ST. CATHARINES, AND TORONTO NAVIGATION COMPANY

The first organized maritime passenger services between Toronto and Port Dalhousie, the latter being located near the northern terminus of the Welland Canal, began in 1878 with the Niagara Falls Line, an enterprise of A.W. Hepburn of Picton, Ontario.

The Hepburn family was a major force behind commercial shipping on the Bay of Quinte as well as on Lake Ontario and the upper St. Lawrence River. From 1860 to 1890, A.W. Hepburn was the second most important shipbuilder in Prince Edward County after John Tait. One winter he had more than 100 workmen in his yard engaged in repair work. His boats were well known, and in his heyday he owned 12 ships: the *Alexandria*, *Empress of India*, *Geronia*, *Niagara*, *Argyle*, *L.S. Porter*, *Aberdeen*, *Water Lily*, *W.M. Egan*, *Fairfax*, *Rob Roy*, and *Riccarton*. In 1905 the family operated under the Ontario and Quebec Navigation Company banner. In 1914 Canada Steamship Lines bought the assets of this company.

One steam sidewheeler provided service between Toronto and Port Dalhousie: the *Empress of India* (built in 1876, official no. 72998). Connections were made at Port Dalhousie East with the Grand Trunk branch, which later became the Grantham Division, and at the foot of Welland Avenue in St. Catharines after locking through the old (second) Welland Canal.

In 1892 Hepburn's monopoly ended with the entrance of the Lakeside Navigation Company and its propeller steamer *Lakeside* (official no. 90778) joining the fray. Letters patent had been granted to Hiram

Aerial view in 1920 of the harbour in Port Dalhousie, Ontario. (Library and Archives Canada PA-030557.)

Steamer *Empress of India* docked in Port Dalhousie harbour, circa 1880. (Niagara Falls Public Library, #102067.)

The steamer *Lakeside* in Port Dalhousie in 1909–10. (Archives of Ontario I0013901.)

and E. Chandler Walker of Walkerville, Ontario; J.H. Smart, N.J. Wigle, A. Cowan, and T. Eddy of Kingsville, Ontario; and J. Ross of Windsor, Ontario, on September 14, 1889. The Walkers were the owners of Hiram Walker and Sons, the Windsor distillery famous for Canadian Club whiskey. The provisional directors of the company (capitalized at $30,000) were the Walkers and Wigle. Supplemental letters patent were granted on December 7, 1900, and May 27, 1901, with capitalization on the latter date raised to $100,000. The *Lakeside* was primarily em-

ployed from the time of its completion until 1892 on the Detroit River and Lake Erie routes, including Cleveland, Ohio, to/from Port Stanley, Ontario. With the possible exception of a portion of the 1894 navigation season, the *Lakeside* served from 1892 onward on Lake Ontario. Details of the *Lakeside* are provided in table 6.1.

Another new competitor entered the arena in 1892: the St. Catharines, Grimsby, and Toronto Navigation Company and its new sidewheel steamer *Garden City*. This ship joined the *Empress of India* and *Lakeside* on the

The steamer *Lakeside* at Toronto's Yonge Street wharf in 1905. (Archives of Ontario I0013966.)

crowded and fiercely competitive Toronto to/from Port Dalhousie run. Early on, all three companies pooled receipts on the route and interactions were amicable. However, in 1894–95, co-operation ceased and a rate war ensued between the three companies.

The St. Catharines, Grimsby, and Toronto Navigation Company gave in first, sending the *Garden City* to Lake Erie to run the Buffalo, New York, to/from Crystal Beach, Ontario, route. This was a lucrative route as well due to the popular Crystal Beach Amusement Park. Details of the *Garden City* (official no. 100035) are available in table 6.2.

At the request in 1896 of several navigation companies, Lakeside Navigation donated a large bell to be placed on the range light tower near the outer end of the

The steamer *Garden City* in Port Dalhousie. (Library and Archives Canada PA-020788.)

east pier at Port Dalhousie. This bell was to be rung by hand during foggy conditions by the lightkeeper in response to fog signals from vessels attempting to make the harbour. It replaced an unreliable foghorn. Why this was the responsibility of an individual navigation company and not the Canadian government is something this author questions. The answer is not known.

In 1897 W.G. Thornton, R. Hamelin, and N.J. Wigle bought a controlling interest in the Lakeside Navigation Company from the Walkers. W.G. Thornton had been the company solicitor. By the end of 1898, the *Empress*

of India had been withdrawn and Lakeside Navigation was left alone on the lucrative Toronto to/from Port Dalhousie run. It quickly became clear that the little *Lakeside* would not be able to satisfy the voracious consumer demand for transportation to/from Port Dalhousie and, indirectly, Niagara Falls. For the summer seasons of 1899 and 1900, the propeller steamer *Lincoln* (official no. 92735) was chartered to run in conjunction with the *Lakeside* (see table 6.3 for details of the *Lincoln*).

Around 1901 the Lakeside Navigation Company was purchased by a group of investors headed by J.W.

The steamer *Greyhound* (renamed the *Lincoln* in 1899) was leased in 1900 by Lakeside Navigation. This view illustrates its later reincarnation as the *Premier*. (Alpena Public Library 61742.61759.)

Flavelle, J.H. Plummer, and Z.A. Lash, the last named being a Toronto attorney and close associate of William Mackenzie and Donald Mann. They represented New York financiers who owned a number of electric railways in the United States, including the Hudson Valley line. Lash soon became the chairman of the board of the company, which on May 27, 1901, was renamed the Niagara, St. Catharines, and Toronto Navigation Company by a supplemental letters patent. In 1899 the same party had incorporated the Niagara, St. Catharines, and Toronto Railway Company to take over the property of the St. Catharines and Niagara Central Railway.

In 1901 the *Lincoln* was assigned to the Buffalo to/from Crystal Beach run, while the Toronto to/from Port Dalhousie run settled down with the *Lakeside* and *Garden City*. The next year the Niagara, St. Catharines, and Toronto Navigation Company became a wholly owned subsidiary of the Niagara, St. Catharines, and Toronto Railway Company. It was also during 1902 that Lakeside Park, a large amusement area, was built by the Navigation Company. At that time the docking facilities for the Navigation Company were switched to Port Dalhousie West, opposite the old Welland Railway terminals.

In 1903–04 a minor depression caused financial difficulties for the U.S. owners, who sold out to a Toronto group. Two Canadian Northern men joined the board of directors while other directors were associated with William Mackenzie's electric utility promotion. The Canadian Northern Railway now had a 40 percent interest in these properties.

Full control of these properties passed to the Canadian Northern Railway in 1907–08. Now all the directors were Canadian Northern men. From that point on, these properties operated as semi-autonomous units of the Canadian Northern system, and finances were handled, in the peculiar style of the Canadian Northern Railway, by Mackenzie and Mann. It was not until 1915 that these properties were shown as constituent companies of the Canadian Northern system in annual financial statements.

One might ask what the motives were of the Canadian Northern Railway in taking over a small regional electric railway and its affiliated navigation company. These motives changed as the goals of Mackenzie and Mann expanded. The Canadian Northern was initially a regional

The steamer *Dalhousie City* in 1928. (Library and Archives Canada MIKAN 3528123.)

Prairie railway. However, it did not take long for the principals to resolve to make it a transcontinental line in order not to be dependent on competitors providing connections east and west. Canadian Northern development took place concurrently with the expansion and consolidation of public utilities in Ontario. Some men were closely involved in both arenas, among them Mackenzie and others in the inner circle of the Canadian Northern. In carrying out such enormous plans, they made use of things at hand. For example, something might be done by an electric corporation that was to be shared at a later date, perhaps by a railway corporation under arrangements to be finalized later. Such long-range plans were sometimes carried out, sometimes abandoned, and sometimes replaced by others so that there were always corporate "bits and pieces" lying around waiting for their time to come or ignored as being part of a purpose that had not or would not come to pass.

The Niagara, St. Catharines, and Toronto properties exhibited all of these characteristics. Whether by design or by accident, these properties were vital to its owners from two viewpoints, neither having much to do with the provision of marine or electric railway service to the Niagara Peninsula. First, they would help to bring Niagara Falls power to Toronto, the cornerstone of Mackenzie and Mann's utilities empire. Second, they would help to bring Canadian Northern steam trains from Toronto to the Niagara Peninsula, considered essential for long-term prosperity of the railway.

As was commonly seen with other properties after acquisition by the Canadian Northern, an expansion program for the electric railway property was undertaken. Within five years the two longest interurban lines had been built (St. Catharines–Port Colborne by 1911 and St. Catharines–Niagara-on-the-Lake by 1913) and unification of the various components of the railway had been achieved.

Over time, traffic steadily increased, especially with interurban services reaching Niagara Falls. In addition, the new line expanded a new Mecca for the travelling public known as Lakeside Park in Port Dalhousie (see sidebar in this chapter). This translated into the need for a replacement steamer for the *Lakeside*. In 1911 the *Dalhousie City* (official no. 130312), one of the last of the "day boats" to be built for the Great Lakes, was assembled in Collingwood, Ontario. Originally to be named simply *Dalhousie*, the name was changed to resemble that of the *Garden City*. Details of the *Dalhousie City* are available in table 6.4.

During the First World War, a sudden upsurge in passenger business did not occur (unlike the case during the Second World War), but business, generally, was steady. However, late in the war severe coal shortages did compromise all coal consumers, including the maritime industry, such that the *Garden City* was laid up in 1917 and later sold.

The *Dalhousie City* soldiered on alone until 1920 when a unique opportunity arose. The propeller steamer *Northumberland* (official no. 96937) had been built by Swan Hunter & Wigham Richardson in 1891 for the Charlottetown (P.E.I). Steam Navigation Company to provide service across Northumberland Strait between Prince Edward Island and mainland Nova Scotia. This company sold out to the Canadian government in 1916, and by 1920, the *Northumberland* became available for use on the Great Lakes. Of interest, the vessel remained under government ownership and its port of registry continued to be Charlottetown until its demise in 1950. The latter fact was evident to all in the beautiful gold scrollwork on its stern.

After its first season under charter to the Niagara, St. Catharines, and Toronto Navigation Company, running opposite the *Dalhousie City*, the *Northumberland* entered Toronto Dry Dock Company over the winter for an extensive rebuilding. Most cabins were removed, the upper deck was made suitable for the lake excursion trade, and much of the lower deck was converted from freight storage to crew quarters. In 1927 a shade deck was added abaft the funnel, unfortunately ruining the former racy yacht-like appearance. In the late 1930s, extensive fundamental reconstruction work, necessitated by its age, was done. Of interest, the original engine and boilers were retained over its 58-year service life.

By the end of the First World War, the Canadian Northern Railway faced insurmountable financial difficulties emanating from a lack of British capital during the war years. The vast transportation empire came gradually under the control of the Canadian government. The Niagara, St. Catharines, and Toronto Navigation Company and Lakeside Park also found themselves under federal government management in 1918, being absorbed into the Canadian National Railways "family." Company ships soon carried the CANADIAN NATIONAL STEAMERS banner.

During the 1920s, the Navigation Company was the only division of the Niagara, St. Catharines, and Toronto Railway whose business continued to grow throughout the decade. In 1921 and 1929, approximately 185,000 and 270,000 passengers were carried, respectively. Steamer revenues increased in 1925–26 with electrification of the Grantham Division. By 1925 the Grand Trunk had become a component of Canadian National Railways, thus facilitating the transfer of the Grantham Division to the Niagara, St. Catharines, and Toronto Railway. This effort was targeted at a competitor — Canada Steamship Lines. The end result was a half-hour time advantage on the Toronto to/from Niagara Falls route for the Niagara, St. Catharines, and Toronto Navigation/Railway Companies (three and a quarter hours) compared with Canada Steamship Lines via Queenston (three and three-quarter hours).

Originally, vessels docked at the foot of Yonge Street on the old waterfront at a wharf obliterated by landfill operations. Its actual location was northeast of the Harbour Commission Building. After 1927 the Toronto dock was located at the foot of York Street with a waiting room and office space rented from adjacent Terminal Warehouses Limited.

Even during the Depression, business remained reasonably good. The company steamers were smaller and less expensive to operate compared with those of Canada Steamship Lines. This competitive edge became very apparent when traffic fell during the Depression. The

The steamer *Northumberland* docked in Toronto in 1925. (Library and Archives Canada PA-056272.)

Navigation Company was able to maintain a service with two ships with four or five trips daily long after Canada Steamship Lines had been forced to a one-vessel service with the propeller ship *Cayuga* after the 1936 season.

The company was always considerate concerning land transportation for the passengers after their lake crossing. For example, on weekends the last trip of the day was scheduled to arrive in Toronto in the wee hours of the morning and was met by a lineup of Toronto Transportation Commission (TTC) streetcars with routes covering most of the city. The ship's passenger load was radioed ahead to enable the TTC to have an adequate number of cars at hand.

A reduction in passenger services was planned for 1941, due in part to operating deficits in 1939 and 1940. In fact, the Navigation Company and Lakeside Park were offered for sale to a "going concern" in October 1941. A viable offer was received, but the prospective buyer could not raise the necessary funds, which was not surprising due to the Second World War being under way. In August 1943, the sale was again advertised, but no offers were received. The ships and the park were considered one entity. Thus, the disposal of even a single ship would be a devastating blow to the sales effort. Unfortunately, the Navigation Company was no longer particularly profitable. Despite returning a modest profit during the Second World War, increasing labour costs brought about deficits after 1946.

Two-ship operation was continued into the late 1940s, since passenger loadings held reasonably stable. These would have continued longer except for a major disaster that occurred in 1949: the burning of the *Northumberland*. On June 2, 1949, fire destroyed the *Northumberland* in Port Dalhousie. This was one day before the vessel was

SPECIAL-PARTY ARRANGEMENTS

Special-party business was actively sought. For example, 150 such groups, totalling 41,000 passengers, were accommodated in 1947 alone. A complex schedule of reduced mid-week and excursion fares was always in effect. As late as the end of the Second World War, a child's day-return ticket from Toronto to Niagara Falls could be bought for under $1. Despite competitive pressures, relations between Canada Steamship Lines and the Niagara, St. Catharines, and Toronto Navigation Company were cordial. When the occasion required it, one company's tickets were honoured on the other firm's ships and accounted for later. Sometimes, for especially large outings, one of the steamers made special trips from Hamilton to Port Dalhousie. For example, 11 such trips were made in 1947, accommodating more than 8,000 passengers. One of the Cobourg, Ontario, to/from Rochester, New York, railcar ferries (*Ontario No. 1* or *Ontario No. 2*) operated by the Ontario Car Ferry Company (OCFC), which was partly owned by Canadian National Railways, was sometimes borrowed to replace absent company ships on the Toronto–Port Dalhousie run.

LAKESIDE PARK

A 1902 development of the Niagara, St. Catharines, and Toronto Navigation Company, Lakeside Park became an important source of traffic for the navigation company and its affiliated Niagara, St. Catharines and Toronto Railway Company. In 1903 approximately 200,000 visitors entered the park, 90 percent of whom had been conveyed there by either the navigation company or the railway. Early on, the improvements to the park were modest. Booths were erected to lease to concessionaires as well as a baseball diamond, carousel, and change booths near the beach.

Soon cottages began to appear on the bluffs above the park as did streets by which to access them. Stairs were built up from the park to gain access to the streets above. By 1905–06, Lakeside Park was rapidly gaining a reputation as a summer resort with swimming, entertainment, and a growing midway. Many company and church picnics swelled attendance figures.

In the early 1920s, with the arrival of the *Northumberland*, attendance figures soared. In large part this was due to the improvements made by the new owner, Canadian National Railways. The park area doubled from six to 12 acres by filling in a low, swampy area. Licences of vendors considered substandard were not renewed. Tent concessions were forbidden. All enclosures in the park were wooden structures painted in the same green-and-white motif. A grandstand and additional bleachers were erected as well as a 3,000-seat covered picnic pavilion and bathing pavilion with swimsuit and locker rentals. Electric lights were added to extend open hours. Allegedly, a roller coaster (Miller/Baker Deep Dipper) was built in 1922, but no further information is available and it cannot be seen on a 1930 park map.

Canadian National was also a thoughtful employer. Dormitories for employees, a home for the park manager, a committee meeting room, and a residence for musicians while their bands played in the park were all added. A first-aid station with a "mother's rest area" (for changing/feeding of infants) was also built. Several of these buildings were recycled old cottages that were moved to the park when their former owners were upgrading. The Canada Railway News Company (predecessor to CARA) operated the park for a year or two in the early 1920s. Canadian National resumed operations in 1923.

Other additions included an archery range, bandstand, dancing pavilion, miniature golf, picnic shelters, and a huge water slide. In addition to the usual food concessions, the Lakeside Inn Restaurant was located right at the ferry pier. It was run like a fine dining car with hostesses and a steward to greet guests.

Rides included Aeroplane Swings (likely a Traver Seaplane De Luxe), carousel, Caterpillar (by Traver), Dodgem bumper cars, rowboats, water bicycles (in 1933), the Whip (by Mangels) and, possibly, a roller coaster (see above). Rides and games cost 5 to 10 cents each and undercover employees made sure the games were not "fixed" and that everyone won at least something.

The carousel was a four-row Looff brand with two chariots and 74 animals, 42 of them being jumpers. Music was supplied by an Artizan band organ, which might have come from the Crystal Palace in London, England. The ride was likely bought used from Scarboro Beach Park, which closed in the 1920s.

Although attendance dipped during the Depression years, the park continued a booming business even through the Second World War.

However, by 1945, Canadian National wanted to divest itself from amusement park holdings and offered it for sale. There were no buyers. In 1949 the *Northumberland* was destroyed by fire, and due to this and other ship fires (for example, the *Noronic* disaster in Toronto), strict governmental fire regulations for ships were imposed. Canadian National would not pay to upgrade the *Dalhousie City* to meet the new fire code and cancelled the ferry service. Obviously, attendance slipped without a ferry service, and Canadian National increased its efforts to sell the park. Sid Brookston, the park manager, bought the park in 1960. However, with cars available to take people farther afield and pollution in Lake Ontario making swimming unsavoury, if not dangerous, the park's decline was relentless, unstoppable. In 1969 only one picnic was booked. The midway closed that year, and the refreshment stands followed in 1970.

Today the park is a day-use park of the city of St. Catharines. The only survivors of the "good old days" are the picnic pavilion and the restored carousel, which still runs, costing patrons a nickel for a ride, just as in its heyday.

scheduled to begin its summer work. The fire started at about 0600 hours in the aft section. Fresh paint helped the fire spread rapidly despite superhuman efforts on the part of the crew, most being newly signed on. A short time previously there had been some trouble experienced with the electrical circuits, but subsequent investigations failed to trace the origin of the fire to that source. The cause of the fire was never officially established. However, there is some support for a carelessly discarded cigarette in a storage room as being the cause.

The loss of the *Northumberland* left the company with only a single ship, slower than the *Northumberland*, such that it could readily make only two round trips per day. Emergency arrangements were made with Canadian National Railways and Canada Steamship Lines to accommodate special-party commitments that could not be handled by one vessel. The *Dalhousie City* did its best during the 1949 season, making two trips weekdays and three on weekends.

In the twilight years of the steamship service between Toronto and Port Dalhousie, the *Dalhousie City* and *Northumberland* might have begun cancelling mail aboard ship. Whether these ships could be considered Travelling Post Offices or whether these were just examples of pursers' stamps has not been fully resolved. The first cancellation was of type 1E (see images in table 3.4 in chapter 3) with the text CAN.NAT./STEAMERS/N.ST.C.&.T.RY.CO. / steamer name (i.e., STR./DALHOUSIE CITY in 1946, STR./ NORTHUMBERLAND in 1948). The second cancellation was in the format of type 7B (see images in table 3.4 in chapter 3) and was used by only one vessel in 1948. The text read: N.ST.C.&T.NAV.CO./STR.NORTHUMBERLAND.

At the end of 1949 it was decided to end the service. Although the 1949 season loss was slightly less than that in 1948, the reduced service of two round trips on weekdays and three on weekends adversely affected the revenues of Lakeside Park and the connecting interurban. *The Dalhousie City* was sold to Inland Lines Limited of Montreal, leaving Port Dalhousie for the last time on April 21, 1950. Lakeside Park was sold to its former manager, but steadily declined thereafter until closing in 1970.

CANADIAN NORTHERN GREAT LAKES/ST. LAWRENCE RIVER BASIN FREIGHT SHIPPING INITIATIVES

Port Arthur Harbour

The harbour area of Port Arthur, Ontario, was disadvantaged by two realities. First, the lakebed was composed of hard pan and rock, necessitating the building of piers and docks into the open bay and, hence, necessitating the construction of an extensive breakwater for protection. Second, the entire harbour was totally exposed to Thunder Bay except for a small portion in the centre of the waterfront protected by a breakwater.

The frontage of the harbour area was seven and a quarter miles with three rivers emptying into it (McKellar, Mission, and Kaministiquia). Eventually, it was divided into four segments as follows:

- One mile for the Canadian Pacific Railway and Pigeon River Lumber Company.
- Two miles for the municipality of Port Arthur.

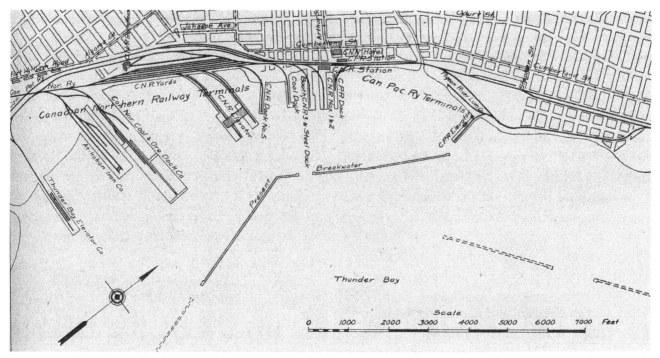

Schematic of Canadian Northern Railway shoreline facilities in Port Authur in 1913. (Canadian Railway & Marine World, April 1913.)

- Three miles for the Canadian Northern Railway.
- One and a quarter miles for various smaller owners.

Early History of Docks in Port Arthur

The first dock in Port Arthur was built by the Thunder Bay Silver Mining Company over the winter of 1867–68 by a Mr. Withrow and 12 experienced builders from Ottawa. It was sited on Mountain Location 4, close to its western boundary, approximately a half mile east of the Current River. It was composed of wooden piers filled with stone, was 180 feet in length, and had a water depth of 10 feet at its end. The first business dock was erected just south of the end of Red River Road (Arthur Street) by James Dickson, acting on behalf of Thomas Marks of Bruce Mines, Ontario, in 1868.

A small dock was built alongside, to the west of the dock described in the previous paragraph, in 1868–69 and was called the "Government" dock. In 1875–76, it was extended by 500 feet. In 1882–83, it was extended a further 400 feet and an "L" addition was constructed for shelter. On the southeast corner of the "L" addition was installed the first lighthouse in Port Arthur. The large Marks dock was built close to the "Government" dock in 1872, with Horne's (hospital) grain elevator being built in association in 1872–73.

This was followed by the No. 5 dock at the foot of Manitou Street, the coal dock of the Lake Superior Dock and Elevator Company a short distance to the north of No. 5, the Clavet dock at the foot of Lincoln Street, the Smith and Mitchell dock at the foot of Park Street, and the Davis dock at the foot of Pearl Street. This now brings us to 1905 and the entry of the Canadian Northern Railway into the affairs of Port Arthur.

Overview of Canadian Northern Lakefront Facilities in the Lakehead

The Canadian Northern Railway entered the Lakehead (Fort William and Port Arthur, Ontario) near the same point as the Grand Trunk Pacific and Canadian Pacific Railways in the suburb of Westfort. From just north of the Canadian Pacific gravity yard, the line swung in a northeasterly direction, continuing on a tangent almost three miles into the heart of Port Arthur. Canadian Northern had only a depot in Fort William, located where the line crossed Victoria Avenue.

Canadian Northern occupied virtually the entire waterfront from Arthur Street to the centre of town, to the extreme southern city border where it abuts Fort William. The depot was located at the foot of Arthur Street, adjoining the shore end of a wharf. The Prince Arthur Hotel was completed in 1910 at the corner of Cumberland and Arthur Streets and had the footprint of an entire city block. The tangent line referred to previously ended in a yard complex to the west of the Canadian Northern elevator complex (see below).

From the depot, various package freight piers could be seen in the immediate foreground. Farther out was the huge grain elevator complex in the harbour supported on a pile-and-concrete pier foundation and approached on both sides by trestlework. Even farther out were the piers of the Atikokan Iron Company and the Canadian Northern Coal and Ore Dock Company. The accompanying site map from the April 1913 issue of *Canadian Railway and Marine World* nicely illustrates the shoreline improvements by the Canadian Northern Railway in Port Arthur.

Canadian Northern Coal and Ore Dock Company and Atikokan Iron Company

Canadian Northern Coal and Ore Dock Company Limited (CNCOD) was incorporated under Ontario letters patent on February 17, 1905, to build and operate coal and ore docks in Port Arthur. Involved in the handling and storage of coal and (iron) ore, it had no role in purchasing, selling, or transporting these entities. The central purposes of the company were to assure a convenient and adequate supply of coal for Canadian Northern locomotives and to, if possible, develop iron ore traffic through Port Arthur. In the context of the latter, the Atikokan Iron Company was incorporated by Mackenzie and Mann under Dominion letters patent on April 14, 1905. Its purposes were to mine ore at company mines 125 miles west of the Lakehead near Atikokan, Ontario (an extension of the Minnesota iron ranges) and to manufacture pig iron at blast-furnace facilities on the waterfront at Port Arthur.

Towers — C. N. R. Coal and Ore Docks, Port Arthur, Ont.

Two early views of the Canadian Northern coal dock in Port Arthur, Ontario. (Toronto Public Library PC-ON 1658 and 917.1312 S594 BR.)

The company was capitalized at $1 million, and the president, vice-president, and plant superintendent were D.D. Mann, J.C. Hunter, and R. Jones, respectively.

Initially, the $500,000 in capital stock of the dock company was divided equally between Mackenzie and Mann and the Pittsburgh Coal Company. By 1911 Mackenzie and Mann had purchased all of the Pittsburgh Coal Company shares. Bonded debt was $1.75 million with a ceiling of $2 million. The president, vice-president, and secretary were H. Sutherland, Z.A. Lash, and L.W. Mitchell, respectively.

The town of Port Arthur paid dearly for CNCOD, the Atikokan Iron Company, and Mackenzie and Mann. The town was to pay a bonus of $200,000 in the form of a bond purchase from the Atikokan Iron Company; provide a minimum of 40 acres of land, valued at $25,000, for free to site the Iron Company; supply sewer connections for a token amount; and grant a taxation exemption on all properties for 20 years (5 Edward VII, chapter 69, assent date May 25, 1905).

The dock company had planned to place a crib pier front on the dock that it was having built. However, in the fall of 1905, a storm swept away all of the cribwork installed to date, due in part to the lack of protection of a breakwater. The company abandoned the idea of a crib pier front in favour of a pile front filled in with stone/rock. The Canadian government, too, decided to erect a temporary breakwater to soften the blows of Mother Nature. Also, in the fall of 1905, a 300-horsepower Robb-Armstrong tandem engine from Robb Engineering was delivered to power the initial dock facilities.

The first section of dock completed in 1906 was 3,000 feet long and 600 feet wide. The site lay between

Two views of the Atikokan Iron Company dock and blast furnace. (Library and Archives Canada PA-021146 and PA-021147.)

the Neebig River and MacIntyre Creek. It was proposed to dredge a channel 200 feet wide and 3,000 feet long from the harbour, which would cross with the dock at its end. The firm of Barnett & Record of Minneapolis, Minnesota, was awarded the contract.

The $13,000 contract for construction of the temporary breakwater was given to the dock company by the federal Department of Public Works in the fall of 1906. The permanent breakwater to be erected by the Canadian government was announced late in 1906. It would be an extension of the current one. However, 1,000 feet from the southwestern end would be removed from the bottom of the existing breakwater before new construction commenced. The new work would be 2,760 feet long (measured on the seaward face of the timber cribwork) and 30 feet wide, with a superstructure of concrete with cribwork block at its southern end (80 feet long and 40 feet wide). The substructure would be built as 29 separate cribs, 27 each being 100 feet long, one being 60 feet long and 30 feet wide, and one being 80 feet long and 40 feet wide. The superstructure would be of concrete block and poured concrete and its top would be eight and half feet above low water level. A berth would be dredged along its entire length to a depth of 26 feet below low water level, followed by placement of a stone foundation.

In 1907 shipments of pig iron from the Atikokan Iron Company to the east by water began in July. On November 5 the Algoma Central and Hudson Bay steamer *Paliki* loaded 2,000 tons destined for the Algoma Steel Company mill at Sault Ste. Marie, Ontario. The iron company also purchased six new Hart-Otis Car Company (Montreal) all-steel dump cars of 50 tons capacity each for use in the transportation of ore from Atikokan to Port Arthur. In late 1908 there was bad news from the iron company. The industrial depression of 1907 and 1908 hit the iron and steel industries particularly hard. It was decided to close down operations and await better market conditions. As time passed without renewed operations and fixed charges could not be met, Mackenzie and Mann obtained a winding-up order from the courts. This was withdrawn only after shareholders obtained sufficient capital to pay off all claims. The facility reopened in August 1909 with an overhauled and improved plant and new superintendent, J.D. Fraser.

In 1910 new coal sheds on the Port Arthur dock were constructed and the filling of the new coal storage yard with soft (bituminous) coal and hard (anthracite) coal was achieved. On December 7, 1911, Barnett & McQueen was contracted to build an extensive addition to the coal dock, commencing in January 1912. This extension, costing $500,000, doubled the company's capacity through the addition of storage for 60,000 tons of hard and 250,000 tons of soft coal. Frontage at the head of the dock was approximately 600 feet. Unloading trackage and three unloading towers extended along this frontage for approximately 450 feet. The area devoted to the coal plant projected for a depth of 2,525 feet from the harbour front. Running through the centre were railway tracks on which cars were loaded with soft coal from various open pockets fed by conveyors from the unloading plant. Beyond these pockets were three storage sheds for hard coal (one being 288 feet by 244 feet and two being 276 feet by 205 feet). These sheds were also served by conveyors and had their own covered coal pockets from which cars could be loaded.

At the shore end was the plant office, and just outside the dock spur line were the track scales. Shed No. 3, with the coal pockets and tracks, was outside but adjoined the area previously mentioned such that at the shore end the plant covered an area of approximately 300 feet by 1,000 feet. The contractors built the foundation, while the dock company did the filling work itself to save money.

Improvements were also made to the south side of the existing dock. Bituminous coal storage was added to the existing dock (250 feet wide by 2,000 feet long). The old anthracite coal shed was removed, while a new 60,000-ton-capacity anthracite shed was added. Additional loading pockets for bituminous coal (144 feet long) and a double pickup storage bridge were built on the south side, while tracks/track scales had to be rearranged. A 2,600-foot-long revetment wall was built along the south side and across the outer edge of the old dock using heavy tongue-and-groove sheet piling.

A 1,000-horsepower steam plant powered the huge facility. Its performance statistics were impressive. Not only was its storage capacity doubled, it could unload a 10,000-ton steamer in only 18 hours while concurrently loading from the same vessel some 225 railcars in 10 hours (or concurrently loading some 175 railcars from the coal piles over the same time period)!

Three Meade-Morrison unloaders equipped with two-ton clamshell buckets could each unload 200 tons per hour. A cable-car system carried coal to the storage bins or sheds. There were two bridges, one with two one-ton hoists and buckets and the other with two two-ton hoists and buckets. Three Ottumwa box car loaders for bituminous coal and one for anthracite coal and an Industrial Works locomotive crane rounded out the dock machinery.

Approximately half of the delivered coal went to supply the needs of Canadian Northern locomotives, while the other half went to coal dealers. About half of the unloaded coal went directly into railcars for immediate delivery, while the other half went into storage on the coal dock.

The final act of the Atikokan Iron Company occurred in 1911. The blast furnace had been operational from August 1909 until 1911. In 1911 a large cast-iron pipe and car-wheel foundry was added to the lakeshore complex to utilize most of the 100 tons of pig iron produced daily. In the end, the very scattered nature of the deposits of magnetite ore at the mine site along with its varied and objectionable phosphorus and sulphur content made the entire operation uneconomic to operate. And so the company folded in 1911.

In contrast, business was so good for the coal operation that in 1913 the dock company proposed to build a new dock to the east of the present one, about 500 feet wide at the head, with storage sheds and loading pockets. However, nothing came of the proposal. Perhaps the tightening money markets due to the clouds of war on the European horizon had something to do with this result.

In the spring of 1915, Barnett & McQueen were contracted to overhaul and repair the coal-handling plant, place 700 lineal feet of solid concrete abutments as foundations for the coal hoists, and face the dock with concrete at an estimated cost of $500,000. This job kept 100 men employed for six months.

All company assets, including waterfront real estate, storehouses, and dock and loading facilities were leased to the Canadian Northern Railway for a period of 25 years, effective January 1, 1916. The annual rental fee was set as the sum of interest and sinking fund charges on its bonded indebtedness. In 1916, with $1.75 million in bonded debt, the rental fee was $122,500. With a rise in bonded debt to its maximum of $2 million, the fee rose to $140,000 per annum.

By 1917 the annual capacity of the coal dock was 1.6 million tons, and storage capacities for soft and hard coal were 500,000 and 250,000 tons, respectively. With the collapse of Canadian Northern's empire, Canadian National Railways acquired all company stock and title on July 20, 1920. Operations ceased in 1926, and the corporate charter lapsed on March 31, 1942.

Other Canadian Northern Docking Facilities in Port Arthur

The Canadian Northern Railway had general freight docks dating back as early as 1902 when the road reached the municipality. One dock was 800 feet long, as attested in a Department of Public Works document describing dredging services provided that year.

By April 1902, Vigers and Company of Port Arthur had been awarded a contract to build an addition to No. 1 dock (100 feet wide by 400 feet long) and erect upon it a shed (52 feet wide by 350 feet long). Two tracks were to be laid upon the dock, which was to handle the company's through freight. The dock was completed the same year.

A steel dock, proposed to Canadian authorities in late 1906, which projected into the water lot between the "extensions" of Lorne and Lincoln Streets into the Port Arthur harbour, was built, as well. It cost $1 million.

Another expansion of general freight dockage occurred in the spring of 1910 when the Thunder Bay Harbour Improvement Company was contracted to expand No. 3 dock. The extension would include a pile foundation and a heavy timber deck and would be 74 feet wide and 250 feet long. After completion a steel-clad freight shed (50 feet wide by 400 feet long) was to be erected on the now-enlarged No. 3 dock.

A package and general freight dock (75 feet wide and 450 feet long) was built during the winter of 1912–13 by the Thunder Bay Harbour Improvement Company under the supervision of and using plans/specifications supplied by the railway. This dock was also intended for unloading steel rails to be used in the construction of the Canadian Northern Railway. Piles were of sound tamarack (40 to 50 feet long), with 12-inch butts (i.e., ends), driven to bedrock and spaced five feet apart. In this location the water was 12 to 20 feet deep with, in places, soft mud covering the lakebed to a depth of up to several feet. Piles were capped by 12-by-12-inch fir running transversely, while longitudinal stringers were fir six inches by 10 inches spaced 24 inches on-centre. Decking was lumber three inches by 12 inches (species not provided). The deck surface was about eight feet above the level of the water.

On July 4, 1914, a section of this dock gave way under a load of approximately 2,100 tons of steel rails recently unloaded from the SS *McKee*. Rails from the *McKee* had been placed in three piles, each about 33 by 66 feet in area. The section of collapse was approximately 75 feet square in area. Two piles of rails, each weighing about 1,050 tons, were carried down with the collapsed dock section.

Of interest, the entire length of the dock was loaded with rails, some piles weighing 1,200 tons or more. After the accident, the dock was emptied as rails were rapidly loaded onto railcars to guard against more loss. Divers helped to salvage rails deposited on the lakebed.

Upon forensic examination, it was determined that the event originated at the east end of the break where the stringers were literally sheared off. Human error certainly played a role here, considering the overloading of the entire dock as well as the haphazard unloading of the contents of the *McKee* into piles that were grossly overweight (more than 2,000 tons). Damages totalled $28,000.

Lakehead Grain Elevators: 1883 to 1904

The first elevator was built to the design of CPR engineers in 1883 and was known as King's Elevator after the lessee Joseph King. It was constructed using a wooden crib technique and was essentially a large wooden warehouse 10 stories tall. All functions were housed in one building with the working house, where grain was received, cleaned, and separated by type and grade, being above the storage bins. It would be the model for subsequent CPR elevators built on the Kaministiquia River (see the map of grain elevators on the Port Arthur waterfront in this chapter).

The next three elevators, CPR Elevators A, B, and C built in 1884–85, 1889, and 1890–91, respectively, were similar in design to King's Elevator. Their respective storage capacities were 1, 1.25, and 1.5 million bushels. Elevator B, built by W.J. Ross, a CPR superintendent, was destined to burn to the ground on May 12, 1904, and be rebuilt with the use of steel, tile, and brick construction.

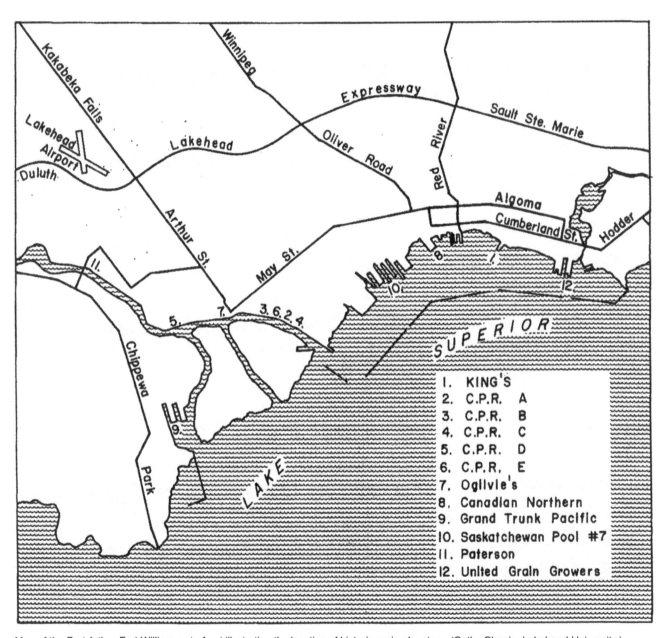

Map of the Port Arthur-Fort William waterfront illustrating the location of historic grain elevators. (Cathy Chapin, Lakehead University.)

Elevator C, erected by J.A. Jamieson, was built as a storage elevator for Elevator A.

Elevator D (CPR) was built in 1897–98 by F.J. Weber of the Steel Storage and Elevator Company of Buffalo, New York. The working house was separated from the storage annex of 24 steel flat-bottomed tanks. Additional storage was added in 1902, and during construction, fire broke out and destroyed the entire elevator complex. It was quickly rebuilt with wood and was later replaced using reinforced concrete.

Elevator E (CPR) was built in 1902–03. In 1903 additional storage was required at King's Elevator. This took the form of circular steel-reinforced concrete bins, utilizing vertical and horizontal steel reinforcement bars ("rebar"), the first successful use of this technique in North America. The initial employment of this practice by Peavey in Duluth, Minnesota, in 1899–1900 had ended in disaster. Construction began in January 1903, and the elevator opened for business on January 3, 1904.

In 1904 Ogilvie's steel elevator was built by MacDonald Engineering Company of Chicago, Illinois, using a patented system of constructing circular bins in clusters. The bins were much smaller in diameter compared with those of the CPR's Elevator E and were conical, not flat-bottomed. In fact, the MacDonald bins were only used as working house storage bins. On May 26, 1906, the elevator slid off its foundation into the Kaministiquia River. However, its bins did not topple. Grain was transferred to other elevators, and the elevator was subsequently dismantled and rebuilt farther back from the river's edge. Due to the distance from the elevator to the loading docks at the water's edge, new loading devices (elevated "steel carriers") had to be created.

It was into this environment that the Canadian Northern Railway, through its Lake Superior Terminals subsidiary, entered the terminal grain elevator world.

Lake Superior Terminals Company Limited

Lake Superior Terminals Company Limited (LSTC) was incorporated under Ontario letters patent on January 4, 1902, to acquire land for and build and operate terminal storage elevators in Port Arthur. Capital stock was $500,000, while bonded indebtedness could be a maximum of $2 million. Capital stock was transferred from Mackenzie and Mann to the Canadian Northern Railway on June 2, 1903. A tract of land 13,140 feet long (most being in Port Arthur's harbour) was acquired and construction began in 1901 (see below). The company was eventually dissolved when its assets were transferred to Canadian National Railways on August 5, 1958.

The LSTC grain elevator in Port Arthur comprised the initial wooden working house, construction of which commenced in 1901 and was completed in 1902, with the tile storage annex finished later in 1902. After completion of the wooden working house (and its enclosed storage bins) by the end of February 1902, the first shipment of grain was received and stored on March 8, 1902.

The wooden working house, which was built offshore, required 7,000 wooden piles and concrete piers to provide an adequate foundation. It was 239 feet long, 72 feet wide, and 157.5 feet tall from the foundation to the gables. The cupola was 41 feet wide and extended the full length of the building. The entire structure was sheathed

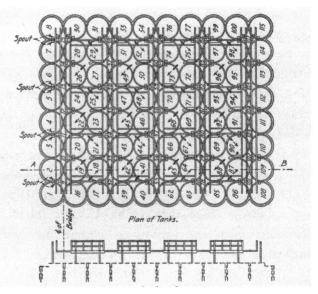

Postcard view of the Canadian Northern grain elevator complex in Port Arthur, Ontario, in 1910. (Toronto Public Library PC-ON 1662.)

Top view of the tile storage tanks of the Canadian Northern grain complex in Port Arthur. (Milo S. Ketchum.)

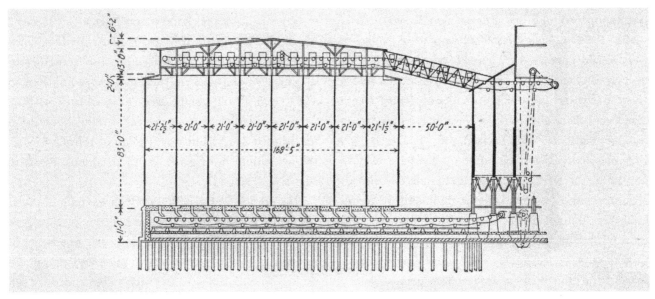

Longitudinal section through the tile storage tanks of the Canadian Northern grain complex in Port Arthur. (Milo S. Ketchum.)

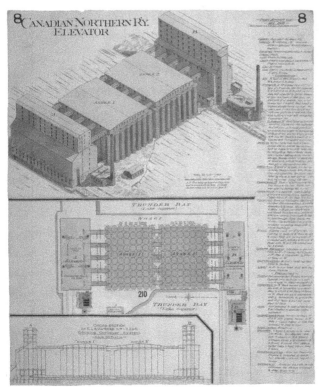

Goad fire insurance map from 1908 illustrating the Canadian Northern grain elevator complex in Port Arthur. (Toronto Public Library M912.13681 I565 Poa15.)

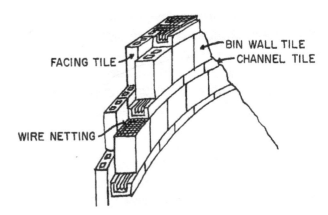

Diagram of construction methodology for the tile storage bins of the Canadian Northern grain elevator complex in Port Arthur. (Carla Tofinetti.)

in corrugated iron. The interior height of the first storey was 24 feet clear to the bin girders. A total of 2.349 million board feet of lumber went into its construction. The capacity of its 60-foot-deep storage bins was 1.5 million bushels.

Like older elevators, railcars still entered the working house. Railway operations were served by one track going into the building and one track outside, next to the building in a one-storey carway. In addition, a freight shed (40 feet wide and 175 feet long) was built on the working house dock.

The working house had five receiving elevators and 10 receiving pits, located so that railcars on both tracks could be unloaded simultaneously. The receiving pits were equipped with automatic power shovels. On the other side of the working house were five cleaning and shipping "legs," each of which was equipped with a no. 9 separator. These "legs" could handle grain from either the working house or the bin annex (see below). Twelve spouts and conveyor belts were used to distribute grain throughout the working house. Five spouts were available to load railcars on either track, with 10 spouts to load ships. Ten hoppers of large capacity received grain from below, after which it was weighed in 10 sets of 1,440-bushel-capacity hopper scales. Working House A, completed in 1902, was demolished in 1926. Working House B was dismantled in 1919 and replaced with a concrete structure in 1920.

Tile construction was a technique used at the beginning of the 20th century as an alternative to building terminal elevators of wood or steel. This was the method selected for the storage bins of the massive Canadian Northern elevator complex on the Port Arthur waterfront in 1902. Barnett-Record semi-porous tile was utilized (see accompanying diagram illustrating the tile construction method). The method was akin to building with concrete blocks, but in this case they were curved and glazed. The glazing process led to these precast blocks being called tiles. The tiles were precast locally in a brickyard and brought to the site. Construction with tile required three different tiles in two sizes with steel reinforcing bars placed in the channel tiles and wire mesh used in the mortar connecting individual tiles. In essence, bins were of double-walled construction.

Bins in the Canadian Northern elevator complex were 21 feet in diameter and 83 feet high. Storage Annex B consisted of 80 circular bins and 63 inter-space bins. For every eight feet in height, each bin would require:

- 378 tiles (12 by 12 by 5 inches).
- 378 channel tiles (12 by 3 by 5 inches).
- 216 facing tiles (outer bins only).
- 336 facing tiles (corner bins only).
- 250 bricks.
- 513 pieces of wire mesh (12 by 4 inches by 375, 48 by 8 inches by 12, and 12 by 1 inches by 126).

When one considers that the average bricklayer of the era could lay 364 tiles per 10-hour working day, the man-hours of labour just building the walls of the storage bins were immense.

The capacity of the total 143-bin complex was slightly over 2.1 million bushels, calculated as follows:

- 48 circular bins at 21,825 bushels = 1,047,600 bushels.
- 32 circular bins at 21,440 bushels = 686,080 bushels.
- 63 intermediate bins at 6,300 bushels = 396,900 bushels.
- Total: 2,130,580 bushels.

This construction method, patented by Johnson and Record, was called "fireproof tile grain storage construction." One purported advantage was the ability to repair damaged bin walls from the exterior without having to remove the grain. The tiles were manufactured by the Kaministiquia Brickyard, founded in 1900. Unlike most local brick, which was unglazed and hence not long-lasting, the Barnett-Record system required glazing. The longevity of this technique is proven, since these storage bins remained in use until the early 2000s.

The elevator storage annexes rested on a pile-and-concrete foundation surrounded by a retaining wall on three sides. Piles were of pine, spruce, and tamarack, each 40 to 50 feet long and eight to 12 inches in diameter.

The entire complex was worked from a single power house. The power house was constructed of brick with a fireproof tile roof supported by steel trusses. Four horizontal tubular boilers (73 inches long by 18 inches in diameter each) supplied steam at 125 psi to two Wheelock steam engines (each with a 22-inch piston diameter and 50-inch stroke).

A later addition in 1904 was a drying house built of brick on a wooden pile-and-concrete foundation. It was located between the elevator complex and the powerhouse.

Its exterior dimensions were 18 by 27 feet with a height of 47 feet. In almost all cases, "rough" grain went to the drying plant before entering the working house or storage bins.

While under construction, it was apparent that Canadian Northern designers and engineers were introducing new ideas into the planning of terminal elevators. Larger in size than any other Lakehead elevator, it was literally planned as a double elevator with two working houses and two storage annexes called A and B. The second working house and storage annex, with a total capacity of 3.5 million bushels, was built beginning in 1904. The entire complex, with a capacity of seven million bushels, was in operation by 1906. With the exception of the first working house (built by J.A. Jamieson of Montreal for $350,000), the entire complex was constructed by Barnett-Record of Minneapolis.

What is quite striking, beyond the sheer mammoth proportions of the complex itself, was the contrast between the old-fashioned appearance of the working houses of wooden crib construction and the modern avant-garde appearance of the tile storage annexes.

After the Winnipeg Grain Exchange established a wheat futures contract that allowed hedging grain purchases, Frank T. Heffelfinger and Frederick T. Wells (sons-in-law of Frank Peavey, the U.S. elevator king) leased the Canadian Northern elevator complex. This was done via the establishment in 1906 of the British American Elevator Company in which Mackenzie and Mann owned 40 percent of the stock. The complex was purchased by the Saskatchewan Wheat Pool in the 1920s and named Saskatchewan Wheat Pool 6. The entire complex was demolished in the early 2000s.

CANADIAN NORTHERN'S FREIGHT SHIPPING INITIATIVES ON THE GREAT LAKES AND ST. LAWRENCE RIVER

The launch of the Canadian Ocean and Inland Navigation Company (COIN), yet another Mackenzie and Mann subsidiary, was announced in December 1900. The firm, capitalized at $200,000, was headquartered in Newcastle, England. The company was the result of discussions between William Petersen of turret steamer fame (see "William Petersen Limited" sidebar) and William Mackenzie when both toured Canadian Northern facilities in the West in the late 1890s. The ownership of five turret vessels was transferred to this firm: the *Turret Chief* (official no. 106605), *Turret Court* (official no. 106608), and *Turret Cape* (official no. 104283) in 1901, and the *Scottish Hero* (official no. 105718) and *Turret Bay* (official no. 104245) in 1902. The *Turret Crown* (official no. 104279) also came under the control of Mackenzie and Mann in 1906, although ownership was vested in another subsidiary company (see below).

The five turrets owned by Canadian Ocean and Inland Navigation were managed by William Petersen Limited of Newcastle. The *Scottish Hero* and *Turret Bay* were too long to pass through the Welland Canal and thus served primarily in the Sydney, Nova Scotia, to/from Montreal/Quebec City coal trade, at least initially. Details of these six vessels are available in tables 6.6 to 6.11, respectively.

In 1903 it was announced that this firm would also operate a steamship line between Rotterdam and Canadian ports of call. It was intended to make this a biweekly

WILLIAM PETERSEN LIMITED

This company was incorporated on November 9, 1900, to take over the assets of and ship management as previously carried out by Petersen, Tate and Company. Petersen et al had started out in 1897, contracting with the Canadian government for a fast freight/passenger service to/from the United Kingdom. They wished to use turret steamers on the route but funding could not be obtained in the British market, since turret ships were so new (see "Turret Steamers" sidebar) and their deposit to the Canadian government was forfeited.

William Petersen Limited was the managing owner of five steamships belonging to four companies. One of these companies was Dominion Turret Line Limited, which was sold to Canadian Ocean and Inland Navigation for £130,000 (£100,000 in cash; 30,000 in shares). In 1902 Petersen sold £80,000 of Canadian Ocean and Inland Navigation securities to Canadian Lake and Ocean Navigation (CLON) for £65,000 in cash and retained management of the turrets *Scottish Hero* and *Turret Bay*. Three turrets (*Turret Cape*, *Turret Court*, and *Turret Chief*) were transferred to the Great Lakes. Canadian Lake and Ocean Navigation then transferred $150,000 in CLON shares as a bonus to Petersen. From 1902 onward, the firm became more and more involved in establishing a steamship line between Canadian and French/Belgian ports, which led to the firm's insolvency in 1906.

service. A key reason for initiating this service was the importation of German-made steel rails for the Canadian railway boom, especially that of the Canadian Northern Railway. The steamships *Toronto* (official no. 113569) and *Aboukir* (official no. 108151) were chartered for this service in 1903.

The Canadian Lake and Ocean Navigation Company (CLON), another Mackenzie and Mann subsidiary, received its letters patent of incorporation on August 27, 1902. Capital stock was set at $3 million. The president in 1902 was A.E. Ames, a prominent Toronto stockbroker, while the secretary was F. Plummer and the board of directors comprised A.E. Ames, F. Plummer, H.M. Pellatt, F. Nicholls, Z.A. Lash, and E.R. Wood. In 1903 J.H. Plummer became president. There were also rumours that George Cox, president of the Canadian Bank of Commerce, was also involved in this firm. Headquarters were located in Toronto.

The turret vessel *Scottish Hero*. (Alpena Public Library 127166.127178.)

A bylaw (no. 4) passed in late 1902 allowed the number serving on the board of directors to range from two to eight, as compared with the previous range of two to seven. In 1903 J.B. Foote became marine superintendent of the firm, serving in this capacity until 1910, while in 1905, J.H. Plummer and F. Plummer became president and secretary, respectively. In 1906 the board of directors was comprised of H.M. Pellatt (president), Z.A. Lash (vice-president), F. Nicholls (vice-president), L. Lukes, H. Sutherland, E.R. Wood, and F. Plummer (secretary/ treasurer and general manager). A general reorganization

was made in 1907 with D.B. Hanna becoming president, Z.A. Lash maintaining his vice-presidency, and a board of directors comprising D.B. Hanna, H. Sutherland, F. Nicholls, E.R. Wood, H.M. Pellatt, Z.A. Lash, N. Marshall, and F.H. Phippen. At that time R.W. and A.B. MacKay of Hamilton became managers of the fleet. In 1910 management was shifted to J.W. Norcross. D.B. Hanna was president until at least 1914 when Canada Steamship Lines started to absorb the company's vessels.

The major reasons for the development of the Canadian Lake and Ocean Navigation Company were:

TURRET STEAMERS

William Doxford and Sons of Sunderland, England, patented an ocean-going cargo ship of radical design in 1891. The primary reason for the development of what became known as the "turret" design" was to save on canal and harbour fees. This result occurred through a reduction in both net tonnage and area of the exposed upper deck to a minimum and, in addition, an increase in cargo area.

From the turn of the bilge to a few feet above the load line, the turret steamer did not differ from the conventional hull form of cargo ships. However, above this point, the side shell plating curved inward to create a narrow deck space called the "harbour deck," which was just a part of the shell plating. From the inner side of the harbour deck, the plating curved to rise perpendicularly to meet the narrow flush upper deck on which were erected the bridge structure and usual deck fittings (winches, derricks, posts, hatches, et cetera). As a result of the narrow deck, the crew quarters were exceptionally cramped and scarcely provided room to turn around, which led to the common saying, "If you walked into a cabin, you had to back out."

The Doxford design did not meet with the approval of the Lloyd's Classification Committee when

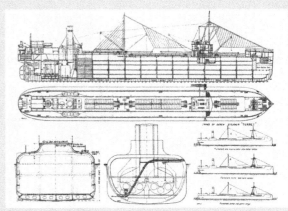

General Arrangement of s. s. TURRET (From L. Gray and J. Lingwood, *The Doxford Turret Ships*. Kendal, England: The World Ship Society, 1975.)

plans were first submitted. That would have been the death knell for this novel design, since non-approval by that committee meant non-insurability. In order to prove the seaworthiness and cargo-carrying advantages of the new design, Doxford, in association with Captain William Petersen, built the first turret vessel, sharing risks and costs equally. This ship, named the *Turret*, won approval from the committee after its first sea voyage when its behaviour in heavy seas and manoeuvrability proved exceptional. The turret design was profitable and gained much favour with owners trading to the Middle East and Far East through the Suez Canal where tolls were levied based on exposed deck area.

During the 1890s and early 1900s, more than 150 turrets were built by Doxford. However, popularity of the design waned after the turn of the century as even larger vessels were needed and the advantage of lower canal and harbour fees was lost due to a change in the basis for calculation of these fees. Surely, one had to expect canal and harbour administrators to look for ways to circumvent this advantage of the turret design. In addition, these vessels were more difficult to unload, since the narrow deck limited the width of the hatches. Like their cousins, the whalebacks, the turret ships had their day and lost their popularity when the need for larger ships and progress rendered them obsolete.

Some of the smaller turrets found their way into the Great Lakes and St. Lawrence River in the early 20th century. When William Petersen Limited secured a contract in 1900 to haul coal from Sydney to Montreal for the Dominion Iron and Steel Company, no fewer than seven turrets were allocated to serve: the *Scottish Hero*, *Turret Bay*, *Turret Bell*, *Turret Cape*, *Turret Chief*, *Turret Crown*, and *Turret Court*. The *Turret Bay* was lost while in Sydney to/from Montreal service when it grounded near St. Paul's Island in the Gulf of St. Lawrence on May 20, 1904, and foundered with 13 fatalities.

The remaining six turrets were purchased by Mackenzie and Mann (Canadian Northern Railway) interests as discussed elsewhere. However, the *Turret Bell* was destined to ground in the St. Lawrence River off Port Hastings on November 11, 1904, and was declared a constructive loss. Thus, five turret steamers were left, which served Mackenzie and Mann and its successors for many years on the Great Lakes as well as on salt water during the First World War.

Capacities of the turret vessels, as with other ships, was draft-dependent, i.e., 3,250 tons capacity for an 18-foot draft and 2,000 tons for a 14-foot draft (the latter being equivalent to 75,000 bushels of wheat). However, among the turret vessels employed on the Great Lakes, their grain-carrying capacities were gargantuan, either 110,000 bushels or 125,000 bushels for the two largest ones (*Scottish Hero* and *Turret Bay*). These capacities exceeded those of usual canallers by twofold or greater. For example, the grain-carrying capacities of package freight steamers such as the *A.E. Ames*, *J.H. Plummer*, and *H.M. Pellatt* were only 55,000 bushels each.

The steamer *Turret Cape*. (Alpena Public Library 142882.142918.)

The steamer *Turret Chief*. (Alpena Public Library 143007.143023.)

The steamer *Turret Court*. (Alpena Public Library 143056.143082.)

The steamer *Turret Crown*. (Alpena Public Library 143103.143128.)

(Below) The steamer *Turret Bay* being loaded in 1895. (McCord Museum II-112706.)

- Ownership of three package freighters on the Great Lakes (the *A.E. Ames* [official no. 114449], *J.H. Plummer* [official no. 114447], and *H.M. Pellatt* [official no. 114446]; see below).
- Management of a small fleet of turret steamers on the Great Lakes (the *Scottish Hero*, *Turret Cape*, *Turret Chief*, *Turret Crown*, *Turret Bay*, and *Turret Court*) in the grain trade from Port Arthur to Georgian Bay ports (especially Depot Harbour, Ontario) whence grain was conveyed farther east by rail.

The relationship of the two shipping companies, especially vis-à-vis management of the turret steamer fleet, is unclear. Although there were rumours concerning the addition of ocean-going vessels in 1903 to carry grain from Montreal (rail terminus from Depot Harbour) to Europe, no such vessels were purchased or chartered other than the steamers *Toronto* and *Aboukir* (see above) and the steamers *Lake Simcoe* and *Lake Erie* (see below).

Early in the 1903 navigation season, attempts were made to secure eastbound cargoes of iron ore or other goods such that westbound cargos of coal from Sydney could be justified and crews kept employed until the grain trade began later in the season. Most such attempts were unsuccessful.

In early 1904, it was announced that the Rotterdam to/from Montreal/Quebec City service would be continued. Toward this end, the steamers *Lake Simcoe* (official no. 113488) and *Lake Erie* (official no. 110631), former Beaver Line ships, were chartered from Elder-Dempster. Of interest, the Canadian government fined the *Lake Simcoe* and its crew $26,000 for allowing 26 Syrians scheduled for deportation to escape. Although the fine was overturned on appeal due to a technicality, the attorney general was prepared to reissue it. The end result is not known. The same vessel/crew was also seized in the United Kingdom for nonpayment of charges for bunker coal ($5,437) and supplies ($3,718). Once the appropriate securities had been posted, the ship was allowed to leave the United Kingdom. There is no evidence that this service continued beyond the end of 1904 or early 1905.

During 1904–05, George Stamp of Newcastle managed the *Turret Crown*, while Jacks and Company of Glasgow, Scotland, managed the *Scottish Hero* and William Petersen Limited managed the other four turret vessels and the three new package freight steamers (see below). The planned renaming of the *Turret Chief* to *Z.A. Lash* and the *Turret Court* to *E.R. Wood* was cancelled for unstated reasons.

Several significant events occurred in 1904, including the loss of the *Turret Bay* on May 20 on St. Paul Island, Cape Breton, Nova Scotia, the end of the managerial relationship with William Petersen Limited, and the maturation of package steamer fleet services with the *A.E. Ames*, *H.M. Pellatt*, and *J.H. Plummer* (for details of these vessels, see tables 6.12 to 6.14, respectively).

During 1905–06, the following were the vessel responsibilities of the four listed corporate parties:

- Canadian Lake and Ocean Navigation: *H.M. Pellatt* and *J.H. Plummer*.
- Canadian Ocean and Inland Navigation: *A.E. Ames*, *Turret Cape*, *Turret Chief*, and *Turret Court*.
- D. Howden, London, England: *Turret Crown*.
- Jacks and Company: *Scottish Hero*.

The package freighter *A.E. Ames* up-bound in Little Rapids Cut, St. Marys River, Michigan, in 1917. (John O. Greenwood.)

This division of responsibility was largely maintained until the founding of Merchants' Mutual Line in 1910, although the *Turret Crown* was managed by additional U.K. managers (H.M. Hubbard, London; H.W. Harding, London).

During the navigation season of 1906, the two Canadian Northern subsidiaries united forces with a new shipping entity: the Montreal and Lake Superior Line. This line was formed in the spring of 1906 by F.H. Plummer, A.B. MacKay, and Captain J.B. Fairgrieve. It operated six vessels during 1906: the three CLON/COIN package freight steamers already noted, the *Wahcondah* (official no. 102577) and *Neepawah* (official no. 102579) of the R.O. and A.B. MacKay interests, and the *Arabian* (official no. 100394) of the F.H. Plummer, A.B. MacKay,

and J.B. Fairgrieve interests. The last three vessels were organized as the New Ontario Steamship Company. Each company operated its own ships. The agreement pertained to joint services only. This firm was dissolved at the end of the 1906 navigation season. That same year Mackenzie and Mann leased the west side of the wharf at Block D, Harbour Square, Toronto, and the freight shed on it from City Council for $3,500 annually.

In 1907 William Petersen Limited was forced to declare bankruptcy. During proceedings, it was noted that Canadian Ocean and Inland Navigation owed the firm £2,500 (which was paid) and that the company had a £9,785 investment, subject to mortgage, in Canadian Lake and Ocean Navigation. Thus, William Petersen Limited had remained involved with Mackenzie and

The package freighter *H.M. Pellatt* aground at The Orchard, Point Iroquois, Michigan, on May 23, 1912. (John O. Greenwood.)

The package freighter *J.H. Plummer* under way on the St. Clair River in 1916. (John O. Greenwood.)

Mann's Great Lakes maritime initiatives long after ceasing to operate the latter company's ships.

Early in 1907, Mackenzie and Mann announced that a dock was to be built at the foot of York Street in Toronto (65 feet wide with two slips, one on each side) that would be used by the Canadian Lake and Ocean and Niagara, St. Catharines, and Toronto Navigation Companies and the Hamilton Steamboat Company.

During the navigation season of 1907, the two Canadian Northern subsidiaries again united forces with a new shipping entity: the Canadian Lake Line. Regular semi-weekly service was provided to Montreal, Prescott, Kingston, Toronto, Hamilton, Cleveland, Windsor, Walkerville, Courtright, Sault Ste. Marie, Port Arthur, and Fort William. F. Plummer was the general manager of the firm. Seven steamers were to be operated in 1907: the three CLON/COIN package freight steamers, the *Arabian*, and three vessels owned by C.H.F. Plummer (the *Morena* [official no. 95226], *Corunna* [official no. 95224], and *Nevada* [official no. 95225]). However, the *Morena* was wrecked on May 19, 1907, off Cape Race, Newfoundland, en route from the United Kingdom and would never serve on the Great Lakes.

In 1908 the Canadian Lake Line became the Canadian Lake Transportation Company, although the latter had already been incorporated on April 12, 1907, with capitalization set at $100,000. J.H. Plummer was president, while C.H.F. Plummer was secretary-treasurer and general manager. Offices were at 18 Wellington Street East in Toronto. Eight steamers were operated during the 1908 navigation season: the three CLON package freight steamers, the *Arabian*, and four steamers owned by the

Canadian Lake Transportation Company: the *Corunna*, *Nevada*, and two new vessels, the *Kenora* (official no. 124235) and *Regina* (official no. 124231).

At some point between the end of the 1908 navigation season and the beginning of the 1909 navigation season, the CLON package freight steamers were withdrawn from management by Canadian Lake Transportation. Apparently, Mackenzie and Mann wanted to use this shipping line as a feeder for the Canadian Northern Railway at Port Arthur or, at least, manage the three CLON vessels with this objective in mind. Management of Canadian Lake Transportation refused these requests and this led to the withdrawal of the CLON vessels.

By 1909 Mackenzie and Mann had secured a controlling interest in Canadian Lake and Ocean Navigation, and the Toronto office of the latter was moved from 10 Wellington Street East to the Canadian Northern Building at 9 Toronto Street. President J.H. Plummer and General Manager F. Plummer resigned. New officers were D.B. Hanna as president, A.J. Mitchell as secretary-treasurer, and F.H. Phippen as general manager. The new board of directors included D.B. Hanna, F.H. Phippen, Z.A. Lash, H. Sutherland, L. Lukes, F. Nicholls, and H.M. Pellatt, all being well-connected to Mackenzie and Mann.

By this time, Canadian Ocean and Inland Navigation had assumed responsibility for the *Scottish Hero*. From this time until their takeover by Canada Steamship Lines or sale, the turret ships continued under the management of Canadian Ocean and Inland Navigation, or in the case of the *Turret Crown*, by Turret Crown Limited, another Mackenzie and Mann subsidiary. Turret Crown Limited had been federally incorporated in 1906 with all directors

being from Mackenzie and Mann. The three package freight steamers became the responsibility of a new line heavily financed and influenced by Canadian Northern interests: the Merchants' Mutual Line (MML).

The Merchants' Mutual Line initially had offices at 8 Wellington Street East in Toronto and its general agents were R.W. and A.B. MacKay. In the 1909 navigation season, this entity operated 11 vessels: the three CLON package freight steamers; the *Acadian* (official no. 124258), *Canadian* (official no. 125427), and *Wasaga* (official no. 117084), owned by the Mutual Steamship Company; the *Beaverton* (official no. 125440) and *Mapleton* (official no. 123961), owned by the Merchants' Steamship Company; the *Edmonton* (official no. 122856) and *Haddington* (official no. 116764), owned by the Mathews Steamship Company; and the *Bickerdike* (official no. 121784), owned by the Montreal and Great Lakes Steamship Company.

Given the success of Great Lakes bulk carrier lines and their seemingly ever-expanding markets, the sector by 1910 was ripe for consolidation. Indeed, the industry might have been undercapitalized, since there was little leverage in many of the lines' corporate structures. Two exceptions to this were CLON and Inland Navigation.

The Merchants' Mutual Line received Dominion letters patent on April 1, 1910, and was capitalized at $750,000. Headquarters were located at 1 Toronto Street in Toronto. Provisional directors included J.S. Lovell, W. Bain, R. Gowans, H. Chambers, and R.M. Coates, all hailing from Toronto. The first president and vice-president (D.B. Hanna and Z.A. Lash, respectively) were Canadian Northern–affiliated. A.J. Mitchell was secretary/treasurer. This company was created to collect the assets of

The package freighter *Beaverton* up-bound in Little Rapids Cut, St. Marys River, Michigan, in 1916. (John O. Greenwood.)

The bulk freighter *Mapleton* down-bound in Little Rapids Cut, St. Marys River, Michigan, in 1913. (John O. Greenwood.)

the Canadian Lake and Ocean Navigation, Canadian Interlake Line, Colonial Transportation, Merchants' Steamship, and Mutual Steamship Companies. In 1910, and for a few years prior to 1910 in the case of CLON, R.W. and A.B. MacKay managed both Canadian Lake and Ocean Navigation and the Merchants' Mutual Line.

In 1910 the Merchants' Mutual Line operated eight vessels: the three CLON package freight steamers; the *Canadian* and *Acadian*, soon to be purchased by MML from the Mutual Steamship Company; the *Beaverton* and *Mapleton*, purchased by MML from the Merchants' Steamship Company; and the *Saskatoon* (official no. 123965), purchased by MML from Colonial

NAMESAKES FOR PACKAGE FREIGHTERS OF CLON/MML

The six vessels owned by the Merchants' Mutual Line had the following namesakes:

- *A.E. Ames*: Namesake was Alfred Ernest Ames, founder of the Toronto stock brokerage firm A.E. Ames & Company, president of the Toronto Stock Exchange in 1897, and investor in numerous maritime activities.
- *Beaverton*: Namesake was the town of Beaverton on the west shore of Lake Simcoe.
- *Mapleton*: Namesake was a combination of "maple" (the symbol of Canada) and "ton" of the former Mathews Line and original owner of the vessel.

- *H.M. Pellatt*: Namesake was Henry Mill Pellatt, an influential Toronto investor in numerous firms, including the Dominion Iron and Steel Company, Richelieu and Ontario Navigation Company, and Toronto Electric Light Company. He also hired architect E.J. Lennox to build Casa Loma, his residence in Toronto.
- *J.H. Plummer*: Namesake was J.H. Plummer, president of Dominion Iron and Steel when this vessel was owned by the Merchants' Mutual Line.
- *Saskatoon*: Namesake was the city of Saskatoon, Saskatchewan.

Transportation. Details of the latter five vessels are available in tables 6.15 to 6.19, respectively. Late in 1910 the firm also began managing the *C.A. Jaques* (official no. 129497), owned by the Jaques Transportation Company.

In 1911 day-to-day operations of both Canadian Lake and Ocean Navigation and the Merchants' Mutual Line were assumed by Captain J.W. Norcross as managing director and Captain H.W. Cowan as operating superintendent. The Merchants' Mutual Line operated 17 vessels during the 1911 navigation season: the *D.A. Gordon* (official no. 129479), owned by the International Steamship Company; the *Bickerdike*; the *A.E. McKinstry* (official no. 129491), owned by the Interlake Transit Company; the *Advance* (official no. 88632), owned by the Montreal Transportation Company; the *Renvoyle* (official no. 126836), owned by Point Anne Quarries; the *Kenora*, *Regina*, and *Tagona* (official no. 128188) of the Canadian Lake Transportation Company (new name: Canadian Interlake Line); and the nine vessels operated in 1910.

The bulk freighter *Saskatoon* near the Soo Locks on the border between Michigan and Ontario in 1910. (John O. Greenwood.)

In 1912 the Merchants' Mutual Line operated its core of six owned steamers (*A.E. Ames, H.M. Pellatt, J.H. Plummer, Beaverton, Mapleton,* and *Saskatoon*), the Canadian Interlake Line fleet (*Acadian, Canadian, Renvoyle, A.E. McKinstry, Calgarian* [official no. 131056], *Hamiltonian* [official no. 131052], and *Fordonian* [official no. 133077], the latter being the first diesel-powered freighter on the Great Lakes), the *D.A. Gordon,* and the *C.A. Jaques* — 15 vessels in total.

The 1912 merger of the Richelieu and Ontario Navigation Company with the Niagara Navigation and Northern Navigation Companies and St. Lawrence River Steam Boat and Thousand Islands Steam Boat Companies presaged massive changes in the Canadian maritime freight industry on the Great Lakes.

The Canada Interlake Line succeeded the Canadian Interlake Line in 1913, with capitalization set at $3 million, bonded indebtedness at $720,000, and mortgage debt at $66,432. In fact, only three of 14 vessels were owned "free and clear." The appraised value of the fleet was $1.85 million. Added vessels included the *D.A. Gordon, Kenora, Regina, Tagona,* and three U.S. vessels purchased from Cleveland-Cliffs (the *Cadillac* [official no. 138230], *Mars* [official no. 131057], and *Pioneer* [official no. 133741]).

Early in the 1913 navigation season, the Merchants' Mutual Line operated 20 vessels: its six owned package freight steamers and the 14 vessels of the Canada Interlake Line (*A.E. McKinstry, Acadian, Calgarian, Canadian, Cadillac, D.A. Gordon, Fordonian, Hamiltonian, Kenora, Mars, Pioneer, Regina, Renvoyle,* and *Tagona*). Later in the season the Merchants' Mutual Line was destined to give up management of the latter 14 vessels.

On June 17, 1913, Canada Transportation Lines Limited was created after the merger of the Richelieu and Ontario Navigation Company and the Canada Interlake Line. Mackenzie and Mann was noticeably absent from the governance structure of the new company, having only one member on the 14-member board of directors (D.B. Hanna, vice-president). This company, capitalized at $25 million, eventually acquired the Lake Ontario and Bay of Quinte Steamboat Company, the Ontario and Quebec Navigation Company, and 80 percent-plus of the Quebec Steamship Company and the Canada Interlake Line, totalling more than 100 vessels! The name was changed "in deference to the wishes of the British investors" to the now-familiar Canada Steamship Lines (CSL). Most of these ships would soon "answer the call

The steamer *Acadian* showing its Merchants' Mutual Line colours. (Historical Collection of the Great Lakes 000060, Bowling Green State University.)

to war," being placed in the Sydney to/from Montreal coal trade or the ocean/coasting trade south of the Gulf of St. Lawrence or to/from the West Indies, especially after freeze-up on the Great Lakes.

In 1914 the Merchants' Mutual Line operated only a small number of vessels, since the Canada Interlake Line had been absorbed into the new behemoth of CSL. Vessels operated were reduced to the original three package freight steamers (*A.E. Ames*, *J.H. Plummer*, and *H.M. Pellatt*) and the three early MML acquisitions (*Beaverton*, *Mapleton*, and *Saskatoon*). In addition, Mackenzie and Mann still controlled four turret steamers (*Scottish Hero*, *Turret Cape*, *Turret Court*, and *Turret Crown*).

The steamer *Canadian* in its Canada Steamship Lines colours. (Historical Collection of the Great Lakes 000761, Bowling Green State University.)

The steamer *Midland King* in the Toronto area in 1937 in Canada Steamship Lines colours. (Historical Collection of the Great Lakes 003595, Bowling Green State University.)

The Merchants' Mutual Line sold out to CSL in 1915, but the CLON/COIN/MML vessels mostly retained their former markings, at least for a time. In fact, the six CLON/MML vessels (*A.E. Ames*, *H.M. Pellatt*, *J.H. Plummer*, *Beaverton*, *Mapleton*, and *Saskatoon*) were informally called the "CSL Freight Division." However, they were all eventually repainted from their CLON/MML livery (black hull, solid black smokestack, and white superstructure) to the CSL livery (red hull, smokestack being red with a black top, and grey superstructure). Interestingly, they would keep their MML bow logo (see Appendix 1) despite repainting. These six vessels plus the *Scottish Hero* were taken over by the CSL subsidiary Merchants' Mutual Lake Line, which was incorporated on August 8, 1913, with a capitalization of $1.5 million.

In 1915 the turret steamers were destined to leave the Great Lakes. Still owned by Canadian Lake and Ocean Navigation and managed by J.W. Norcross, who was now managing director of CSL in Montreal, they were chartered for wartime service in the Gulf of St. Lawrence and St. Lawrence River. The *Turret Cape* and *Turret Crown* were chartered by the Nova Scotia Steel and Coal Company of New Glasgow, Nova Scotia, to haul coal from North Sydney to St. Lawrence River ports. The *Scottish Hero* was chartered by the Dominion Iron and Steel Company of Sydney for a three-year period. Due to its size, it would once again have to be cut into two to pass through the Welland Canal, with the halves rejoined in a St. Lawrence River port. Ashtabula, Ohio, was the site of its "halving." The *Turret Chief* was sold in 1915, after its salvage, to A.B. MacKay, leaving what was left of the CLON fleet. The *Scottish Hero* and *Turret Cape* were sold to CSL in 1916. The *Turret Crown* was sold to the Coastwise Steamship and Barge Company of Vancouver, British

The steamer *Midland Queen*. (Historical Collection of the Great Lakes 003597, Bowling Green State University.)

Columbia, in 1916 for war work in the Pacific Ocean. In the fall of 1916, Canadian Northern Steamships purchased six vessels from the Merchants' Mutual Lake Line (i.e., CSL): the *A.E. Ames*, *H.M. Pellatt*, *J.H. Plummer*, *Beaverton*, *Mapleton*, and *Saskatoon*. However, they were to be operated by CSL. In the fall of 1917, the steamers *A.E. Ames*, *H.M. Pellatt*, and *Beaverton* entered dry dock for overhaul/refit for ocean war service. The *J.H. Plummer* was too expensive to refit for ocean service, so it remained on the Great Lakes. The steamers *Mapleton* and *Saskatoon* were engaged in the coal trade (Sydney to/ from Saint John, New Brunswick, and Montreal), while the *Mapleton* was also employed in the Lake Erie ports to/ from Montreal coal trade.

On occasion other vessels were chartered or arrangements were made to operate other vessels in conjunction with the Canadian Northern Railway or the freight shipping lines affiliated with Mackenzie and Mann. For example, in early 1906, the *Midland King* (official no. 116661) and *Midland Queen* (official no. 110991) were chartered to haul grain at the opening of the navigation season from Fort William to Montreal (one vessel) and Fort William to Kingston (one vessel). They were also chartered to haul grain on several occasions that season from Fort William to Depot Harbour. Details of these two vessels are available in tables 6.20 and 6.21, respectively.

During the 1907 navigation season, the Canadian Northern Ontario Railway chartered the steamer *Seguin* (official no. 94763), operated by the Parry Sound Transportation Company, to carry freight and passengers between Parry Sound, Ontario, and Port Arthur, with intermediate stops, on a weekly round-trip basis. This vessel required extensive remodelling and refitting in order to accommodate passengers. Table 6.22 illustrates details of this vessel.

That same navigation season the Georgian Bay Navigation Company of Parry Sound operated a biweekly service in conjunction with the Canadian Northern Ontario Railway between Parry Sound and Sault Ste. Marie, with calls also at intermediate ports. Service was provided by the steamer *Mabel Bradshaw* (official no. 117085). Of interest, Georgian Bay Navigation had attempted to change the name of the vessel to *Killarney*, after the picturesque Georgian Bay village of the same name. However, the Canadian government rejected the request due to an existing vessel named *Killarney Belle* (official no. 97114). The existence of two such similar names could have led to much confusion, hence, the justification for the rejection.

The steamer *Renwick* aground in Cornwall, England, in 1903. (Author's Collection.)

The steamer *Seguin*, formerly of Parry Sound Transportation, in Canada Steamship Lines colours. (Historical Collection of the Great Lakes 004980, Bowling Green State University.)

The *Renwick* (official no. 97954) came under the Mackenzie and Mann umbrella from 1907 until its untimely demise in 1911. Again, a separate subsidiary company was set up by 1911 to own and manage this vessel (the Renwick Company based in Toronto). From 1907 to 1911, the vessel was owned by Robert Horne-Payne of Brentwood, England, a well-known Canadian Northern Railway/Mackenzie and Mann associate. Details of this vessel are available in table 6.23.

LAKE ST. JOHN AND SAGUENAY NAVIGATION COMPANY

The Quebec and Lake St. John Railway was the best-known of Quebec's colonization railways. It began as a 25-mile-long wooden railway running between Quebec City and Gosfield, and opened for business in 1870. The rail line served primarily to supply wood for heating and the building trades in Quebec City. When its wooden rails failed, bankruptcy ensued. In 1880 it was reorganized to build from Quebec City to Lake St. John. Encountering numerous financial difficulties, the main line, nevertheless, reached Roberval in 1888. A branch to Chicoutimi was completed in 1892. The road cost $8.7 million, 45 percent of which was supplied by federal and provincial grants and municipal bonuses.

The Quebec and Lake St. John Repatriation and Colonization Society had, for years, sought French-speaking immigrants and repatriated French Canadians from the United States to colonize the Saguenay region. In 1905 the society proposed to provide some new steamers for Lake St. John and the

Interior of the sidewheeler *Mistassini*. This appears to be a builder's photograph or, at least, very early in the vessel's commercial existence. (Library and Archives Canada PA-033185.)

rivers flowing into the lake (Métabetchouan, Mistassini, Ashuapmushuan, Péribonka, and others). Suggested vessels were flat-bottomed sternwheelers, since their shallow draft would allow access farther up the shallow rivers flowing into the lake.

At approximately the same time it was announced that a company was being formed at Roberval, capitalized

at $50,000, to carry on a general navigation business on Lake St. John and adjacent waters over an aggregate 200 miles in routes. At a meeting on January 17, 1906, the following were elected as company officers: H.J. Lyons, president; J.G. Scott, first vice-president (as well as general manager and secretary of the Quebec and Lake St. John Railway); R. Dupont, second vice-president and

Postcard view of the sidewheeler *Mistassini* on Lake St. John, Quebec. (Author's Collection.)

managing director (as well as colonization officer of the Quebec and Lake St. John Railway); F.X. Laroche, third vice-president; T.L. Marcoux, secretary and traffic superintendent; and H.B. Locke, purchasing agent. Other directors included J.L. Guay, L. Lindsay, and H. Gagne.

A report in *Railway and Marine World* in February 1906 stated that orders had been placed with the Polson Iron Company of Toronto for two shallow-draft, flat-bottomed sternwheelers, one being 65 feet long and 17 feet wide and the other being 100 feet long and 20 feet wide. There is no evidence that either vessel was produced, based on a review of the shipbuilder's records for 1906. However, a small steel tow/tugboat — the *Pikouagami* — was built for the Quebec and Lake St. John Railway by Polson Iron Works in 1906 (see below). It was also mentioned in the same report that consideration was being

given to the initiation of a line of freight and passenger steamers along the Saguenay River between Chicoutimi and Rivière-du-Loup, but nothing came of this idea.

Thus was formed the Lake St. John and Saguenay Navigation Company, granted Quebec letters patent on March 15, 1906. Company headquarters were located in the Eulage Ménard Building in Roberval, Quebec. The company requested a provincial subsidy for five years for the maintenance of its services on Lake St. John and its tributary waters. The principal justification for the request was the allegation that the company would promote colonization in the area. Company steamers would operate on the following routes during the navigation season of 1906, with all originating at Roberval: Grande Décharge, 36 miles; Honfleur, 33 miles; Mistassini, 46 miles; Péribonka, 32 miles; Saint-Félicien, 20 miles;

Havre de Roberval, P. Q.

Postcard view of the *Mistassini* (1) and *Le Pikouagami* (2) in 1908 or 1909. (Saguenay Historical Society P2-S7-P00221-2.)

Saint-Gédéon, 28 miles; and Saint-Jérôme, 21 miles. However, there were a number of other vessel owner/operators on Lake St. John who could claim similar justification for provincial subsidies. In fact, subsidies for the provision of water transportation on Lake St. John had also been provided to three other individuals:

- $2,000 to Alexandre Morin ($300 for each of 1903 and 1906, $400 for 1904, and $1,000 for 1905) for the routes of La Pipe to/from Saint-Jérôme to/from Saint-Gédéon (1903, 1904, 1906) and La Pipe to/from Roberval, Roberval to/from Saint-Méthode, and Saint-Félicien to/from Mistassini (1905).
- $400 to P.J. Dery in 1904 for the route Roberval to/from Saint-Félicien to/from Saint-Méthode to/from Mistassini.

- $1000 to Édouard Niquette ($200 in 1906 and $400 in each of 1904 and 1905) for the route Roberval to/from Péribonka to/from Honfleur.

In any case, the company was provided with a five-year provincial subsidy of $2,500 annually for providing passenger/freight service on the lake. Destinations served included Chambord, Grande Décharge, Honfleur, La Pipe, Mistassini, Péribonka, Roberval, Saint-Félicien, Saint-Gédéon, Saint-Jérôme, Saint-Méthode, and Saint-Prime.

Later in 1906 it was reported that the company was negotiating the purchase of a passenger steamer to operate on the Saguenay River. It had operated a fleet of five vessels over the 1906 navigation season: four steam sidewheelers (*Le Roberval* [official no. 116226], *Le Colon* [official no. 103147], *Mistassini* [official no. 100854], and *Péribonka* [official no. 100470]), as well as a tugboat (*Marie Alma* [official no. 111498]). Tables 6.24 to 6.28 provide details regarding these vessels.

The relationship between the company and the Quebec and Lake St. John Railway is unclear as sources support no connection (except for the leasing of the *Pikouagami* [official no. 125991], a sternwheeler owned by the railway, in 1907 [see table 6.29]), ownership by the railway of several vessels, and ownership of the company by the railway.

By the fall of 1907, both the railway and navigation company had come under majority stock control of Mackenzie and Mann. The importance of the railway in the eyes of Mackenzie and Mann resided in the excellent access and terminals in Quebec City. Mackenzie and

Photograph of the sidewheeler *Le Roberval*. (Saguenay Historical Society P2-S7-P06558-3.)

The sidewheeler *Le Colon* on the Mistassini River in Quebec. (Saguenay Historical Society P2-S7-P07034-2.)

Mann also acknowledged the excellent potential of the region served in the areas of pulp and paper, hydroelectric power, and tourism. However, the officers of Mackenzie and Mann were railway men, not small-scale steamboat enthusiasts. When the Lake St. John and Saguenay Navigation Company lost the confidence of the population that it had served in less than two years through failing to meet its commitments, which led to complaints of a monopoly and a resulting legal inquiry, Mackenzie and Mann was not there to bail it out.

In December 1907, it was announced that the company had suspended operations "for the present." Apparently, the vessels were being operated by other parties (the *Pikouagami* by the Quebec and Lake St. John Railway, the *Mistassini* by Hotel Roberval, *Le Roberval* by the Péribonka Pulp Company, and the *Marie Alma* by M. Déry of Quebec City).

Also in late 1907 the provincial government published the subsidies granted to vessel owners/operators on Lake St. John, as previously discussed. For the Lake St. John and Saguenay Navigation Company, these amounts for 1906 and 1907 were $2,500 and $4,017, respectively. The 1907 award was greater, since the five-year grant had been terminated that year, effective at the end of the navigation season, and extra monies were provided to "pay certain claims" (i.e., wrap up operations). The company's charter was not annulled by the provincial government until 1977–78.

Thus, it appears that the losses of the provincial subsidy as well as the confidence of the public it served led to the premature departure of the Lake St. John and Saguenay Navigation Company. The Canadian Northern Railway did not mourn its loss.

The sidewheeler *Péribonka* at the Roberval dock in Quebec. (Collection Jean Gagnon, Centre d'archives de la MRC du Doumaine-du-Roy.)

Table 6.1
Lakeside (official no. 90778)

Builder:	William Lane in Windsor, Ontario, in 1888.
Hull Material:	Wood.
Engine:	Fore and aft compound (19- and 32-inch piston diameters, 26-inch stroke) built by Kerr Brothers, Walkerville, Ontario.
Boiler:	One. In 1920 it was replaced by a firebox, 9 feet x 14.2 feet, built by Bertram Engine Works, Toronto.
Dimensions:	121 feet long x 26 feet wide x 9.3 feet deep.
Propulsion:	Steam screw (single).
Tonnage:	348/220 (gross/net).
Passenger Capacity:	No data.
Freight Capacity:	No data.
Miscellaneous:	Rebuilt as a tug in 1920 (118.4 feet long x 25.9 feet wide x 9 feet deep; 200 gross/77 net tons). Laid up in 1911 at Muir's Pond, Port Dalhousie, Ontario.

Owners	Dates
Lakeside Navigation Company (Niagara, St. Catharines, and Toronto Navigation Company)	1888–1911
M.J. Hogan	1911–20
J.E. Russell (name changed to *Joseph L. Russell*)	1920–29
Sin Mac Lines	1929

Incidents

- On October 2, 1897, the *Lakeside* struck and carried away all of the gates of Lock No. 1 of the old Welland Canal, causing considerable damage to the vessel and requiring a week's stay in dry dock to effect repairs.
- The *Lakeside* sank next to the dock at Port Dalhousie, Ontario, because its sea cock(s) had been left open by mistake. The vessel was raised on March 25, 1905.

Disposition

- On November 15, 1929, vessel foundered off Point Peter in Lake Ontario while towing a barge. Crew was rescued by the steamer *Glenella*.

Table 6.2
Garden City (official no. 100035)

Builder:	Redway (Toronto) in 1892.
Hull Material:	Steel.
Engine:	Steeple compound (28- and 54-inch piston diameters and 48-inch stroke).
Boilers:	Two. Fireboxes, 6.25 feet by 16 feet each, built by S.F. Hodge and Company, Detroit.
Dimensions:	177.9 feet long x 26.1 feet wide x 10 feet deep.
Propulsion:	Steam sidewheeler.
Tonnage:	637/401 (gross/net).
Passenger Capacity:	No data.
Freight Capacity:	No data.

Owners	Dates
Lakeside Navigation Company (Niagara, St. Catharines, and Toronto Navigation Company)	1892–1922
J. Rinfret	1922–33
J.H. Beaudoin	1933–35
J.L. Lachance Ltée	1935

Disposition
• Scrapped in 1935.

Table 6.3

Lincoln (official no. 92735)

Builder:	Melancthon Simpson in Hamilton, Ontario, in 1888 as *Greyhound*.
Hull Material:	Wood.
Engine:	Steeple compound.
Boiler:	One.
Dimensions:	130 feet long x 25.2 feet wide x 9 feet deep.
Propulsion:	Steam screw (single).
Tonnage:	337/219 (gross/net).
Passenger Capacity:	800 (1906).
Freight Capacity:	No data.
Miscellaneous:	In 1898–99, vessel was rebuilt and renamed *Lincoln*. Rebuilt in 1904. Rebuilt in Collingwood in 1906.

Incidents

- On March 9, 1904, vessel was holed by ice and sank at the dock in 40 feet of water. Raised and rebuilt.
- Burned at the King's Dock on April 6, 1905.
- In August 1906, vessel was stranded on Pelee Island.

Disposition

- Burned at Bruce Mines, Ontario, on November 13, 1920. Abandoned.

Per Historical Collection of the Great Lakes (Bowling Green State University)

Owners	Dates
Gooderham and Worts Brewing	1888–99
R.W. Hamelin (name changed to *Lincoln*)	1899–1902
A.G. Knowles	1902–06
Pelee Island Transit (name changed to *Premier*)	1906–07
Doty Engine Works	1907–08
W.C. Fremline	1908–13
St. Joseph Island and Sault Line	1913–16
E. Stubbs	1916–20

Per Thunder Bay National Marine Sanctuary Collection (Alpena Public Library)

Owners	Dates
H.A. Simpson	1892–1898
R.H. Hamelin and W.G. Thurston (name changed to *Lincoln* in 1899)	1898–1901
A.G. Knowles	1901–03
A. Cowan, A & J McCormick	1903–04
Pelee Island Navigation	1904–05
F.W. Doty	1905–06
Doty Engine Works (name changed to *Premier*)	1906–08
W.C. Fremline	1908–09
T.J. Wilcox	1909–14
E. Stubbs et al.	1914–17
Captain T.W. Climie	1917–20
Climie and Stubbs	1920

Table 6.4
Dalhousie City (official no. 130312)

Builder:	Collingwood Ship Building Company, Collingwood, Ontario, in 1911 (hull no. 30).
Hull Material:	Steel.
Engine:	Triple expansion (18-, 28.5-, and 38-inch piston diameters x 30-inch stroke), 1520 ihp.
Boilers:	Two.
Dimensions:	199.8 feet long x 37 feet wide x 13.9 feet deep.
Propulsion:	Steam screw (single).
Tonnage:	1,256/752 (gross/net).
Passenger Capacity:	1,050.
Freight Capacity:	No data.
Miscellaneous:	Bow stove in after collision with pier in Port Dalhousie, Ontario.

Owners	Dates	Disposition
Niagara, St. Catharines, and Toronto Navigation Company	1911–50	• On November 13, 1960, vessel burned in the Lachine Canal followed by dismantling in 1961.
Lake Shore Lines Ltd. (name changed to *Island King II*)	1950–60	
Buckport Shipping	1960	

Table 6.5

Northumberland (official no. 96937)

Builder:	Swan Hunter & Wigham Richardson, Wallsend, England, in 1891 (hull no. 955).
Hull Material:	Steel.
Engines:	Two triple expansion (17.5-, 27.5-, and 46-inch piston diameters x 33-inch stroke), 2,500 ihp.
Boilers:	Two.
Dimensions:	220 feet long x 33 feet wide x 20.3 feet deep.
Propulsion:	Steam screw (double).
Tonnage:	1,255/519 (gross/net).
Passenger Capacity:	No data.
Freight Capacity:	No data.
Miscellaneous:	Plied route of Pointe-du-Chêne, New Brunswick, to Summerside, Prince Edward Island (35 miles). Chartered to Niagara, St. Catharines, and Toronto Railway on June 13, 1920.

Owners	Dates
Charlottetown Steam Navigation Company	1891–1916
Government of Canada (Railways/Canals)	1916–36
Government of Canada (Transport)	1936–50

Incidents

- March 1894: Charlottetown Steam Navigation Company announced that it would abandon mail service between the mainland and Prince Edward Island unless the Canadian mail subsidy was increased (the company had had annual losses of $30,000 over previous three years).
- February 3, 1931: While in New Zealand, vessel sent via wireless the urgent need for medical assistance after a catastrophic earthquake on North Island had knocked out all other communications.

Disposition

- June 2, 1949: Burned at the dock in Port Dalhousie, Ontario, while fitting out. Scrapped in 1950 in Port Weller, Ontario.

Table 6.6

Turret Chief (official nos. 106605 [Canadian], 170538 [U.S.])

Builder:	W. Doxford and Sons, Sunderland, England, in 1896 (hull no. 248).
Engine:	Triple expansion (20-, 34-, and 57-inch piston diameters and 39-inch stroke), 208 nhp, 1,100 ihp at 60 rpm.
Boilers:	Originally, two water-tube (each 10 feet x 12.3 feet) at 200 psi by Babcock and Wilcox, London, England. Reboilered in 1915 with two Scotch (each 11 feet x 14 feet).
Dimensions:	253 feet long x 44 feet wide x 20 feet deep.
Propulsion:	Steam screw (single).
Tonnage:	1,881/1,197 (gross/net) (as ship); 1,731/1,688 (gross/net) (as steam barge).
Freight Capacity:	3,200 tons.
Miscellaneous:	Brought to the Great Lakes in 1907. Salvaged and rebuilt in Port Arthur, Ontario, in 1914 after grounding near Copper Harbor, Michigan, in 1913. Requisitioned by British Admiralty in 1914 for war service and served as a munitions transport ship between the United Kingdom and Archangel, Russia. Returned to the Great Lakes in 1922. Grounded again and abandoned yet again in Lake Huron in 1927. Salvaged and converted to a lightering barge. In 1930 the vessel came under U.S. ownership and licensure.

Incidents

- Grounded at Four Mile Point on the St. Lawrence River near Kingston, Ontario. Was aground on May 10, 1903.
- Grounded near foot of Galops Rapids at Waddell's Point, near Brockville, Ontario, on the St. Lawrence River on July 12, 1904. Released by tugboat *Mary* with little damage.
- After grounding east of Copper Harbor, Michigan, at the tip of the Keweenaw Peninsula in Lake Superior on November 7, 1913, vessel was abandoned to the insurers. However, despite being stuck on rocks nearly 100 feet inland, vessel was successfully salvaged using hydraulic jacks and released about July 14, 1914, followed by rebuilding. Captain Paddington was censored by the Dominion wreck commissioner for errors in judgment and negligence in contributing to the wreck.
- Grounded on Saddlebag Island in False Detour Channel in Lake Huron on November 16, 1927. Vessel was abandoned but later salvaged by T.L. Durocher and converted to a lightering barge.

Disposition

- The barge *Salvor* broke away from its tow/tugboat *Richard Fitzgerald* in a gale and foundered on Lake Michigan off Muskegon, Michigan, on September 26, 1930 (11 fatalities).

Per Gray & Lingwood

Owners	Dates
Dominion Turret Line (Petersen, Tate, and Company, managers)	1896–1901
Canadian Ocean and Inland Navigation (W. Petersen, manager; to be renamed *Z.A. Lash* in 1903 but cancelled; Petersen management cancelled in 1904)	1901–15
Entente Steamship Company (Leopold Walford and Company, managers; name changed to *Vickerstown* in 1915; name changed to *Jolly Inez* in 1918)	1915–24
H.W. Cowan	1924
International Waterways Navigation	1924–27
Walford Lines Limited (Leopold Walford Shipping Company, managers; wrecked near De Tour, Michigan, on November 16, 1927, but salvaged and rebuilt as the barge *Salvor*)	1927–30

Per Thunder Bay National Marine Sanctuary Collection (Alpena Public Library)

Owners	Dates
W. Petersen Limited (Swan, Petersen, and Company)	1896–1907
Canadian Lake and Ocean Navigation	1907–13
Canada Steamship Lines	1913–14
Entente Steamship Company (Leopold Walford and Company)	1914–15
British government (war service, name changed to *Vickerstown* in 1915 and *Jolly Inez* in 1918)	1915–22
International Waterways Navigation	1922–28
T.L. Durocher and Company (name changed to *Salvor* in 1930)	1928–30

Table 6.7

Turret Court (official no. 106608)

Builder:	W. Doxford and Sons, Sunderland, England, in 1896 (hull no. 249).
Engine:	Triple expansion (20-, 34-, and 57-inch piston diameters and 39-inch stroke), 203 nhp, 1,100 ihp at 60 rpm; 10.5 knots speed.
Boilers:	Originally, two water-tube (each 10 feet x 12.3 feet) at 200 psi, built by Babcock and Wilcox, London, England. Reboilered in 1915 with two Scotch (each 11 feet x 14 feet) at 180 psi.
Dimensions:	253 feet long x 44 feet wide x 20 feet deep.
Propulsion:	Steam screw (single).
Tonnage:	1,879/1,179 (gross/net).
Capacity:	3,200 tons; two hatches (each 14.5 feet x 60 feet) over two cargo compartments.
Miscellaneous:	Brought to the Great Lakes in 1898. British Admiralty requisitioned vessel in 1915 for saltwater service. Operated in the river and lake trade in the 1920s. Machinery was condemned in 1930 and was converted to a salvage barge. As latter, the vessel was laid up at Sorel, Quebec, for a long time before being scrapped.

Disposition

- Scrapped in Hamilton in 1940.

Per Thunder Bay National Marine Sanctuary Collection (Alpena Public Library)

Owners	Dates
W. Petersen	1896–1907
Canadian Lake and Ocean Navigation	1907–13
Canada Steamship Lines	1913–16
Turret Steamship Company (Dominion Iron and Steel Company)	1916–25
International Waterways Navigation	1925–30
Sincennes-McNaughton Lines	1930–40
Steel Company of Canada, Hamilton	1940

Per Gray & Lingwood

Owners	Dates
Petersen, Tate and Company	1896–98
Dominion Turret Line (Petersen, Tate, and Company, managers)	1898–1901
Canadian Ocean and Inland Navigation (W. Petersen, manager; to be renamed *E.R. Wood* in 1903 but cancelled; Petersen management cancelled in 1904)	1901–14
Canadian Lake and Ocean Navigation	1914–15
Turret Steamship Company (Dominion Iron and Steel Company, managers)	1915–16
Oriental Navigation Company (USA)	1916–17
Turret Steamship Company (Dominion Iron and Steel Company, managers)	1917–26
Turret Steamship Company (British Empire Steel Corporation, managers; Dominion Shipping Company, managers in 1927)	1926–31
Inland Waters Navigation Company	1931–35
Sincennes McNaughton Tugs (rebuilt as a barge in 1937)	1935–40

Table 6.7 Cont'd

Incidents

- On July 29, 1898, hit Black's Bridge on the Lachine Canal in Quebec, damaging it.
- On August 5, 1899, steam steering gear failed and, veering to port, vessel collided with steamer *Ramillies*, 1.5 miles below Pointe-à-la-Citrouille lighthouse, Batiscan, Quebec.
- In mid-September 1902, vessel stuck fast in the Queenstown Street Bridge over the Welland Canal. Ran between the pier and open bridge and became wedged in place, blocking vehicular and ship traffic for hours until vessel could be cleared (reported September 19, 1902).
- In early November 1902, vessel grounded in harbour of Port Arthur, Ontario (reported November 6, 1902).
- Stuck in Welland Canal (no details available, reported June 3, 1903).

- On July 22, 1903, collided with the steamer *Waverly*, sending latter to the bottom. Occurred near Harbor Beach, Michigan. Turret's steering gear was alleged to have broken while the vessel was overtaking the *Waverly*.
- In early December 1904, vessel grounded at Whitefish Point, Michigan, and, once freed, proceeded to Owen Sound, Ontario, for repairs (reported December 6, 1904).
- On May 8, 1907, vessel was prevented from departing from harbour in Fort William, Ontario, by ice floes for 24 hours. Freed by the icebreaker *Whalen*.
- Alleged to have collided with and sunk the barge *Acadia* in Montreal's harbour (date uncertain).

Table 6.8

Turret Cape (official no. 104283)

Builder:	W. Doxford and Sons, Sunderland, England, in 1895 (hull no. 234, launched April 23, 1895).
Engine:	Triple expansion (21.5-, 36-, and 59-inch piston diameters and 39-inch stroke), 217 nhp, 1,100 ihp at 70 rpm; eight to 10 knots speed.
Boilers:	Two water-tube (each 11 feet x 12.5 feet) at 180 psi; six furnaces (grate surface area of 110 square feet and heating surface area of 4,588 square feet). Built by Babcock and Wilcox, London, England.
Dimensions:	253 feet long x 44 feet wide x 19.4 feet deep.
Propulsion:	Steam screw (single).
Tonnage:	1,827/1,142 gross/net (1895); 2,079/1,158 gross/net (1941).
Freight Capacity:	3,200 tons; two hatches, each being 14.7 feet x 32 feet, over three cargo compartments.
Miscellaneous:	Brought to the Great Lakes in 1907. Rebuilt in 1912 after grounding in Lake Huron. Requisitioned by the British Admiralty in 1915 for saltwater service. In the 1920s, vessel operated in lake/river trade. Converted into a steam barge in Port Dalhousie, Ontario, in 1928 (1,796 gross tons). Engines were condemned in 1930. Lay idle until converted in 1937 into a barge for flour storage. Converted into a bulk freighter in 1941 in Montreal for the bauxite (aluminum) trade between British Guyana and Port Alfred, Quebec (had diesel engine and pilothouse aft; four hatches, each 14.5 feet x 35.1 feet in size). Converted to a suction dredge in 1943 for the Demerara River but soon reverted to the Demerara-Trinidad bulk trade. Returned to Great Lakes in 1949. After inactivity at the Lakehead for several years, was sold for scrap.

Incidents

- Outbound from Montreal to Avonmouth (Bristol), England, grounded on south shore of Île d'Orléans on Vallière Bank on November 22, 1897. The *Lord Stanley* was sent from Quebec to assist.
- Grounded on the mudbank near Four Mile Point on May 7, 1903. Released on May 8. Entered government dry dock to have hull overhauled on May 9.
- Grounded on Goose Island in the St. Lawrence River on September 18, 1904, and required temporary repairs and a visit to a Cleveland, Ohio, dry dock.
- Struck lower east wall of Lock 3 in the Welland Canal in 1906.
- Ran into Crawford's Wharf and tore up one section, circa November 7, 1908. No damage to vessel. Caused by human error.
- In a blinding snowstorm, vessel grounded on the Middle Bank near Cove Island, Lake Huron, on November 18, 1911. Striking at 2315 hours, ship was pounded for hours before sinking on the ledge, bow sticking up in the air. The entire crew sheltered there for 48 hours before being rescued, all being nearly dead from exhaustion and exposure. Vessel remained there all winter. Salvaged in the spring of 1912 by Reid Wrecking of Sarnia, Ontario/Port Huron, Michigan. Refloated on May 16, 1912. Proceeded to Collingwood, Ontario, for repairs totalling $30,000; four weeks later, vessel returned to service.
- Steering gear became disabled on October 23, 1915, near Point Iroquois, Lake Superior. Had to be towed into Sault Ste. Marie for repairs.

Table 6.8 Cont'd

Per Gray & Lingwood		Per Thunder Bay National Marine Sanctuary Collection (Alpena Public Library)	
Owners	**Dates**	**Owners**	**Dates**
Turret Steam Shipping Company (Petersen, Tate, and Company, managers)	1895–189?	Turret Steam Shipping Company (W. Petersen Ltd.)	1895–1907
St. Bade Trading Company (Petersen, Tate, and Company, managers)	189?–1901	Canadian Lake and Ocean Navigation	1907–13
Canadian Ocean and Inland Navigation (Petersen, Tate and Company, managers; management ceased in 1904)	1901–14	Canada Steamship Lines	1913–16
Canadian Lake and Ocean Navigation	1914–15	Turret Steamship Company (Dominion Iron and Steel Company)	1916–17
Cape Steamship Company (Canada Steamship Lines, manager; management changed to Dominion Iron and Steel Company in 1917 and British Empire Steel Corporation in 1926)	1915–27	Cape Steamship Company (Dominion Iron and Steel Company)	1917–25
		International Waterways Navigation (R.W. Campbell and J.E. Russell)	1925–37
Inland Waters Navigation (converted to a steam barge in 1928)	1927–41	Fort William-Montreal Navigation (Robin Hood Flour Mills)	1937–41
Saguenay Terminals (propulsion changed to six-cylinder Sulzer oil engine)	1941–48	Saguenay Terminals (name changed to Sunchief in 1948 and Walter Inkster in 1949)	1941–49
Sarnia Steamships (R. Scott Misener, manager; name changed to Sunchief)	1948–49	Colonial Steamships	1951–56
Colonial Steamships (R. Scott Misener, manager; name changed to Walter Inkster)	1949–58	A. Newman and Company	1956–59
Scott Misener Steamships	1958–59		

Disposition

- Scrapped in Port Dalhousie in 1959.

Table 6.9
Scottish Hero (official no. 105718)

Builder:	W. Doxford and Sons, Sunderland, England, in 1895 (yard no. 235).
Engine:	Quadruple cylinder running to triple crankshafts (19.5-, 27.5-, 39-, and 55-inch piston diameters and 42-inch stroke), 285 nhp, 1,000 ihp at 60 rpm, 10 knots speed.
Boilers:	Three Scotch (each 10.5 feet x 11 feet) at 210 psi. Six furnaces (grate surface area of 110 square feet and heating surface area of 3,900 square feet). Built by Collingwood Ship Building Company.
Dimensions:	297 feet long x 40 feet wide x 22 feet deep.
Propulsion:	Steam screw (single).
Tonnage:	2,202/1,402 (gross/net).
Freight Capacity:	3,800 tons. Four hatches (two being 12.7 feet x 32 feet, one being 12.7 feet x 16 feet, and one being 12.7 feet x 14 feet) over four cargo compartments.
Miscellaneous:	Cut in half at Lévis, Quebec, in 1907 to allow transit to Great Lakes where halves were rejoined. In 1916 the British Admiralty requisitioned vessel for saltwater service. In 1917 the vessel was cut in half at Ashtabula, Ohio, to allow transit to lower St. Lawrence River where halves were rejoined.

Incidents

- Emerged from Davis's dry dock on October 20, 1899.
- Grounded in foggy conditions 22 miles east of Halifax on April 30, 1905; repairs being made thereafter.
- In late October 1908, while up-bound opposite Point Iroquois, Michigan, a dangerous fire was spotted on shore and vessel stopped to render aid. Five men volunteered to take the yawl boat to shore to assist in pitch darkness and heavy seas. Finding they could make no headway, they returned the half-water-filled boat to the vessel. First mate made sure the other four crew members had been safely deposited on the deck before he was hauled up. However, his strength gave out while he was being hauled up and he fell and drowned.
- Grounded at entrance to Midland, Ontario, harbour on May 3, 1911, and was badly damaged.
- Driven ashore in Mud Lake (near Sault Ste. Marie) during the terrible November 1913 storm. When vessel arrived at the Soo on November 11, 1913, its fore topmast was gone.

Disposition

- Shelled and sunk by German submarine *U-155* on June 10, 1917 (440 miles west by south of Fastnet, i.e., southwest tip of Ireland). One fatality.

Table 6.9 Cont'd

Per Gray & Lingwood		Per Thunder Bay National Marine Sanctuary Collection (Alpena Public Library)	
Owners	Dates	Owners	Dates
Scottish Line (McIlwraith, McEachern, and Company, managers)	1895–99	Scottish Line	1895–99
Scottish Hero Steamship Company (Petersen, Tate, and Company, managers)	1899–1902	Scottish Hero Steamship Company (McIlwraith, McEachern and Company, managers)	1899–1907
Canadian Ocean and Inland Navigation (W. Petersen, manager; Jacks and Company assumed managerial role in 1904; no manager listed after 1906)	1902–14	Canadian Lake and Ocean Navigation	1907–13
Canadian Lake and Ocean Navigation	1914–15	Canada Steamship Lines	1913–17
Merchants' Mutual Line (Canada Steamship Lines, manager)	1915–17	Hero Steamship Company	1917

Table 6.10

Turret Bay (official no. 104245)

Builder:	W. Doxford and Sons, Sunderland, England (yard no. 220, launched March 8, 1894).
Engine:	Triple expansion (23-, 37-, and 60-inch piston diameters and 42-inch stroke), 233 nhp.
Boilers:	Two water-tube (each 11 feet x 12.5 feet) at 200 psi.
Dimensions:	297 feet long x 40 feet wide x 22 feet deep.
Propulsion:	Steam screw (single).
Tonnage:	2,211/1,376 (gross/net).
Freight Capacity:	3,800 tons.

Owners	Dates
Guildford Steamship Company (Petersen, Tate, and Company, managers)	1894–1901
Canadian Ocean and Inland Navigation (W. Petersen, manager)	1901–04

Incidents

- A June 28, 1897, newspaper report announced that the vessel was aground near Champlain on the St. Lawrence River.
- In 1900 the pilot (Joseph Larochelle, no. 80) aboard the vessel ran it ashore on Goose Island on the St. Lawrence River. Was found guilty of negligence and was suspended from piloting for nine months.

Disposition

- On May 20, 1904, vessel wrecked on rocks off St. Paul's Island in the St. Lawrence River while proceeding from Sydney, Nova Scotia, to Montreal with a coal cargo in fog. Thirteen fatalities of 22-man crew.

Table 6.11

Turret Crown (official no. 104279)

Builder:	W. Doxford and Sons, Sunderland, England, in 1895 (hull no. 233).
Engine:	Triple expansion (22-, 36-, and 59-inch piston diameters and 39-inch stroke), 217 nhp, 1,100 ihp at 60 rpm.
Boilers:	Originally, two water-tube (each 11 feet x 12.5 feet) built by Babcock and Wilcox, London, England. Reboilered with two Scotch (each 11 feet x 14 feet) at 180 psi. Six furnaces (grate surface area of 116 square feet and heating surface area of 4,557 square feet). Built by Western Dry Dock and Shipbuilding, Port Arthur, Ontario.
Dimensions:	253 feet long x 44 feet wide x 19.4 feet deep.
Propulsion:	Steam screw (single).
Tonnage:	1,827/1,142 (gross/net).
Freight Capacity:	3,200 tons. Three hatches (each 68 feet in one dimension) over three cargo compartments.
Miscellaneous:	Brought to Great Lakes in 1907. Requisitioned by British Admiralty for saltwater war service in 1915. Operated late in the war in the Pacific despite ownership in Toronto. Returned to Great Lakes in 1922.

Incidents

- On June 8, 1895, vessel was involved in a minor collision off Cape Rosier, Gaspé, Quebec.
- On June 12, 1903, vessel grounded on a shoal near the old ship channel between Nine Mile Point and Amherst Island in Lake Ontario at approximately 1100 hours. Was released on June 13 and entered dry dock for light repairs on June 20.
- On July 4, 1904, the *British Whig* (Kingston) newspaper reported that to avoid a collision with the steamer *Russia* and the barge *Oneonta* the captain of the *Turret Crown* ran his ship at full speed into an unoccupied dock in Port Huron, Michigan. Damage was extensive, but if either vessel had been hit, either would have been cut in two (actual date of event unknown).
- On October 19, 1905, Captain Malcolm Cameron of the *Turret Crown* was fined $5 plus court costs (or could spend 15 days in jail) for assaulting a deckhand who had knocked down the female cook. He paid the fine.
- On October 25, 1905, the *Turret Crown* collided with the Pioneer Steamship Company's *Martin Mullen* in the port of Lorain, Ohio, due to the former vessel improperly steering from its course while passing up the harbour. The latter vessel was struck 30 to 40 feet back from the bow on the starboard side, producing $6,000 in damages. Owners of the *Turret Crown* agreed to put up a $9,000 bond for any damages awarded.
- Per a report in the September 22, 1906, issue of the *British Whig*, the captain of the *Turret Crown* was fined $1,000 in a Superior, Wisconsin, court for an infraction of marine regulations (i.e., upon arrival from a foreign port, the hold must be inspected before loading). Apparently, the elevator company started loading without his knowledge. The September 29 *British Whig* reported that the fine had been rescinded and he had been issued a warning.
- Trying to outrace a northwestern gale and snow on November 27, 1906, vessel missed the Grand Marais, Minnesota, harbour and grounded to the west. Was easily released by the steamer *Favorite* and proceeded to Cleveland for repairs.
- Collided with the steamer *William H. Mack* near Whitefish Point, Michigan, in fog on May 4, 1913. Despite considerable damage near the boiler house to the starboard, vessel limped into Sault Ste. Marie, Ontario, where it settled to the bottom in 12 feet of water. After temporary repairs were made, vessel was brought to Collingwood, Ontario, for permanent repairs.
- The May 8, 1913, issue of the *British Whig* announced that the *Turret Crown* was ashore at Fort William, Ontario, while the May 12 issue announced that the vessel had been released.
- On October 9, 1922, vessel grounded on Cove Island and was subsequently salvaged.

Table 6.11 Cont'd

Per Gray & Lingwood	
Owners	Dates
Turret Steam Shipping Company (Petersen, Tate, and Company, managers)	1895–1902
G.M. Stamp	1902–04
D.A. Howden	1904–05
H.M. Hubbard	1905–07
Turret Crown Steamship Company (H.W. Harding, manager)	1907–15
Coastwise Steamship and Barge Company	1915–18
Commonwealth Steamship Company (Universal Transportation Company, managers)	1918–22
W.J. and S.P. Herival	1922–24
W.J. McCormack	1924

Per Thunder Bay National Marine Sanctuary Collection (Alpena Public Library)	
Owners	Dates
W. Petersen	1895–1907
Canadian Lake and Ocean Navigation	1907–13
Canada Steamship Lines	1913–15
Turret Crown Steamship Company (H.W. Harding, manager)	1915–16
Coastwise Steamship and Barge Company	1916–18
Commonwealth Steamship Company	1918–21
W.J. and S.P. Herivel	1921–22
A.B. MacKay	1922–24
Captain W.C. Jordan	1924

Disposition

- Vessel grounded on Meldrum Point, Manitoulin Island, on November 11, 1924, becoming a construction total loss. Destroyed by storms over the winter of 1924–25, vessel was salvaged for its metal between 1925 and 1945 (sources conflict).

Table 6.12
A.E. Ames (official no. 114449)

Builder:	Northumberland Ship Building Company, Newcastle, England (yard no. 109) in 1903.
Engine:	Triple expansion (20.5-, 33-, and 59-inch piston diameters and 36-inch stroke), 175 nhp, 1,250 shp at 83 rpm; 11 knots speed. Built by Wallsend Slipway and Engineering Company Limited in England.
Boilers:	Two Scotch (each 10.3 feet x 13.5 feet) at 180 psi. Six furnaces (grate surface area of 108 square feet). Built by Wallsend Slipway and Engineering Company Limited.
Dimensions:	245 feet long x 37 feet wide x 24 feet deep.
Propulsion:	Steam screw (single).
Tonnage:	1,637/1,020 (gross/net).
Freight Capacity:	1,800 tons. Five hatches (one being 10 feet x 14 feet and four being 14 feet x 20 feet), 24 feet on centre, over two cargo compartments; two cargo booms; side ports on both sides for wheeled/trucked cargo.

Owners	Dates
W. Petersen Limited	1903–1905
Canadian Ocean and Inland Navigation	1905–11
Merchants' Mutual Line	1911–18
Canada Steamship Lines	1918–21
Société Belge d'Armement Maritime SA (name changed to *Breughel*)	1921–24
Société Félcampoise de Navigation (name changed to *Ginette Le Borgne*)	1924–25
Charles Le Borgne	1925–40

Incidents

- Struck and damaged Grand Trunk Railway bridge at Port Colborne, Ontario (trains were detoured until repairs were completed). Reported on October 28, 1903.
- Struck a rock. Dranelly Wrecking divers assessed damage. Reported on November 20, 1911.
- Struck and severely damaged Grand Trunk Railway bridge in Hamilton, Ontario, on May 18, 1912. Harbour was blocked for about one week.
- Grounded at Salmon Point, about 40 miles west of Kingston, Ontario, on July 4, 1913, and was released on July 9. Immediately proceeded to a U.S. dry dock for repairs.
- Grounded at Farrow's Point on the St. Lawrence River during August 1915. Forepeak and ballast tank no. 1 filled with water, so vessel was docked at Port Arthur, Ontario, on September 9, 1915.

Disposition

- Hit a mine west of Sardinia off San Pietro Island on September 13, 1940, and foundered.

Table 6.13

H.M. Pellatt (official no. 114446)

Builder:	Russell and Company, Greenock, Scotland, in 1903 (yard no. 511).
Engine:	Triple expansion (21-, 35-, and 57-inch piston diameters and 36-inch stroke), 196 nhp, 1,250 shp at 83 rpm; 11 knots speed. Built by D. Rowan and Company, Glasgow, Scotland.
Boilers:	Two Scotch (each 10.3 feet x 13.5 feet) at 180 psi. Six furnaces (grate surface area of 110 square feet). Built by D. Rowan and Company, Glasgow.
Dimensions:	240 feet long x 37 feet wide x 22 feet deep.
Propulsion:	Steam screw (single).
Tonnage:	1,591/1,038 (gross/net).
Freight Capacity:	1,700 tons. Four hatches (each being 16 feet x 20 feet), 24 feet on centre, over two cargo compartments; two cargo booms; side ports on both sides for wheeled/trucked cargo.

Owners	Dates
W. Petersen Limited	1903–05
Canadian Ocean and Inland Navigation	1905–11
Merchants' Mutual Line	1911–17
Canadian Northern Steamships	1917–18
Canada Steamship Lines	1918–20
Société de Belge d'Armement Maritime SA (name changed to *Memling*)	1920–1924/25
Compagnie Charles Le Borgne (name changed to *Nicole Le Borgne*)	1924/25–1934
Giuseppe Pagan (name changed to *Giuliana Pagan*)	1934–35
Aurora SA di Navigazione (name changed to *Scillin Secondo*, shortened to *Scillin* in 1937)	1935–by 1941
Fratelli Bianchi Società di Navigazione	by 1941–1942

Disposition

- Sunk by Royal Navy submarine HMS *Sahib* on November 14, 1942, nine miles north of Kuriat, Tunisia, killing nearly all of more than 800 Allied (non-Axis) prisoners of war aboard. This incident was concealed from the public for years.

Incidents

- Grounded on June 4, 1904, hard against the head of Harsen's Island in the St. Clair River.
- Grounded on May 22, 1906, while entering the lift lock at the Cardinal Canal on the St. Lawrence River.
- R.M. Brownie fell backward into the ship's hold and died instantly (reported June 8, 1906).
- Grounded on/near Calumet Island near Kingston, Ontario, and was released by the steamer *Donnelly* (reported on August 23, 1907).
- Collided with the steamer *John Hanlon* and latter sank at the Toronto Bay Street ferry docks. The *John Hanlon* was struck on its starboard side near the stern. Collateral damage to the sideway and roadway was severe. The *John Hanlon* was pushed up to the edge of the pier, then slid back into the water and sank. Occurred in the early-morning hours of June 30, 1909. The crew members of the *H.M. Pellatt* were found entirely at fault in Admiralty Court.
- Grounded on Round Island near Sault Ste. Marie in dense fog on July 11, 1909.
- Collided with the steam yacht *Cygnet* in an unnamed St. Lawrence River canal on August 12, 1911. Was seized in Montreal on August 14, 1911, on a $10,000 damage claim.
- Grounded at Iroquois, Ontario, below Prescott in the St. Lawrence River on September 19, 1911, and was released on October 6.
- Grounded heavily near Point Iroquois, Michigan, on May 22, 1912. Salvage tugs required three days to release vessel (cost $18,977).
- While being towed from Buffalo, New York, to Ashtabula, Ohio, was run down by the railcar ferry *Pere Marquette No. 15* (latter ran between Conneaut, Ohio, and Port Stanley, Ontario), causing severe damage (date unknown).

Table 6.14

J.H. Plummer (official no. 114447)

Builder:	Whitworth, Armstrong and Company, Newcastle, England, in 1903 (yard no. 740).
Engine:	Triple expansion (20.5-, 33-, and 54-inch piston diameters and 36-inch stroke), 175 nhp, 1,250 shp at 81 rpm; nine knots speed.
Boilers:	Two Scotch (each 10.3 feet x 13.5 feet) at 180 psi. Six furnaces with grate surface area of 108 square feet.
Dimensions:	246 feet long x 37 feet wide x 22 feet deep.
Propulsion:	Steam screw (single).
Tonnage:	1,582/992 (gross/net).
Freight Capacity:	1,800 tons. Five hatches (one being 10 feet x 14 feet and four being 14 feet x 20 feet), 24 feet on centre, over two cargo holds; two cargo booms; side ports on both sides for wheeled/trucked cargo.

Owners	Dates
W. Petersen Limited	1903–05
Canadian Lake and Ocean Navigation	1905–11
Merchants' Mutual Line	1911–17
Canadian Northern Steamships	1917–18
Canadian Maritime Company	1918–20
Société Belge d'Armement Maritime SA (named changed to *Van Eyck*)	1920–23
Kirkwood Line (name changed back to *J.H. Plummer*)	1923–24
Coastwise Steamship and Barge (J. Griffiths and Sons, managers; name changed to *Amur*)	1924–46
Cia de Vapores Sino-Americana SA (name changed to *Far Eastern Carrier*)	1946
Tung An Shipping Company (name changed to *Tung An*)	1946–49

Incidents

- Suffered unknown damage in September-October 1903, necessitating a visit to dry dock in Superior, Wisconsin.
- Collided with the propeller ship *Dorothy* in the Soulanges Canal in Quebec in August 1905.
- At 1815 hours on September 18, 1914, grounded in fog off Kingston, Ontario. Had to have one-third of load lightered off before vessel could be released. Able to resume journey on September 21. Two shell plates replaced later ($4,000 repair).
- Collided with the propeller ship *Algonquin* on May 7, 1914, in heavy fog.

Disposition

- Wrecked off China on April 10, 1949 (six miles southwest of Shaweishan, Yangtze River).

Table 6.15
Canadian (official no. 125427)

Builder:	W. Dobson and Co., Newcastle, England (yard no. 154, launched July 9, 1907).
Engine:	Triple expansion (19-, 32-, and 52-inch piston diameters and 36-inch stroke), 1,200 ihp at 86 rpm. Built by Wallsend Slipway Company, England.
Boilers:	Two Scotch (each 10 x 13 feet) at 180 psi. Six furnaces (grate surface area of 204 square feet and heating surface area of 6,000 square feet). Built by Wallsend Slipway Company.
Dimensions:	248 feet long x 43 feet wide x 23 feet deep.
Propulsion:	Steam screw (single).
Tonnage:	2,214/1,444 (gross/net).
Freight Capacity:	2,800 tons. Six hatches (each being 9 feet x 27 feet) over three cargo compartments.

Owners	Dates
Mutual Steamship Company (J.W. Norcross, manager)	1907–13
Canada Interlake Line (J.W. Norcross, manager)	1913–14
Canada Steamship Lines (U.K.)	1914–16
Canada Steamship Lines (CN)	1916–60

Incidents

- In a November 5, 1908, newspaper, it was reported that arrest warrants for smuggling were issued and that the lighter *Reliance* was seized in connection with the rescue of the grounded *Canadian*. It appears that large quantities of canned goods, tea, and sugar were jettisoned overboard by the crew members of the *Reliance*, who subsequently returned and picked up the goods. Taking the goods back to the U.S. Soo, the crew of the *Reliance* divided the booty among themselves without paying duty.

Disposition

- Scrapped in the second quarter of 1960 in Hamilton, Ontario.

Table 6.16
Acadian (official no. 124258)

Builder:	Clyde Shipbuilding and Engineering Co., Port Glasgow, Scotland (yard no. 278, launched February 20, 1908).
Engine:	Triple expansion (18-, 30-, and 50-inch piston diameters and 36-inch stroke).
Boilers:	Two Scotch (each 10 x 13 feet) at 180 psi. Six furnaces.
Dimensions:	248 feet long x 43 feet wide x 24 feet deep.
Propulsion:	Steam screw (single).
Tonnage:	2,305/1,457 (gross/net).
Freight Capacity:	2,732 tons. Six hatches (each 9 feet x 27 feet) over three cargo compartments.

Owners	Dates
Mutual Steamship Company	1908–13
Canada Interlake Line	1913–16
Canada Steamship Lines (U.K.)	1916–18

Incidents

- Two captains of the *Acadian* died on the vessel: Neil Morrison in August 1911 after falling into the hold and J. Whiteside one year earlier after being hit by a derrick in Port Arthur, Ontario.
- Grounded in a gale near Thunder Bay, Ontario, on Sulphur Island on November 11, 1913. Could not be salvaged until February 1914 after which vessel was delivered to Great Lakes Engineering Works (Ecorse, Michigan) to complete repairs costing $98,000.

Disposition

- Torpedoed by German submarine UB-117 on September 16, 1918, 11 miles southwest by west off Trevose Head, England (25 fatalities).

Table 6.17
Beaverton (official no.125440)

Builder:	R. Stephenson and Company, Hebburn, England (yard no. 118, launched April 16, 1908).
Engine:	Triple expansion (17-, 28-, and 46-inch piston diameters and 33-inch stroke), 950 shp at 84 rpm. Built by North Eastern Marine Engineering, Wallsend, England.
Boilers:	Two Scotch (each 11 feet x 12 feet) at 185 psi. Four furnaces. Built by North Eastern Marine Engineering, Wallsend.
Dimensions:	249 feet long x 43 feet wide x 21 feet deep.
Propulsion:	Steam screw (single).
Tonnage:	2,012/1,357 (gross/net).
Freight Capacity:	3,000 tons. Six hatches, 24 feet on centre, over three cargo compartments. Two cargo booms.

Owners	Dates
Merchants' Steamship Company	1908–10
Merchants' Mutual Line	1910–14
Merchants' Mutual Lake Line	1914–17
Canadian Northern Steamships	1917
Canada Steamship Lines (U.K.) (Leopold Walford Ltd., managers)	1917–19
Canada Steamship Lines (CN)	1919–60

Incidents

- Vessel became stuck in the Thorold gate of the Welland Canal (reported on May 20, 1912).
- Dan Brown, a steward on the *Beaverton*, fell down a hatch, resulting in injuries (reported on September 18, 1913).
- The steamers *W.B. Ketchem* and *Beaverton* collided in the Welland Canal on September 24, 1913, the latter being on its first voyage since being in the repair shops of Kingston Ship Building Company for one month.

Disposition

- Scrapped on September 13, 1960, in Hamilton, Ontario.

Table 6.18

Mapleton (official no. 123961)

Builder:	Sunderland Shipbuilding Company, Sunderland, England (yard no. 253, launched April 6, 1909).
Engine:	Triple expansion (17-, 28-, and 46-inch piston diameters and 33-inch stroke), 950 shp at 84 rpm. Built by North Eastern Marine Engineering, Sunderland.
Boilers:	Two Scotch (each 11 feet x 12 feet) at 185 psi. Four furnaces (grate surface area of 60 square feet and heating surface area of 2,750 square feet). Built by North Eastern Marine Engineering, Sunderland.
Dimensions:	250 feet long x 43 feet wide x 16 feet deep.
Propulsion:	Steam screw (single).
Tonnage:	1,782/1,139 (gross/net).
Freight Capacity:	3,000 tons. Six hatches, 24 feet on centre, over three cargo compartments. Two cargo booms.

Owners	Dates
Merchants' Steamship Company	1909–10
Merchants' Mutual Line	1910–14
Merchants' Mutual Lake Line	1914–17
Canadian Northern Steamships	1917
Canada Steamship Lines (U.K.)	1917–23
Canada Steamship Lines (CN)	1923–46
British government (name changed to *Eastern Med* in 1948)	1946–50

Incidents

- Grounded on Gravel Island on August 3, 1909, and was released on August 4 after being lightened by removal of 500 tons of cargo. Proceeded to Great Lakes Engineering Works (Ecorse, Michigan) by August 18, 1909, for repairs, taking one week in dry dock.
- Struck stone abutment between Locks 24 and 25 of the Welland Canal and started to leak on October 8, 1909. Into dry dock on October 21 for repairs.
- Saved crew of sinking propeller ship *F.A. Meyers* on December 18, 1909.
- Grounded in Montreal's harbour on October 10, 1912, and was later released.
- Collided with propeller ship *George C. Howe* in the Welland Canal in July 1913.
- In late 1913, while passing through the Welland Canal, vessel struck the wall of the Humberstone Bridge near Port Colborne, Ontario, causing damage to its forward plates.
- On November 19, 1913, vessel grounded on Drummond Island, Lake Huron, in dense fog.
- On April 30, 1915, while leaving the Welland Canal for Ashtabula, Ohio, vessel struck a submerged boulder in the channel about 800 feet from the end of the pier.

Disposition

- Vessel burned November 22, 1950, at Adabiya (Port Suez) while loading oil drums and was scrapped at La Spezia, Italy, on February 24, 1953.

Table 6.19

Saskatoon (official no. 123965)

Builder:	Sunderland Shipbuilding Company Limited, Sunderland, England (yard no. 256, launched February 25, 1910).
Engine:	Triple expansion (17-, 28-, and 46-inch piston diameters and 33-inch stroke), 800 shp at 76 rpm. Built by North Eastern Marine Engineering, Newcastle, England.
Boilers:	Two Scotch (each 11 feet x 12 feet) at 185 psi. Four furnaces (grate surface area of 66 square feet and heating surface area of 2,750 square feet). Built by North Eastern Marine Engineering, Newcastle.
Dimensions:	250 feet long x 43 feet wide x 19 feet deep.
Propulsion:	Steam screw (single).
Tonnage:	1,798/1,148 gross/net (1910); 1,752/1,029 gross/net (1940).
Freight Capacity:	2,500 tons. Six hatches (each being 12 feet x 27 feet), 24 feet on centre, over three cargo holds. Two cargo booms.
Miscellaneous:	Converted to a tanker in 1940 by Marine Industries Limited, Sorel, Quebec. Reduced to a floating loading station in 1971–72.

Incidents

- Grounded near Portneuf Light in the St. Lawrence River on July 24, 1914.
- Damaged the lower gates of the south Lock No. 1 of the Lachine Canal ($10,000 in damages) on October 21, 1922.
- In summer 1926, vessel was blown against a bridge in Port Arthur, Ontario, leading to a bent funnel and damaged plates that were repaired during the following winter layup.
- Due to fierce late fall storms, vessel was laid up in Windsor, Ontario, over the winter of 1927–28.
- On May 11, 1928, vessel grounded near the infamous ledge of rock about 200 feet off Lucille Island on the Rock of Ages reef (off southern point of Isle Royale in Lake Superior).

Owners	Dates
Colonial Transportation	1910
Merchants' Mutual Line	1910–14
Merchants' Mutual Lake Line	1914–17
Canadian Northern Steamships	1917–18
Canadian Maritime Company (E. Heinz, London, England, manager)	1918–20
E.J. Heinz	1920–22
Interlake Navigation	1922–27
Canada Steamship Lines (name changed to *Rosemount*)	1927–35
Manseau Shipyards	1935–40
Branch Line (name changed to *Willowbranch*)	1940–45
British government (name changed to *Empire Tadpole*)	1945–46
Bulk Storage Company	1946–47
Basinghall Shipping Company (name changed to *Basingcreek*)	1947–50
Canadian Coastwise Carriers (name changed to *Coastal Creek*)	1950–52
Coastalake Tankers	1952–68
Hall Corporation of Canada (name changed to *Creek Transport*)	1968–72
McNamara Corporation, J.P Porter Company, and Richelieu Dredging Corporation (name changed to *Île de Montréal*)	1972–76

Disposition

- Vessel scrapped sometime between 1976 and 1985 at Montmagny, Quebec, by the Nittolo Metal Company.

Table 6.20
Midland King (official no. 116661)

Builder:	Hull was from Polson Iron Works, subcontracted to Collingwood Ship Building and Engineering Company (hull no. 4). Launched August 19, 1903.
Engine:	Triple expansion (20-, 33.5-, and 55-inch piston diameters and 40-inch stroke), 1,000 ihp at 85 rpm. Built by Bertram Engineering Works, Toronto.
Boilers:	Two Scotch (each 12 feet x 14 feet) at 177 psi. Six furnaces (grate surface area of 126 square feet and heating surface area of 4,400 square feet). Built by Bertram Engineering Works, Toronto.
Dimensions:	367 feet long x 48 feet wide x 28 feet deep.
Propulsion:	Steam screw (single).
Tonnage:	3,965/2,450 (gross/net).
Freight Capacity:	5,500 tons (at least 218,000 bushels of grain). Ten hatches, each nine feet wide, 24 feet on centre over four cargo compartments.
Miscellaneous:	Vessel was chartered in March 1906 by Canadian Lake and Ocean Navigation for charters from Fort William, Ontario, to Montreal, Quebec, and Kingston, Ontario, at the opening of the navigation season and also for several charters from Fort William to Depot Harbour on Georgian Bay. At the onset of the Great Depression (December 1932), vessel was laid up until 1937 sale to Steel Company of Canada (Stelco). Steering gear was placed in the steamer *Robert P. Durham*.

Owners	Dates
Midland Navigation Company	1903–1910/13
Inland Lines or Richelieu and Ontario Navigation*	1910/13–1913/14
Canada Steamship Lines	1913/14–1937
Steel Company of Canada	1937/38

*Conflicting records.

Incidents

- Grounded near De Tour, Michigan, in late October 1908. Still held fast on November 3.
- Collided with the steamer *Glenfinnan* southeast of Passage Island, Lake Superior, on May 18, 1922, suffering $20,000 worth of damage.

Disposition

- Vessel scrapped in Hamilton, Ontario, in 1937 or 1938.

Table 6.21

Midland Queen (official no. 110991)

Builder:	Caledon Shipbuilding and Engineering Company, Dundee, Scotland (hull no. 160, launched January 7, 1901).
Engine:	Triple expansion (18-, 30-, and 50-inch piston diameters and 36-inch stroke), 800 ihp at 75 rpm.
Boilers:	Two Scotch (each 10 feet x 12.5 feet) at 170 psi. Four furnaces.
Dimensions:	249 feet long x 43 feet wide x 21 feet deep.
Propulsion:	Steam screw (single).
Tonnage:	1,993/1,349 (gross/net).
Freight Capacity:	At least 3,000 tons. Hatches 24 feet on centre.
Miscellaneous:	In its very early years, vessel was chartered to the Canadian government to serve as a lighthouse tender. It was chartered in March 1906 by Canadian Lake and Ocean Navigation for charters from Fort William, Ontario, to Montreal, Quebec, and Kingston, Ontario, at the opening of the navigation season and also for several charters from Fort William, Ontario, to Depot Harbour on Georgian Bay. Chartered March 10, 1915, by the Nova Scotia Steel and Coal Company and the Dominion Steel and Coal Company (for Montreal to/from Sydney, Nova Scotia, coal trade). Vessel was first laker lost to enemy action in the First World War. Made one successful round trip with war supplies sent to the United Kingdom, but on the next eastbound voyage it was "sent to the bottom."

Incidents

- On its way to the Great Lakes for the first time from its builder in October 1901, vessel grounded in the Soulanges Canal near Montreal. Vessel went into Detroit dry dock to make temporary repairs, requiring replacement of 24 plates at a cost of $20,000. Required more permanent repairs in Collingwood, Ontario, dry dock in February 1902.
- On July 9, 1904, vessel ran aground in fog about one mile from Kincardine, Ontario. Was released on July 11 by two tugs, then proceeded to Goderich, Ontario, for temporary repairs.
- On October 4, 1904, vessel collided with the Canada Atlantic Transit steamer *Ottawa* off Cariboo Island, Lake Superior, at night in heavy fog. Both required dry-dock repairs, especially the *Midland Queen* with a badly twisted stem and many cracked plates.

- On May 1, 1906, vessel collided with the steamer *William G. Mather* in the Detroit River off Amherstburg, Ontario. Went to Wyandotte, Michigan, for repairs.
- On May 26, 1906, in a storm at night, vessel missed the Port Colborne, Ontario, breakwater and grounded east of it. Once lightered, vessel was released, reloaded cargo, and set off for its destination (Kingston, Ontario).
- On November 2, 1907, the second mate got his right foot caught in a winch, crushing it badly.
- On June 24, 1911, a longshoreman laid down on the deck near the rudder chains to rest after many hours of loading pipe. He was fatally crushed in his sleep.

Owners	Dates
Midland Navigation Company	1901–10
Inland Lines	1910–13
Canada Steamship Lines	1913–15

Disposition

- Sunk by surface gunfire from German submarine U-28 on August 4, 1915, 70 miles southwest by west of Fastnet, Ireland. No deaths, but an interesting incident was noted in the autobiography of the submarine captain: Georg-Gunther von Forstner, *The Journal of Submarine Commander von Forstner* (New York: Houghton-Mifflin, 1917). A crew member had apparently been forgotten or had slept through the bombardment and was now alone on the sinking ship. He was so scared that he dared not leave the ship despite its precarious state. When beckoned by the German submarine crew to swim to them, he refused and swore at them profusely. The ship then pitched violently forward and stood nearly erect with its nose in the water and the crew member hanging on for dear life. With a shrill, whistling sound, the vessel slid below the surface along with the crew member. Usually, this would mean certain death due to the suction generated by the sinking vessel. But not this time! Suddenly, a loud detonation was heard and an explosion of compressed air within the ship sent barrels, boards, debris, and the marooned crew member sky-high into the air. Falling back into the sea, no worse for wear, the crew member swam to the submarine crew and was promptly turned over to his mates in one of the lifeboats that had returned to get him.

Table 6.22
Seguin (official no. 94763)

Builder:	Polson Iron Works in Owen Sound, Ontario, in 1890 (hull no. 24).
Engine:	Triple expansion (17-, 28-, and 46-inch piston diameters and 30-inch stroke), 116 nhp, 550 ihp at 86 rpm.
Boilers:	Two Scotch (each 10.3 feet x 10 feet) at 160 psi.
Dimensions:	207 feet long x 34 feet wide x 13 feet deep.
Propulsion:	Steam screw (single).
Tonnage:	818/556 gross/net (1890); 1,141/771 gross/net (1910).
Freight Capacity:	1,200 tons. Five hatches, each being 9 feet x 11 feet, 24 feet on centre over two cargo compartments (1910).
Miscellaneous:	Operated as a lighthouse tender by the Department of Marine and Fisheries in 1898 and 1905. Rebuilt in 1907 and chartered by Canadian Northern Ontario Railway for that navigation season. Rebuilt in 1910 as a double-decked package steamer. Laid up in 1927 in Hamilton, Ontario, and later in Kingston, Ontario. Engines went to the tugboat *J.E. McQueen* (ex-*Stoic*, ex-ferry *Essex*).

Owners	Dates
Parry Sound Transportation Company (J.B. Miller and W.H. Smith)	1890–1916
A.B. MacKay	1916–18
Canada Steamship Lines (name changed to *Mapleboro* in 1920, *City of Montreal* in 1926, and *Arvida* in 1927)	1918–37
Manseau Shipyards	1937–39
Marine Industries	1939–44

Incidents

- In September 1891, vessel struck a rock in Georgian Bay near Owen Sound, Ontario.
- In November 1891, Captain Sims fell into the hold in Port Huron, Michigan, and broke his collarbone.
- On April 28, 1897, vessel grounded on the bottom at Germania Park near Buffalo, New York, but was released the same day.
- In the July 1899 gale on Lake Erie, vessel was driven ashore near Ashtabula, Ohio, but was released the same day.
- On May 30, 1900, in dense fog, vessel grounded a half mile west of McGulpin's Point near Mackinaw City, Michigan, but was released the same day.
- On June 27, 1900, vessel lost its deck load of lumber during a heavy sea into Lake Michigan 20 miles off Chicago.
- On August 5, 1902, vessel collided and sank the steamer *City of Venice* off Rondeau, Ontario. The *City of Venice* was struck amidships and was penetrated halfway through, sinking in less than 15 minutes with three dead and several injured.
- On November 14, 1906, vessel collided with and sank the barge *Sir Isaac Latham Bell* at its dock in the St. Clair River.
- On June 12, 1909, vessel ran aground near Farran's Point on the St. Lawrence River but was released by June 15.
- On July 11, 1909, vessel's machinery broke down and it was forced to put back into port in Kingston, Ontario.
- On May 7, 1910, vessel grounded on the foot of Fighting Island in the Detroit River near Amherstburg, Ontario.
- On June 13, 1910, vessel collided with the tug *Golden City* in the Welland Canal and the latter sank.

Disposition

- Vessel scrapped in Sorel, Quebec, in 1944.

Table 6.23
Renwick (official no. 97954)

Builder:	Tyne Iron Shipbuilding, Willington Quay, England, in 1890 (yard no. 84, launched November 27, 1890).
Engine:	Triple expansion (13.5-, 22.5-, and 36-inch piston diameters and 27-inch stroke), 70 nhp. Built by North Eastern Marine Engineering, Wallsend, England.
Boiler:	One Scotch. Built by North Eastern Marine Engineering, Wallsend.
Dimensions:	180 feet long x 28 feet wide x 14 feet deep.
Propulsion:	Steam screw (single).
Tonnage:	664/402 (gross/net).
Freight Capacity:	No data.
Miscellaneous:	Sir John Gunn sold this vessel to R.M. Horne-Payne of Walbrook, London, England, on May 14, 1906. Horne-Payne, a financier, was heavily invested in Mackenzie and Mann projects and became a director of several Canadian Northern companies.

Owners	Dates
Fisher, Renwick and Company, Newcastle, England	1890–92
Renwick Steamship Company, U.K.	1892–1902/04
Sir John Gunn	1902/04–1906
R.M. Horne-Payne (Renwick Company [H.W. Harding, manager])	1906–07
Renwick Company, Toronto (Mackenzie and Mann)	1907–11

Incident

- Grounded in Cornwall, England (Falmouth), in 1903.

Disposition

- Sank after colliding with the French vessel *St. Pierre-Miquelon* off County Harbour Island, Nova Scotia, on December 27, 1911 (three fatalities).

Table 6.24

Le Roberval (official no. 116226)

Builder:	T. du Tremblay, Roberval, Quebec, in 1902.
Engines:	Two horizontal, 12-inch cylinder diameter, 30-inch stroke, built by F.X. Drolet, Quebec City (50 rhp).
Boiler:	No data.
Dimensions:	86 feet long x 23 feet wide x 4 feet deep.
Propulsion:	Steam sidewheeler to steam propeller (single).
Tonnage:	126/71 (gross/net).
Passenger Capacity:	No data.
Freight Capacity:	No data.
Miscellaneous:	Used only intermittently. Rebuilt as a steam propeller by Price Brothers. Hull survives and is being restored.

Owners	Dates
Lake St. John and Saguenay Navigation	1902–07
Péribonka (Roberval) Pulp Company	1907–12
La Banque Nationale	1916–19
Quebec Saguenay Pulp Company	1921
Price Brothers	1927–28

Disposition
• File closed in the summer of 1928 as "wrecked."

Table 6.25

Le Colon (official no. 103147)

Builder:	H.J. Beemer, Roberval, in 1894.
Engines:	13-inch piston diameter, 12-inch stroke, 11 rhp. Built by Carrier, Laine, and Company, Lévis, Quebec.
Boiler:	No data.
Dimensions:	79 feet long x 24 feet wide x 4 feet deep.
Propulsion:	Steam sidewheeler (? tug).
Tonnage:	173/109 (gross/net).
Passenger Capacity:	200.
Freight Capacity:	No data.

Owners	Dates
E.F. Wurtele	1894–1908
B.A. Scott	1910–13
Quebec Development Corporation	1916–22

Disposition
• File closed in 1917 (?) as "condemned."

Table 6.26

Mistassini (official no. 100854)

Builder:	H.J. Beemer, Roberval, in 1891.
Engine:	17.5- and 35-inch piston diameters and 48-inch stroke, 200 rhp. Built by Doty Engine Works, Toronto.
Boiler:	No data.
Dimensions:	130 feet long x 22 feet wide x 8 feet deep.
Propulsion:	Steam sidewheeler.
Tonnage:	249/157 (gross/net).
Passenger Capacity:	400.
Freight Capacity:	No data.
Miscellaneous:	Badly damaged in a fire at the Roberval wharf on July 21, 1899 ($50,000 loss, uninsured). Rebuilt in 1900. Mistassini is derived from the Cree word *mista-assini*, meaning "large stone," which refers to the irregular 10-foot-high boulder located at the outlet of the Mistassini River into Lake St. John.

Owners	Dates
E.F. Wurtele	1891–1901
Quebec and Lake St. John Railway	1906
B.A. Scott	1916–21

Disposition
• File closed in 1929 as "broken up."

Table 6.27
Péribonka (official no. 100470)

Builder:	H.J. Beemer, Roberval in 1888
Engine:	Compound, two cylinders (13- and 16-inch piston diameters and 32- and 40-inch stroke [sources differ]), 28 rhp. Built by Carrier, Laine, and Company, Lévis, Quebec.
Boiler:	No data.
Dimensions:	90 feet long x 22 feet wide x 6 feet deep.
Propulsion:	Steam sidewheeler.
Tonnage:	179/113 (gross/net).
Passenger Capacity:	No data.
Freight Capacity:	No data.
Miscellaneous:	Rebuilt in 1892.

Owners	Dates
E.F. Wurtele	1894–1904
Quebec and Lake St. John Railway	1906
E.F. Wurtele	1907
B.A. Scott	1910–12
Quebec Development Corporation	1916–21

Disposition
• File closed in 1936 as "broken up."

Table 6.28
Marie Alma (official no. 111498)

Builder:	J. and P. Dery, Roberval, Quebec, in 1900.
Engine:	Eight-inch cylinder diameter, eight-inch stroke (?).
Boiler:	No data.
Dimensions:	64 feet long x 14 feet wide x 5 feet deep.
Propulsion:	Steam screw (single).
Tonnage:	52/36 (gross/net).
Miscellaneous:	Lake St. John tow/tugboat.

Owners	Dates
J. Déry	1900–13
Martel and Dufour	1917

Disposition
• File closed in 1921 as "broken up" in 1915.

Table 6.29

Pikouagami (official no. 125991)

Builder:	Polson Iron Works, Toronto, in 1906.
Engine:	Two horizontal, seven-inch cylinder diameter, 30 inch stroke.
Boiler:	No data.
Dimensions:	65 feet long x 18 feet wide x 4 feet deep.
Propulsion:	Steam sternwheel to steam screw (single).
Tonnage:	57/36 (gross/net).
Miscellaneous:	*Pikouagami* is a Native Canadian word meaning "flat lake," which is descriptive of shallow Lake St. John. Vessel possessed a steel frame and machinery consistent with use as a tow/tugboat. The ship was assembled in Roberval, Quebec. Vessel was leased to Lake St. John and Saguenay Navigation Company in 1907. The *Pikouagami* had its trial sailing on June 28, 1906, from Saint-Félicien, Quebec. Was blessed by Father Paradis after a banquet chaired by provincial Minister of Colonization Prévost on July 3. Nicknamed "La Barouette" (play on the word *brouette*, meaning wheelbarrow, due to its square back). Drew less than 20 inches of water since it had no keel, but even the slightest wind could be threatening. Converted to a propeller tug for the McLaren mill at Pointe-Bleue, Quebec.

Owners	Dates
Quebec and Lake St. John Railway	1906–09
Captain G. Lindsay	1909–?
McLaren Mill	?

Incidents

- In its first season, vessel hit a rock in the Ashuapmushuan River.
- In 1908 vessel was overloaded at Mistassini with several hundred boxes of blueberries in addition to the usual load and ran aground on a sandbar downriver.
- In 1908 the vessel hit a rock on the Ashuapmushuan River and sank.
- In 1909 the vessel was holed by a tree trunk at the entrance to the Mistassini River while hauling 400 bags of flour. Crew stuffed one bag in the hole and proceeded to be towed home.

Disposition

- Vessel burned in 1928 to a total loss.

EPILOGUE

In the end, few of the maritime assets of the Grand Trunk Pacific and Canadian Northern Railways helped to jump-start the maritime arm of successor Canadian National Railways. Exceptions included the Niagara, St. Catharines, and Toronto Navigation Company and the western coastal vessels of the Grand Trunk Pacific Coast Steamship Company. In part, this was due to the savage losses incurred during the First World War with the unlimited submarine warfare practised by the Central Powers in the Atlantic Ocean and Mediterranean Sea. To a degree, this was also due to the nature of some of the maritime activities of these new transcontinental ships (i.e., vessels used short-term in the construction of railway infrastructure).

Furthermore, a lack of planning of where the maritime arms would fit into the overall strategic goals and plans of the umbrella corporate structures of the two lines perhaps contributed, as well. This latter comment applies especially to Mackenzie and Mann and the Canadian Northern Railway, wherein disparate properties were sometimes acquired seemingly "without rhyme or reason." Both companies can be accused of establishing maritime arms far too early, the obvious exceptions being those maritime activities used in the construction of railway infrastructure. Both had the example of the Canadian Pacific Railway, which for the most part proceeded with the establishment of its maritime services well after its railway infrastructure had been constructed and refined or revised. Of course, the CPR had the luxury of a monopoly on transportation services for quite some time, while the Grand Trunk Pacific and Canadian Northern did not. In addition, the CPR created its maritime arm to complement the railway in establishing the "All-Red Route" from Britain to Asia.

It could be argued that in the Edwardian era the business outlook was so bright that Charles Hays and the board of directors of the Grand Trunk Railway and Mackenzie and Mann of the Canadian Northern Railway felt that any forays into the maritime arena would still be richly rewarded. Alas, it was not meant to be.

The story of the maritime arms of the Grand Trunk Pacific and Canadian Northern should not, however, be considered only one of gloom, doom, and failure. Their "experimentation" with a wide variety of maritime services, despite stiff competition in most quarters, provided valuable lessons for the infant Canadian National Railways, since leaders of this newest Canadian transcontinental had to decide what maritime services to establish/continue and where. The experiences of the maritime arms of these two predecessor lines, in direct competition with well-entrenched shipping interests in the transatlantic, western coastal, and Great Lakes/St. Lawrence River Basin trades, served Canadian National Railways well.

Canadian National did not enter either the transatlantic or trans-Pacific shipping arenas. It became involved in the Canada-Bermuda-Caribbean trade with its "Lady Boats," where competition was modest. Although the railway developed a freight-shipping arm, it did so largely as a result of operating most of the fleet of the Canadian Government Merchant Marine Limited (CGMML) from 1919 to 1936. When Prime Minister Sir Robert Borden had to decide which "crowd" (his terminology) would operate the vessels until Canadian National Railways was fully formed and operationalized in 1919, he selected the Canadian Northern "crowd." In his mind, unlike the "dithering and floundering" Grand Trunk management, the Canadian Northern

trio of William Mackenzie, Donald Mann, and D.B. Hanna (the last eventually becoming chief operating officer of CGMML) had decided to boldly go into the steamship business. And so the government's 63 vessels were turned over to the Canadian Northern Railway. However, these operations proved to be a rocky road over the longer term, in part because of deficiencies in ship design and selection of trade routes. One thing was certain: there would be no competition for the Great Lakes/St. Lawrence River Basin trade, not with the behemoth Canada Steamship Lines and other stiff competition already in place.

Canadian National also became heavily involved in shipping services (especially ferries) between the maritime provinces of Nova Scotia, New Brunswick, Prince Edward Island, and (after 1949) Newfoundland, another arena wherein competition was modest. Although Canadian National continued the western coastal services established by Grand Trunk Pacific, it did so principally to support the terminus of Prince Rupert as well as to take advantage of the tourist trade to northern British Columbia and Alaska. The Canadian Northern car ferry operations between the Lower Mainland and Vancouver Island also continued under Canadian National.

Far from being failures as widely perceived, the maritime arms of the Grand Trunk Pacific and Canadian Northern Railways illustrated the great breadth of possibilities of maritime operations available to Canadian railways in the early 20th century. They also considerably eased the decision-making process of the early Canadian National Railways leadership with respect to implementing a rational and complementary maritime arm for this government-owned railway.

APPENDIX 1

HOUSE FLAGS AND FUNNELS OF SHIPPING LINES
MENTIONED IN THE TEXT

Shipping Line	House Flag Description[a]	Funnel Description
Alaska Steamship Company	Red with a centred white-bordered black disk bearing a white letter "A" (1895–1970).	Yellow with a black top.
Allan Line	Red pennant over a tricolour of red, white, and blue.	Red with black top (red section bisected with a narrow black band, and a moderate white band divides red from black top).
Beaver Line	White with a blue border and a black beaver in the centre.	Black with two narrow white bands and a black top.
Canadian Inland and Ocean Navigation Company	None found.	All black.
Canadian Lake and Ocean Navigation Company	None found.	All black.
Canadian Northern Steamship Company	Blue and white pennant divided vertically (blue to flagpole side). On blue side, divided horizontally by red stripe into equal portions. On each blue portion, corners joined by white stripes (saltires). Red ball centred on white side.	Buff with a dark blue top.
Canadian Pacific Line	Red-and-white-checkered pattern.	Buff with a black top (1906–21).

Cunard Steamship Company	Red with yellow lion in centre holding a globe.	Red with black top and two thin black bands dividing red into three equal parts.
Dominion Coal Company Limited	Red with centred black diamond.	Black with red band with centred black diamond.
Dominion Line	Red with centred white diamond containing a blue ball (changed between 1903 and 1909 to the same in a pennant shape).	Red with black top and one white band (red between black top and white band).
Donaldson Line	Tricolour of red, white, and blue with a blue letter "D" centred in the white stripe.	Black with one white band (1880–1967).
Elder Dempster	White swallowtail with tapering edges, red St. George's cross bearing a yellow Royal Crown in centre.	All yellow (1890–1989).
Fisher, Renwick & Company/Fisher Renwick	Blue/white alternating horizontal bands (four blue, three white) with black centred letters "F.R.&C" or "F.R." on middle white band.	Black with three moderately thick white bands (both).
Furness-Withy	A pale blue swallowtail pennant. In upper hoist is a white letter "F" and centre bears a black disk with two horizontal stripes of different widths.	All black (1865–1921).
Grand Trunk Pacific Coast Steamships	Red with centred white disk bearing a green maple leaf with white letters "GTP."	Black with a white disk bearing a green maple leaf with white letters "GTP" and black with a red-bordered black disk bearing a green maple leaf with white letters "GTP."
Hamburg-America Line	Blue and white diagonally quartered (no cross stripes, and top and bottom quarters in white and side quarters in blue) with a black anchor in centre. Superimposed on anchor is a yellow shield bearing black letters "H.A.P.A.G."	All buff (1889–1927).
Lakeside Navigation Company	Pennant/swallowtail. Dark background colour with two light stripes following along top and bottom but set in from edge. Light-coloured letters "LAKESIDE" along central axis (specific colours unknown).	All black.
Mackenzie Brothers Steamship Company	White and red diagonally quartered with black letters "M," "B," "S," and "CO" in quarters from top to bottom.	All black.
Manchester Liners	White with centred red oval bearing white letters "ML."	Same as Dominion Line except band is black, not white.
Merchants' Mutual Line[b]	None found.	All black.
New York and Continental Line	None found.	Black with four narrow white bands (and black top).
Niagara, St. Catharines, and Toronto Navigation Company	None found.	All black.
Northwest Transport Line	None found.	Same as New York and Continental Line.

Pacific Coast Steamship Company	Blue with a centred white diamond bearing a red Maltese cross.	All black.
Union Steamships of British Columbia	Orange and light blue diagonally quartered with black letters "U," "S," "S," and "CO" in quarters (top to bottom).	Red with black top.
Uranium Steamship Company	Blue and white diagonally-quartered with white letters "U," "S," "S," and "C" in quarters (top to bottom).	Black to yellow with black top (changed in 1914).

[a]House flags are rectangular unless otherwise specified.

[b]Ships bore, on upper forward portion of hull near bow on both sides, a white disk bearing a black centred letter "M."

DEFINITIONS

Diagonally quartered = Where colour immediately preceding "diagonally quartered" is colour of corner-to-corner stripes.

St. George's cross = Red vertical cross on a white background.

Tricolour = Rectangular flag with three vertical or horizontal, equal-sized stripes (order of colour is left to right or top to bottom).

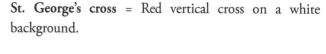

Pennant =

Swallowtail =

APPENDIX 2

Scale-Modelling GTP/CNoR Vessels/Maritime Infrastructure

For those readers interested in scale-modelling the vessels or maritime infrastructure covered in this book, there are a limited number of resin, plastic, and wood kits available in the traditional scales of HO, N, O, et cetera.

Vessels

- **Blue Jacket Ship Crafters (Searsport, Maine):** Small and large barges (HO scale: cat. KH0307 and KH0306, respectively). Small barge is suitable for N scale as well. Both can be built as car floats.
- **Frenchman River Model Works (Langdon, North Dakota):** Generic 45-foot harbour tug (HO scale: cat. 131), 169-foot, three-track car float (HO scale: cat. 152), 24-foot and 45-foot generic steam tugs (O and ON30 scale: cat. 175 and 136, respectively).
- **Inter-Action Enterprises (Salmon Arm, British Columbia):** *C.R. Lamb* sternwheeler from Kamloops, British Columbia, area (HO scale: cat. HO-7032).
- **Model Shipways (Tobyhanna, Pennsylvania):** Tug *Taurus* (HO scale: cat. MS2021).
- **Model Tech Studios (North Hampton, New Hampshire):** Small generic harbour tug (HO scale: cat. S0040), small (three- to four-car capacity) and large (six- to eight-car capacity) car floats (HO scale: cat. S0151 and S0149, respectively).
- **N Scale Ships (www.nscaleships.com):** Duluth, Missabe, and Iron Range tug *Edna G* (no cat. no.).
- **Sea Port Model Works (Hampton, New Hampshire):** Generic 53-foot harbour steam tug (HO scale: cat. H125-HO), 81-foot steam tug *Exeter* (HO scale: cat. H116-HO).
- **Sylvan Scale Models (Parkhill, Ontario):** Generic 260-foot Great Lakes package freighter (HO scale: cat. HO-1050;

N scale: cat. N-2050), generic 81-foot steam tug (HO scale: cat. HO-1025; N scale: cat. N-2025), 45-foot steam tug (O scale: cat. O-3122), two-track (eight-car capacity) car float (N scale: cat. N-2066).

- **Train Troll (Westerley, Rhode Island):** Car transfer barge (two tracks, up to six-car capacity) based upon CPR 1890–1910s barges (HO scale: cat. HO-103).
- **Walthers (Milwaukee, Wisconsin):** Generic three-track car float and car float apron (HO scale: cat. 933-3152 and 933-3068, respectively).

COAL DOCK

No kits are available for a Great Lakes coal dock, although, in HO scale, the Walthers ore dock (cat. 933-3065) could be used as the basis for "kit-bashing" one.

GRAIN ELEVATORS

A plethora of grain elevator kits exist in multiple scales, although extensive "kit-bashing" would have to be done to replicate the early 20th-century Port Arthur elevators.

- **Altoona Model Works (Martinsburg, Pennsylvania):** HO, S, and O scales (no cat. numbers).
- **American Model Builders (St. Louis, Missouri):** O scale: cat. 472; HO scale: cat. 115, 121, 166; N scale: cat. 606, 610, 621, 651.
- **Bergen National Laser (Waldwick, New Jersey):** N scale (no cat. numbers).
- **BH Models (Henderson, Kentucky):** HO scale: cat. 159-407 (no longer made).
- **Branchline Trains (Vernon, Connecticut):** HO scale: cat. 689, N scale: cat. 889.
- **Campbell Scale Models (Central Point, Oregon):** HO

scale: cat. 384, N scale: cat. 445.
- **GC Laser (Genoa City, Wisconsin):** HO scale: cat. 19017, 19071, 14202, 14203; N scale: cat. 04202, 04204; Z scale: cat. 53203.
- **Heljan (Denmark):** HO scale: cat. 806.
- **Kanamodel (Coquitlam, British Columbia):** HO scale: cat. 1017-1021 (five versions) and N scale: cat. 6017-6021 (five versions); grain complex in HO scale: cat. 1022-1026 (five versions) and N scale: cat. 6022-6026 (five versions).
- **Korber Models (Milford, Ohio):** O scale: cat. 315.
- **Lionel (Concord, North Carolina):** O scale: cat. 6-81628.
- **Micro Trains (Talent, Oregon):** Z scale: cat. 79990912.
- **Microfigs (Brantford, Ontario):** Z scale (no cat. no. and no longer made).
- **Osborn Model Kits (Angus, Ontario):** HO scale: cat. RRA-1067, N scale: cat. RRA-3067.
- **Plastruct (City of Industry, California):** HO scale: cat. KIT-1025, O scale: cat. KIT-3025.
- **Quality Craft Models (Northumberland, Pennsylvania):** N scale (no longer made).
- **Sidetrack Laser Manufacturers (Newburg, Oregon):** HO scale (no cat. number).
- **Suncoast Models (Artesia, California):** HO scale: cat. 3060.
- **Walthers (Milwaukee, Wisconsin):** HO scale: cat. 933-3022, 933-3036, 933-3096; N scale: cat. 933-3225, 933-3238.

BLAST FURNACE AND RELATED

- **Minitrix (TRIX) (Germany):** HO scale: cat. 66101, N scale: 66120.
- **Walthers (Milwaukee, Wisconsin):** HO scale: cat. 933-2973, N scale: cat. 933-3249.

PLANS

- **Bearco Marine Models (Madison, Ohio):** Several blast furnace, coke plant plans in a variety of scales.
- **Dundee City Archives (Scotland):** *Midland Queen* (scale[s] unknown).
- **Glasgow (Scotland) City Archives:** *Volturno*, *Cairo* (*Royal Edward*), and *Heliopolis* (*Royal George*) (scale[s] unknown).
- **Marine Museum of the Great Lakes (Kingston, Ontario):** A variety of ship plans are available for the following vessels: *Dalhousie City*, *Beaverton*, *Saskatoon*, *Scottish Hero*, *Turret Cape*, *Turret Crown*, *Turret Chief*, *Turret Court*, and *Midland King* (layout plans generally in 1:48, 1:96, and 1:192 scales and close-ups in 1:2 to 1:24 scales).
- **Mystic Seaport Museum (Mystic, Connecticut):** 1905 Mackenzie River sternwheeler (Miscellaneous Commercial Power Collection, file 13.33, scale[s] unknown) (basis for scratch-building/"kit-bashing" the Foley, Welch and Stewart and Canadian Northern sternwheelers).
- **Royal Museums Greenwich, National Maritime Museum (London, England):** *Avoca*, *Jelunga*, and *Raglan Castle* (1:24, 1:48, 1:96 scales).

- **ScaleModelPlans.com:** Grain elevator plans in N, HO, OO, and O scale.
- **The Model Dockyard (Redruth, England):** 1902 sternwheeler *Mount Royal* (Marine Modelling Magazine Plans) in 1:72 scale (cat. MAR2406) and Paddlewheels and Props (Maineville, Ohio): 1906 Columbia River sternwheeler *G.K. Wentworth* in 1:24 and 1:48 scales and 1912 sternwheeler freight boat *W.H. Bancroft* (from Seattle, Washington; served on Copper River in Alaska) in 1:48 scale. Steam tug (Harold Underwood Powered Steam Plans in 1:96 scale) (basis for scratch-building/"kit-bashing" the tug *Lorne* and Canadian Tugboat Company vessels).
- **TheModelShipwright.com:** Steam tug *Hercules* (1907) (basis for scratch-building/"kit-bashing" the tug *Lorne* and Canadian Tugboat Company vessels).
- **Tyne & Wear Archives (Newcastle, England):** *J.H. Plummer* (1:8 scale).

Appendix 3

Glossary of Nautical Abbreviations and Terms

Abaft: Toward the stern relative to some other object/position.

Aft: Area behind the mid-portion of the vessel (i.e., toward the rear or stern).

Bowsprit: A spar, projecting from the bow, used for the forestay (i.e., rigging holding up the mast[s]) and other rigging.

Brace: Line rigged to the end of a yard arm used to change the angle of a square sail to the wind.

Brake Horsepower (bhp): Calculated as indicated horsepower minus frictional losses within the engine (e.g., bearing drag, rod, and crankshaft windage losses, oil film drag, et cetera). Measured at the crankshaft.

Bulwarks: Extension of the ship's side above the level of the weather deck.

Capstan: Vertical-axled rotating drum-like mechanism that applies force to ropes, cables, and hawsers. Operates on the same principle as a windlass, which is horizontally axled. Can be powered electrically, hydraulically, or via steam or internal combustion engine. May have a gearbox to increase torque.

Fore: Area ahead of the mid-portion of the vessel (i.e., toward the front or bow).

Forecastle: Superstructure at or immediately aft of the bow or crew's quarters in forward part of the ship.

Gross Tonnage: Total volume of a vessel expressed in units of 100 cubic feet (gross ton), with open structures, deckhouses, tanks, et cetera, exempted.

Hawser: Thick cable or rope for mooring to a dock/wharf/ other vessel or towing.

Indicated Horsepower (ihp): Theoretical capability of the engine (i.e., no adjustment for frictional losses).

Jib-Boom: A spar extending the bowsprit.

King Post: An upright post with cargo-handling or fuelling-rig devices attached to it.

Net Tonnage: Taxable gross tonnage of a vessel (calculated as the volume of the vessel's revenue-earning space).

Nominal Horsepower (nhp): Horsepower derived from the size of the engine and piston speed (only accurate at a pressure of seven pounds per square inch).

Official Number (no.): Ship identifier number assigned by the vessel's country of registration. In terms of international recognition, national official numbers have been supplanted today by IMO ship identification numbers. Issued by Britain and the United States beginning in 1855 and 1866, respectively.

Plates: Metal sheets forming the exterior of the hull.

psi: Pressure in pounds per square inch.

Salvor: Vessel engaged in marine salvage (i.e., recovering a vessel, its cargo, or other property after a shipwreck or other maritime casualty).

Screw: Propeller.

Shaft Horsepower (shp): Calculated as brake horsepower minus frictional losses in transmission (e.g., bearings, gears, oil drag, et cetera). Measured at the output shaft of the transmission assembly.

Snatch Block: Component of a block-and-tackle system of two or more pulleys with rope/cable threaded between them. Used to pull/lift heavy loads.

Stem: Vertical reinforced member at front of bow.

Travelling Post Office (TPO): The sorting of mail within a vessel while it is sailing to its destination.

SOURCES

BOOKS

Affleck, E.L. *A Century of Paddlewheelers in the Pacific Northwest, the Yukon, and Alaska*. Vancouver: Alexander Nicholls Press, 2000.

Anderson, S. *Lawrence of Arabia: War, Deceit, Imperial Folly, and the Making of the Modern Middle East*. New York: Anchor Books, 2004.

Ashdown, D. *Railway Steamships of Ontario*. Erin, ON: Boston Mills Press, 1988.

Basberg, B.L., J.E. Ringstad, and E. Wexelsen. *Whaling and History: Perspectives on the Evolution of the Industry*. Sandefjord, Norway: Sandefjordmuseene, 1993.

Bennett, N.V., compiler. *Pioneer Legacy: Chronicles of the Lower Skeena River*. Vol. 1. Terrace, BC: Dr. R.E.M. Lee Hospital Foundation, 1997.

Bonsor, N.R.P. *North Atlantic Seaway: An Illustrated History of Passenger Services Linking the Old World with the New*. New York: Arco Publishing Company, 1975.

Burdett, R.J., ed. *Fort William Industrial and Commercial Review*. Fort William Industrial Bureau. Fort William, ON: Times-Journal Press, 1913.

Clapp, F.A. *Spratt's Ark: A History of Joseph Spratt's Unique Vessel*. Seattle: Puget Sound Maritime Historical Society, 1997.

Downs, A. *Paddlewheels on the Frontier: The Story of British Columbia and Yukon Sternwheel Steamers*. Sidney, BC: Gray's Publishing, 1972.

Gardiner, R., ed. *Conway's All the World's Fighting Ships, 1906–1921*. Annapolis, MD: U.S. Naval Institute Press, 1985.

Gilbert, M. *The First World War: A Complete History*. New York: Henry Holt, 1994.

Gillham, S. "The Niagara, St. Catharines and Toronto Navigation Co." In *Ten Tales of the Great Lakes*. St. Catharines, ON: Stonehouse Publications, 1983.

"Granaries." In *Encyclopaedia Britannica*, 11th ed. (1911), vol. 12: 336–41.

Gray, L., and J. Lingwood. *The Doxford Turret Ships*. Kendal, U.K.: The World Ship Society, 1975.

Greenwood, J.O. *The Fleet Histories Series*. Vol. 10, *The Fleets of: Misener, Soo River, Reoch, International-Harvester, Keystone, Lake Tankers, Lloyd Tankers, Merchants Mutual Line, Minto Trading, Masaba Steamship, Western Navigation, Pine Ridge Coal, and Spanish River/Abitibi Power*. Cleveland: Freshwater Press, 2003.

Guay, D.R.P. *Hiram Walker's Railroad: The Lake Erie & Detroit River Railway*. Windsor, ON: Walkerville Press, 2015.

Hagelund, W.A. *Whalers No More: A History of Whaling on the West Coast*. Madeira Park, BC: Harbour Publishing, 1987.

Heal, S.C. *Always Ready: Tugboats Along the Coast, the Evolution of an Industry*. Vancouver: Cordillera Books, 2003.

Hendrickson, R. *The Ocean Almanac*. Garden City, NY: Main Street Books, 1984.

Henry, T. *Westcoasters: Boats That Built B.C.* Vancouver: Harbour Publishing, 2001.

Ketchum, M. *The Design of Walls, Bins, and Grain Elevators*. 1st ed. New York: McGraw-Hill, 1907.

Laister, P. *Mariner's Memorabilia: A Guide to British Shipping Company China of the 19th and 20th Centuries*. Vols. 1 and 2. Self-published, 2006.

Large, R.G. *The Skeena: River of Destiny*. Surrey: Heritage House, 1996.

Leonard, F. *A Thousand Blunders: The Grand Trunk Pacific Railway and Northern British Columbia*. Vancouver: University of British Columbia Press, 1995.

Lloyd's Book of House Flags and Funnels of the Principal Steamship Lines of the World and the House Flags of Various Lines of Sailing Vessels. London, U.K.: Lloyd's Royal Exchange, 1912.

Ludlow, L.M. *Catalogue of Canadian Railway Cancellations and Related Transportation Postmarks*. Tokyo: Self-published, 1982.

Marc, J. *Pacific Coast Ship China*. Victoria: Royal British Columbia Museum, 2009.

Mills, J.M. *The Niagara, St. Catharines and Toronto Railway*. Toronto: Upper Canada Railway Society and Ontario Electric Railway Historical Association, 1967.

_____. *Niagara, St. Catharines and Toronto Railway: An Illustrated History of Electric Transit in Canada's Niagara Peninsula*. Montreal: Railfare DC Books, 2007.

Muralt, D.E. *The Victoria and Sidney Railway: 1892–1919*. Victoria, BC: BC Railway Historical Association, 1992.

Musk, G. *Canadian Pacific: The Story of the Famous Shipping Line*. Newton Abbot, U.K.: David & Charles Limited, 1981.

Newell, G.R., ed. *H.W. McCurdy Marine History of the Pacific Northwest: An Illustrated Review of the Growth and Development of the Maritime Industry from 1895, the Date of Publication of the Last Such Comprehensive History/Lewis & Dryden's Marine History of the Pacific Northwest*. Seattle: Superior Publishing, 1966.

Oliff, R. *Fastest to Canada: The Royal Edward from Govan to Gallipoli*. Kettering, U.K.: Silver Link Publishing, 2004.

Oxford, W. *The Ferry Steamers: The Story of the Detroit-Windsor Ferry Boats*. Erin, ON: Boston Mills Press, 1995.

Regehr, T.D. *The Canadian Northern Railway: Pioneer Road of the Northern Prairies, 1895–1918*. Toronto: Macmillan Canada, 1976.

Report and Hearings of the Select Committee Appointed to Investigate Certain Charges Under House Resolution 543. U.S. Congress, House of Representatives. Washington, DC: U.S. Government Printing Office, 1911.

Rushton, G. *Whistle Up the Inlet: The Union Steamship Story*. Vancouver: J.J. Douglas, 1974.

Skinner, D.E, and L. McDonald. *Alaska Steam: A Pictorial History of the Alaska Steamship Company.* Anchorage: Alaska Geographic Society, 1984.

Tennant, A.J. *British Merchant Ships Sunk by U-Boats in World War One.* Penzance, U.K.: Periscope Publishing, 2006.

Turner, R.D. *The Klondike Gold Rush Steamers. A History of Yukon River Steam Navigation.* Winlaw, BC: Sono Nis Press, 2015.

_____. *The Pacific Empresses. An Illustrated History of Canadian Pacific Railway's Empress Liners on the Pacific Ocean.* Victoria: Sono Nis Press, 1981.

_____. *The Pacific Princesses: An Illustrated History of the Canadian Pacific's Princess Fleet on the Northwest Coast.* Victoria: Sono Nis Press, 2004.

_____. *Sternwheelers and Steam Tugs: An Illustrated History of the Canadian Pacific Railway's British Columbia Lake and River Service.* Victoria: Sono Nis Press, 1984.

_____. *Vancouver Island Railroads.* Victoria: Sono Nis Press, 1997.

Twigg, A.M. *Union Steamships Remembered.* Campbell River, BC: Self-published, 1997.

Webb, R.L. *On the Northwest: Commercial Whaling in the Pacific Northwest, 1790–1967.* Vancouver: University of British Columbia Press, 2011.

_____. *West Whaling: A Brief History of Whale-Hunting in the Pacific Northwest.* Vancouver: Vancouver Maritime Museum, 1984.

Wise, J.E, and S. Baron. *Soldiers Lost at Sea: A Chronicle of Troopship Disasters.* Annapolis, MD: Naval Institute Press, 2004.

Wooley, P.W, and T. Moore. *The Cunard Line: A Pictorial History 1840–1990.* Coltishall, U.K.: Ship Pictorial Publications, 1990.

Young, J.E. *Historical Facts: Grain Elevator Construction and Shipping, Lakehead Harbour 1883–1965.* Port Arthur, ON: Lakehead Harbour Commission, 1965.

NEWSPAPERS

Chilliwack Progress.

Philadelphia Inquirer.

Portland Canal Miner.

Prince Rupert Daily News.

Prince Rupert Evening Empire.

Prince Rupert Optimist.

"Railway By-Law. The Proposed Plan of Railway and Ferry Connection Fully Discussed." Victoria, BC: Colonist Presses, 1900.

San Francisco Call.

Sidney and Islands Review.

Vancouver Daily News Advertiser.

Vancouver Daily Province.

Vancouver Daily World.

Victoria Daily Colonist.

Victoria Daily Times.

PERIODICALS

Alaska Hearings Before the Committee on the Territories. House of Representatives, 67th Congress, First Session, HR 5694. Washington, DC: U.S. Government Printing Office, 1921.

Annals of the American Academy of Political and Social Science 55 (September 1914): 60.

Annual Report of the Department of Marine and Fisheries, Parliament, Dominion of Canada. Multiple years. Ottawa: Various printers.

Atlantic Royals: *Royal Edward* and *Royal George.* Canadian Northern Steamships Advertising Brochure. Undated.

British Columbia Gazette. Various issues.

British Columbia Lumberman. Various issues.

Canadian Railway and Marine World. Multiple years and issues. Toronto: Acton Burrows.

Clapp, F.A. "Canadian National Railways British Columbia Transfer Barge Services, Part I of II." *Sea Chest* 41, no. 2 (2009): 51–75.

——. "Mackenzie Brothers Limited: Steamship Owners and Operators, Vancouver, B.C." *Sea Chest* 28 (September and December 1994): 3–16 and 81–88.

Daily U.S. Consular and Trade Reports, no. 3697 (January 28, 1910): 10.

Dilley, A. "'The Rules of the Game': London Finance, Australia, and Canada, c. 1900–14." *Economic History Review* 63, no. 4 (November 2010): 1003–31.

DiMatteo, L. "Booming Sector Models, Economic Base Analysis, and Export-Led Economic Development: Regional Evidence from the Lakehead." *Social Science History* 17, no. 4 (Winter 1993): 593–617.

Dunn, S.O. "Water Transportation in Its Relation to the Railways." In *Water Transportation: A Symposium* (January 19, 1922). *Proceedings of the American Society of Civil Engineers* 48, nos. 1–4 (1922): 281–86.

Farrell, D. "Keeping the Local Economy Afloat: Canadian Pacific Navigation and Ship Owning in Victoria." *Northern Mariner* 6, no. 1 (1996): 35–44.

Green, F.W., ed. *Green's Marine Directory of the Great Lakes.* Multiple vols. Cleveland, OH: Self-published.

Green, M.T. "The Canadian North-Eastern Railway." *Canadian Rail*, no. 442 (September-October 1994): 167–71.

Green, M.T., and R.D. Turner. "Stewart, B.C. and the C.N.E.R." *Canadian Rail*, no. 459 (July-August 1997): 104–08.

Harbour & Shipping, Vancouver. Various issues.

Hearings Before the Committee on the Merchant Marine and Fisheries. War Emergency — Admission of Foreign Shipping to the Coastwise Trade. House of Representatives, 65th Congress, HR 5609. Washington, DC: U.S. Government Printing Office, 1917.

Lloyd's Register of British and Foreign Shipping. Multiple years. London, U.K..

Lower, J.A. "The Construction of the Grand Trunk Pacific Railway in British Columbia." *British Columbia Historical Quarterly* 4, no. 3 (July 1930): 163–81.

Mackenzie, K.S. "C.C. Ballantyne and the Canadian Government Merchant Marine, 1917–1921." *Northern Mariner* 2, no. 1 (January 1992): 1–13.

McKellar, P. "The Thunder Bay Harbour." *Annual Proceedings of the Thunder Bay Historical Society* (5th Annual Report, 1915): 19–21.

Merchant Vessels of the United States. Bureau of Navigation, Treasury Department (1884–1902) or Department of Commerce and Labor (1903–12). Multiple years. Washington, DC: U.S. Government Printing Office.

Monthly U.S. Consular and Trade Reports 87, no. 332 (May 1908): 53.

North and South via Pacific Coast Steamship Co. Alaska and Other Points of Interest. Pacific Coast Steamships advertising brochure (1896).

Railway and Marine World. Multiple years and issues. Toronto: Acton Burrows.

Railway and Shipping World. Multiple years and issues. Toronto: Acton Burrows.

Records of the Department of Justice, Record Group 13. Vol. 1310. Royal Commission on Insurance, Transcripts of Hearings. Vol. 1. Ottawa: Library and Archives Canada, 1906: 335–36.

Rogers, F.C. "Hard Luck: The Mackenzie Brothers Steamship Company." *Western Mariner* 5, no. 1 (March 2007): 34–37.

Russell A.L. "A Brief History of Port Arthur Harbour." *Annual*

Proceedings of the Thunder Bay Historical Society (6th Annual Report, 1916): 21–26.

Sager, E. "Shipping Industry of British Columbia from 1867–1914." *Northern Mariner* 3, no. 3 (1993): 61–66.

Salmon, M.S. "'This Remarkable Growth': Investment in Canadian Great Lakes Shipping, 1900–1959." *Northern Mariner* 15, no. 3 (2005): 1–38.

Sample, W.C. "Dock Design and Construction in Fort William and Port Arthur." *Canadian Engineer* 24 (May 1, 1913): 643–48.

Sellers, H. "The Early History of the Handling and Transportation of Grain in the District of Thunder Bay." *Annual Proceedings of the Thunder Bay Historical Society* (1st Annual Report, 1909–10): 21–26.

Stafford, S. "The Railway Builders." *Annual Proceedings of the Thunder Bay Historical Society* (8th Annual Report, 1917): 21–23.

Vervoort, P. "Lakehead Terminal Elevators: Aspects of Their Engineering History." *Canadian Journal of Civil Engineering* 17 (1990): 404–12.

THESES

McMahon Haugland, M.L. "A History of the Alaska Steamship Company." Seattle: University of Washington, 1968.

Schuthe, G.M. "Canadian Shipping in the British Columbia Coastal Trade." Vancouver: University of British Columbia, April 1950.

WEBSITES

www.alpenapubliclibrary.org/greatlakesmaritimelanding
www.cefresearch.ca
www.cimorelli.com
www.clydesite.co.uk
www.db.library.queensu.ca/marmus/mills
www.desfilms.com
www.encyclopedia-titanica.org
www.greatlakes.bgsu.edu/vessel
www.heritage-ships.com
www.maritimehistoryofthegreatlakes.ca
www.merchantnavyofficers.com
www.mhs.mb.ca/docs/steamboats/index.shtml
www.miramarshipindex.org.nz
www.norwayheritage.co
www.paulinedodd.com
www.photoship.co.uk
www.royaledward.net
www.searlecanada.com
www.shipslist.com
www.simplonpc.co.uk
www.unioncastlestaffregister.co.uk
www.westcoastferries.ca
www.wrecksite.eu

INDEX

LISTING OF VESSELS

Abbreviations: AL = Allan Line, ASS = Alaska Steamship Co., AWH = A.W. Hepburn, BSC = Boscowitz Steamship Company, CIL = Canadian Interlake Line, CLON = Canadian Lake & Ocean Navigation Company, CNCOD = Canadian Northern Coal & Ore Dock Company, COIN = Canadian Ocean & Inland Navigation Company, CPR = Canadian Pacific Railway, CPSS = Canadian Pacific Steamships, CSL = Canada Steamship Lines, CTC = Canadian Tugboat Company, DonL = Donaldson Line, E&N = Esquimalt & Nanaimo Railway, MBL = Mackenzie Brothers Limited, MML = Merchant's Mutual Line, MSC = Mutual Steamship Company, MSSC = Merchants' Steamship Company, MTC = Montreal Transportation Co., M&M = Mackenzie & Mann, NiNC = Niagara Navigation Co., NStC&TN = Niagara, St. Catharines & Toronto Navigation Co., PCSS = Pacific Coast Steamship Co., PSNC = Puget Sound Navigation Co., R&O = Richelieu & Ontario Navigation Company, RAL = Russian American Line, RORO = Roll-on, Roll-off, StL&CSN = St. Lawrence & Chicago Steam Navigation Co., SNTC = Sidney & Nanaimo Transportation Company, USSBC = Union Steamships of BC, VTR&F = Victoria Terminal Railway & Ferry Company.

VISIT US AT

Dundurn.com
@dundurnpress
Facebook.com/dundurnpress
Pinterest.com/dundurnpress